Malte Faber · John L.

With the Cooperation of
Reiner Manstetten

Evolution, Time, Production and the Environment

Second, Revised and Enlarged Edition

With 75 Figures

Springer-Verlag

Berlin Heidelberg New York
London Paris Tokyo
Hong Kong Barcelona
Budapest

Authors

Professor Dr. MALTE FABER
Alfred-Weber-Institut für Sozial- und Staatswissenschaften
der Universität Heidelberg
Grabengasse 14, 69117 Heidelberg, FRG

Dr. JOHN L. R. PROOPS
Department of Economics and Management Science
University of Keele
Staffordshire ST5 5BG, United Kingdom

With the Cooperation of

Dr. REINER MANSTETTEN
Alfred-Weber-Institut für Sozial- und Staatswissenschaften
der Universität Heidelberg
Grabengasse 14, 69117 Heidelberg, FRG

ISBN 3-540-58044-1 Springer-Verlag Berlin Heidelberg New York Tokyo
ISBN 0-387-58044-1 Springer-Verlag New York Heidelberg Berlin Tokyo

Preface to the Soft Cover Edition

This book has not only been used as a text in the Department of Economics at the University of Heidelberg, but also in interdisciplinary environmental courses at Keele University. We were therefore glad when Dr. Müller of Springer-Verlag offered to publish a soft cover version of the second edition, to make the text economically more accessible to students.

Heidelberg and Keele, July 1994   Malte FABER
                                              John PROOPS

Preface to the Second Edition

This second edition is brought about by two factors. First, the initial printing sold out much more rapidly than we expected.

Second, several colleagues have been kind enough to suggest that this book not only has a contribution to make to ecological economics, but also has relevance to economics general. Thus our distinction between genotypic and phenotypic evolution may be used to characterise not only economic sectors, but also whole economies, and in particular economic schools of thought. For instance, the Austrian subjectivist school deals explicitly with ignorance and the emergence of novelty, and may therefore be used to analyse genotypic development. In contrast, neoclassical economics deals principally with phenotypic development.

When Dr. Müller of Springer-Verlag suggested the production of a second edition, we were therefore pleased that this book might remain available. Several readers and in particular reviewers of the first edition remarked, in one way or the other, that they had questions concerning several of our concepts, such as genotype, phenotype, ignorance, surprise, novelty, knowledge, predictable and unpredictable processes etc. Of course, all these concepts are of importance for evolution in general and for invention and innovation of new techniques in particular. We therefore considered some modifications and extensions of the original text, but on the advice of colleagues, have restricted ourselves to correcting mistakes that crept into the first edition and to two extensions of the text, one major, one smaller.

To enlarge the horizon of our conceptual approach we have supplemented Chapter 2 and added a new Part, Part IV, on ignorance. Since Reiner Manstetten contributed to this chapter and also to the whole revision of the first edition we have mentioned him in the title.

Concerning the order in which the Parts of this book may be read, our comment in the preface to the first edition, that several orderings are possible, still holds. In particular, while Part IV draws upon the concepts of evolution and time in Parts II and III, it can also be taken as a self-contained unit.

Finally, we note that the book has proved also to be a useful text for a course on "The Philosophical Foundations of Ecology and Economics" at the graduate level at the Department of Economics at the University of Heidelberg.

For advice on typos, and other errors of expression and substance, we are grateful for their close reading of the first edition to Christoph HELLE, Frank JÖST, Rainer LEISTEN, Georg MÜLLER and Stefan SPECK. For further assistance in the preparation of this edition we wish to acknowledge Stefan SPECK.

For allowing us to draw upon previously published material, we thank the publishers of Kyklos, Ecological Economics, The Seoul Journal of Economics, Environmental Values and Springer Verlag.

Heidelberg and Keele, November 1992   Malte FABER
                                                    John PROOPS

Preface to the First Edition

This book is a contribution to the foundations of ecological economics. Its aim is the conceptualisation and modelling of long-run interactions between the economy and the environment. It is addressed to all those who share our concern with the impact of human activity on the global ecosystem, irrespective of their disciplinary background. In it we synthesize the research we have been doing separately and together during the last two decades.

We deal with a wide range of issues: a new concept of evolution, time irreversibility, the emergence of novelty, ignorance, and structural change.

We have adapted and extended Neo-Austrian capital theory to formalise the above conceptualisation. From this we have developed a method of simulating the long-run interaction of consumption, capital accumulation, resource use, pollution and its abatement.

We use a verbal approach except in Part IV, where we use some mathematics; this we restrict to high school algebra and elementary calculus. Further, we have attempted to make the individual chapters straightforward in their development. However, because of its range in concepts and methods, and its interdisciplinary nature, we believe that our book as a whole may not be found easy reading.

Partly from the nature of the subject, the ordering of Parts II, III and IV is rather arbitrary, and readers may wish to experiment with the order in which this material is taken. Those with an interest mainly in conceptualization in ecological economics may prefer to read Part IV in a cursory manner, while those whose primary interest is modelling may wish turn to Part IV straight after reading the introduction in Part I.

Very many colleagues and friends have influenced our thinking over a number of years, and many have been kind enough to comment on material now included in this book. For their assistance we thank them. For particular assistance in the preparation of this book we are pleased to acknowledge the critical comments and contributions of Alexander GERYBADZE, Frank JÖST, Marco LEHMANN-WAFFENSCHMIDT, Reiner MANSTETTEN, Peter MICHAELIS, Brigitte RÜGER, Matthias RUTH, Georgia SEATON, Armin SCHMUTZLER and Gunter STEPHAN. For allowing us to draw upon previously published material, we thank the publishers of Kyklos, Ecological Economics, The Seoul Journal of Economics and Springer-Verlag.

Heidelberg and Keele, February 1990   Malte FABER
John PROOPS

Biographical Notes

Malte Faber was born in 1938 in Düsseldorf, Germany. He studied Economics and Mathematics at the Free University of Berlin. He then took his MA in Mathematical Economics at the University of Minnesota, USA. His PhD was on Stochastic Programming, from the Technical University of Berlin, where he also became Privatdozent in Economics. Since 1973 he has been Professor in Economic Theory at the University of Heidelberg. He has published widely in capital theory, public choice, the role of the entropy concept in environmental economics, input-output analysis applications to the management of water, waste and carbon dioxide emissions, and the conceptual foundations of ecological economics. He has served as an adviser on environmental matters to the Federal and State governments of the Federal Republic of Germany.

John Proops was born in 1947 in Bristol, United Kingdom. He studied Physics and Mathematics at the University of Keele, and Engineering Physics at McMaster University, Canada. During a period as a lecturer in mathematics in Northern Nigeria he became interested in economics and development. He returned to the University of Keele to take his PhD on the application of concepts from modern thermodynamics to the structural evolution of economic systems. Since 1977 he has been a Lecturer, Senior Lecturer and Reader in Mathematical and Environmental Economics at Keele University. He has published on energy modelling, input-output analysis, regional economics, the application of concepts of thermodynamics in economic analysis, and the conceptual foundations of ecological economics.

Reiner Manstetten was born in 1953 in Würselen, Germany. He studied philosophy, German philology and music at the Universities of Cologne, Freiburg and Heidelberg. He took his M.A. and his PhD in medieval philosophy at the Department of Philosophy at the University of Heidelberg. Since 1985 he has been an assistant at the Department of Economics in Heidelberg.

The authors have been working jointly for the past ten years on time, evolution, the foundations of ecological economics, capital theory and the application of input-output analysis to the CO_2 problem.

Contents

Part V. Production and Innovation 135

8 Economy-Environment Interactions in the Long-Run 137

9 Production, Accumulation and Time: A Neo-Austrian Approach 149

Part VI. Final Thoughts

12 Policy Implications and the Need for Interdisciplinary Research

List of Figures

List of Tables

Part I

Aims

1 Introduction

1.1 The Nature of the Book

The major problems in the world may be classified into three groups. These are peace, north-south development, and the preservation of the ecosystem. Obviously all three areas are interrelated, as is shown, for example, by the role of oil and OPEC, and the nature of rainforest destruction. Of these three problem areas we feel the one with the greatest potential for long-term harm is the destruction of the ecosystem by economic activity. Therefore, in this book we shall be concerned with the long-run interactions between the economy and the natural environment.

This endeavour comprises two main parts:

1. A conceptualization of interactions in the world appropriate to long-run considerations.

2. A technique of modelling economy-environment interactions which is consistent with and supported by the above conceptualization.

We shall return to a discussion of our methods of conceptualization and modelling in Section 1.3, below.

We now turn in more detail to the nature of the problem we are addressing.

1.2 The Nature of the Problem

The 'problem' of economy-environment interactions in the long-run is probably as old as humankind. There is ample evidence that even hunter-gatherer societies may change their natural environment through their economic activity. For example, the entry of humans into the Americas about 12,000 years ago was followed by massive extinctions of many species of large mammals, it is assumed through over-hunting [CROSBY 1986]. The experience in Australia was similar when humans arrived there approximately 40,000 years ago. There is also evidence that for many thousands of years these first Australians extensively modified their ecosystem with the use of fire, to improve their hunting possibilities [BLAINEY 1975]. Thus we see that the notion of humankind in 'harmony' with nature is but one of the myths with which we construct our world view [PROOPS 1989].

The rise of agriculture over the past few thousand years has seen dramatic and extensive remodelling of the natural environment. For example, in Europe we are accustomed to many upland areas supporting only grasses and heathland plants. These areas, however, are not 'natural', but the result of woodland clearing by neolithic farmers, and have been maintained for thousands of years by the grazing of domesticated animals [HOSKINS 1973].

The rate at which the natural environment was affected in the hunter-gatherer and agrarian periods was relatively slow. With the development of industrialization over the past few hundred years, there has been a huge change in the rate, the scale and the nature of economy-environment interactions.

For agrarian societies the principal structural material was wood, and the principal fuel was also wood. That is, these economies were dependent almost entirely on renewable natural resources.

Early industrialization led to a growing use of metals as structural materials, but the use of wood as the principal fuel continued. The metals were themselves derived from non-renewable ores, though their smelting used great quantities of the renewable resource of wood.

Late industrialization brought the shift towards the use of non-renewable resources (coal, oil, gas) as the major fuels.

This evolution of economic structure and economy-environment interactions had two main sources. First, the depletion of natural resources, and second, the invention of new techniques of production. The new techniques were brought into use because, in the circumstances then obtaining, they were technically 'superior'. However, these new techniques were often more capital intensive, and requiring of greater investment of labour and time for their establishment and operation. As such they were also more 'roundabout'.

This interdependent development of agriculture, industry and the natural environment is particularly clear for England from the late middle ages. During this period the forest cover was rapidly denuded through the growth of agriculture and the rise of iron smelting using charcoal. This resulted in a shortage of wood, and the subsequent rapid increase in the price of wood and charcoal led to the search for alternative techniques of smelting, using alternative fuels. It is very significant that it was coal, as transformed into coke, that provided the alternative fuel, for at this time non-renewable fuel resources became, for the first time, central to human welfare and economic activity.

From this shift, from a fundamentally renewable resource based economy to one more and more dependent on non-renewable resources, springs much of the dynamics of modern economic activity, and many of the modern environmental problems. This can be illustrated by examining the process of industrialization during earlier centuries, and the present relationship between economies and their resource bases.

Returning to the development of the use of coke in iron smelting, this led to a rapid growth in coal mining. However, just as the natural world is a constraint on smelting when the technology permitted only the use of charcoal, so too were natural constraints soon encountered in coal mining. As coal mining progressed, and coal mines became ever deeper, the problem of groundwater flooding set limits on coal extraction. Again, the impact of economic activity on the environment generated a problem, and this problem in turn generated a search for the means of its circumvention, through the search for powerful and efficient water pumps.

The basic conceptual structure that we abstract from such historical experience may be represented by a 'triangle of causation', as illustrated in Fig. 1.1.

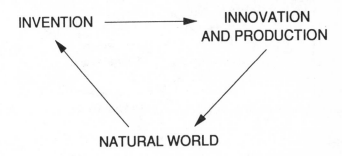

Fig. 1.1. The economy-environment 'triangle of causation'.

The interpretation of this figure is as follows. A new technique becomes available which, in some way, affects the natural environment through resource depletion and/or pollution. This new technique will in turn allow a restructuring of economic activity, over time. This bringing into use of the newly invented technique and its ramifying effect throughout the economy is the process of innovation. This innovation will impact upon the environment to a greater and greater extent, until the effect on the environment itself becomes a threat to economic activity in general, and the use of that technique in particular. This 'natural constraint' will generate a search for new techniques that are not subject to the currently obtaining constraints imposed by the natural environment.

If a new invention occurs, whose innovation will impact upon the environment, this triangle of causation will begin again. However, one should be aware that Fig. 1.1 may be improved in two ways as a representation of the historical process.

1. Fig. 1.1 suppresses the time axis. If we introduce time fully then the process emerges not as closed cycle, but as helix or spiral, as shown in Fig. 1.2.

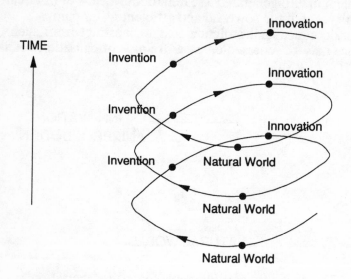

Fig. 1.2. The 'spiral of causation' over time.

2. However, the history of technological development cannot be described by such a single helix. An illustration of this complex process is the search for suitable water pumps for the deep workings of coal mines, mentioned above. The initial development of the steam pump can mainly be attributed to this requirement. The further development of steam engines led in turn to quite different applications of this technology, the outstanding one being the improvement in transport systems. The introduction of steam powered ships and steam locomotives gave rise not only to two new industrial sectors, but opened the path to completely novel and unpredictable economic activities.

Thus it is important to realize the following concerning the spirals of causation as shown in Fig. 1.2.

(a) These spirals can come to an end, because no appropriate invention becomes available.

(b) There exist different spirals at different stages in the same industry, between industries and between economies.

(c) Inventions in one spiral can, as in the case of the steam engine, generate other 'spin-off' spirals, with their own dynamics, as shown in Fig. 1.3.

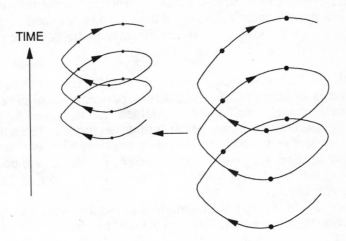

TIME

Fig. 1.3. Invention giving rise to a 'spin-off' spiral.

With respect to these disequilibrating effects, the above analysis is in the spirit of SCHUMPETER's [1912/1934] ideas on innovation and structural change. However, unlike SCHUMPETER, the emphasis of our study is not on the creativity of the entrepreneur, but on the interface between the natural world and the economy.

It is apparent that the recursive relationships between economic development and the natural environment are far from simple. However, three major elements may be identified.

1. The use of non-renewable natural resources is clearly irreversible in time, and a given technology using finite non-renewable resources must, sooner or later, cease to be viable.

2. The invention, and subsequent innovation, of new techniques offers the means of sustaining economic activity in the face of declining stocks of natural resources. This can be achieved both by allowing available resources to be used more effectively (i.e. resource saving inventions), and by allowing resources that had no economic value to become useful in the production process (i.e. resource substituting invention). It is clear that invention is a time irreversible process, as by its very definition invention involves novelty.

3. The production process has a certain time structure. This is particularly clear when the innovation of a newly invented technique is considered. Before innovation there is a certain stock of capital goods, with certain characteristics. The first stage in the innovation process is the building up of a stock of new capital goods, appropriate to the new technique. This is a process which is directed towards a certain end, or telos, and exhibits also a teleological irreversibility, to be described in detail below.

Our considerations show that there are certain characteristics of historical developments concerning the interaction between economies and the natural environment which can be explained (i.e. modelled ex post) and may also be used for prediction of the future (i.e. modelled ex ante). There are other occurrences which, though they may explain developments ex post, cannot, by their very nature, be predicted. To this class of occurrences belong all those which involve novelty, such as invention, and also those involving ignorance.

We now turn to the way we intend to analyse the evolutionary process of interaction between economies and the environment.

1.3 The Nature of the Method
1.3.1 Conceptualization

Regarding the conceptual framework needed for this task, considerable groundwork is necessary. In particular we shall seek a firmly based conceptualization of (a) evolution and (b) time. To this end we have found that an interdisciplinary approach is necessary. Thus in this book we shall draw freely on concepts from biological and physical science, as well as from economics.

A first step is to give production processes a physical underpinning. During the last two decades it has become evident that to this end it is useful to take recourse to thermodynamics, and in particular to the First and Second laws of thermodynamics. The First Law is necessary for a firmly grounded materials balance approach. The Second Law can be applied to problems of energy use, resource extraction and pollution. Here, GEORGESCU-ROEGEN's [1971] pioneering work should be recognised as paving the way for later developments. It is also important in respect to two aspects of time irreversibility mentioned, as will be discussed in Part III.

Further aspects of irreversibility can be comprehended through the development of far-from-equilibrium thermodynamics, especially by the path-breaking work of PRIGOGINE [1962]. These ideas allow one to see invention as an irreversible but unpredictable process. As mentioned in the previous section, clearly by its nature, invention introduces novelty.

Besides these two concepts of irreversibility, humankind knows a third kind of irreversibility. This occurs in general if one has an end, or telos, to be reached over time. The related endeavours to achieve that telos are connected with this third kind of irreversibility. An illustration is of an enterprise aiming to establish a new branch in another country. After having built the appropriate factory, with its process specific capital stock, it may be that a change in the demand conditions means the plant could yield only large losses. Thus all the investment is irreversibly lost. To summarise, a process which is directed towards a specific end is always endangered by a social kind of irreversibility, irrespective of the two other physical irreversibilities mentioned above.

These considerations of the irreversibilities of processes, both natural and social, are naturally related to considerations of the dynamics of processes and the extent to which such dynamics may be predicted. That is, we are led to an analysis of the evolution of systems. The concept of evolution has, so far, been applied most widely and fruitfully in biological science. We are led to the conclusion that the concept of evolution is also applicable to the physical and social sciences, and this application of the concept reveals, we hope clearly, why the understanding of physical dynamics has been able to advance so rapidly, while long-term biological dynamics (over periods of millenia or longer) is still and will remain difficult to treat. Most importantly, it demonstrates why economic dynamics has so far been of little value for the long-run and of questionable value for the short-run.

In particular, our conceptualization of time and evolution has led us to a dichotomising of processes. The first category includes those processes which *do not* involve the emergence of novelty, and are therefore, in principle, predictable. The second category includes those processes which *do* involve the emergence of novelty, and are therefore, in principle, unpredictable. However, it will be shown in detail that this simple dichotomy is insufficient, as many processes in the real world cannot be predicted in practice, even though they may be predictable in principle. For this reason we introduce a third category, which includes those processes of which we are ignorant.

In the light of the above discussion we refer again to Fig. 1.1 and its triangle of causality. It is clear that the effect of a newly emerged technique on the wider economy (cf. INVENTION → INNOVATION AND PRODUCTION: Fig. 1.1) is predictable in the above sense. Less predictable, because of the possibility of ignorance, is the impact of such innovation on the natural environment (cf. INNOVATION AND PRODUCTION → NATURAL WORLD: Fig. 1.1). However, what is not predictable even in principle, is the nature of novel inventions that may occur in response to environmental degradation (cf. NATURAL WORLD → INVENTION: Fig. 1.1). Thus our conceptualization allows us to distinguish the long-run processes which in principle may be modelled and lead to prediction, from those which in principle cannot be modelled and are unpredictable. In addition there are processes of which we are ignorant, either because we simply do not know of their existence, or because the processes are too complex to analyse. Such processes may or may not exhibit novelty.

The problem of ignorance is of importance for environmental problems. We therefore will analyse 'ignorance' in philosophy and science, particularly with respect to the conceptualization, study and solution of environmental problems. We do this within an evolutionary context.

We first turn our attention to the nature and sources of 'ignorance'. Here we deal with surprise and distinguish between 'risk', 'uncertainty' and 'ignorance'. We then offer a categorization of ignorance, and use these categories to assess the role of science as a means of reducing ignorance. We note that to proceed with science several 'acts of faith' are necessary. We conclude with a discussion of the importance of an attitude of openness in philosophy and science, especially regarding environmental problems. It follows from our analysis that the free will to carry through flexible long-run environmental policies, and to adhere to them, is of particular relevance in a world of 'ignorance'.

1.3.2 Modelling and Simulation

Regarding an appropriate method of modelling, the above conceptual work has led us to the conclusion that conventional 'neoclassical' economics requires further enrichment to more fully take into account these aspects of evolution and irreversibility in time. The Austrian theory of capital, founded by BÖHM-BAWERK [1889/1891] stressed the temporal structure of production, and that production is roundabout. The latter implies that it takes time to achieve an end or telos. It was these two features of Austrian capital theory which led to its 'rebirth' [HICKS 1973a] in the nineteen seventies, as neo-Austrian capital theory.

The main feature of neo-Austrian capital theory is that it acknowledges that in the world it takes time to convert primary factors first into intermediate goods, then into final consumption goods. In particular it takes time to build up stocks of capital goods. The neo-Austrian approach is therefore suited to consider the irreversible nature of environmental and resource processes. Hence, it allows the analysis of the predictable long-run effects of environmental pollution and resource extraction.

The neo-Austrian approach is particularly apt for the modelling of SCHUMPETER'S notion of innovation and the resultant structural change of an economy. Neo-Austrian capital theory is therefore not focussed on semi-stationary states, or steady-states, but on unbalanced states. HICKS [1973b:81-150] has dubbed such states the 'traverse' of an economy. The time structure of production, the building up and down of stocks of capital goods, of pollution and of natural resources, is of importance [FABER, NIEMES and STEPHAN, 1987].

Any approach to capital accumulation and resource use must, explicitly or implicitly, make an assumption about the nature of intertemporal choice. In a world with no chance for the emergence of novelty it would be appropriate to model such intertemporal choice taking regard of the indefinite future. However, if one's notion of the world allows for the emergence of novelty in production processes, then the incorporation of consumption possibilities of the distant future in the decision about today's capital accumulation and resource use is clearly inappropriate. Because of the emergence of novelty, one might model the decision making process as continuing over time, thereby allowing the potential impact of new techniques to be included as these occur.

The procedure we use to this end is of 'rolling myopic plans'. (The term 'myopic' derives from 'myopia', the technical term for being 'short-sighted'). When allied to the temporal structure of capital accumulation and resource use implicit in neo-Austrian capital theory, this gives a framework for modelling and simulation which explicitly includes the first and third kind of irreversibility. It also allows for the second type of irreversibility, the emergence of novelty.

The combination of a neo-Austrian capital approach, and the use of rolling myopic plans for the decision process, gives a model with the following three advantages:

1. The description of the production process, involving as it does the replacement of old techniques by emerging new techniques, reflects well the historical experience of industrialization.

2. The model allows a rich temporal structure to the processes described, their evolution allowing for all three types of irreversibility.

3. The model lends itself to simulation in a remarkably straightforward fashion.

This last point has encouraged us to simulate the long-run interaction of economic development with the natural environment, through invention and innovation. This model involves consumption and capital accumulation, with the corresponding resource use and pollution.

The results from these simulations are encouraging in two respects. First, the time profiles of the use of resources and the accumulation of capital and of pollution are qualitatively in line with historical experience. Second, the results of such simulations encourage the testing of detailed historical data, and the establishment of scenarios of the use of resources and the production of pollution in the future.

1.4 The Contents of the Book

In Part II of this book we explore and develop the concept of evolution. In Chapter 2 we review the development of this concept in biological science, particularly noting the distinction between the evolution of the realization (phenotype) of a system, and the evolution of its potentialities (genotype). These concepts are further developed in Chapter 3, where it is shown that they are equally applicable to physical and economic systems. Particular stress is laid on how certain types of evolution are in principle predictable, while other types are in principle unpredictable.

In Part III we turn to a discussion of time and the problem of irreversibility. In Chapter 4 we discuss how time has been treated in economic analysis to date. In this chapter we develop the three types of time irreversibility, mentioned above, which we use throughout the remainder of the book. In Chapter 5 we show that the problem of time irreversibility has already been encountered in natural science, and we suggest how lessons learned there point the way for developments in economics. In Chapter 6 we show that concepts of time irreversibility may be combined with certain conceptual elements of economic theory to allow a typification of various schools of economic thought.

Part IV of this book addresses the problem of 'ignorance' in philosophy and science with respect to the conceptualization, study and solution of environmental problems. This Part contains only one chapter, Chapter 7, but this is rather long. There we develop, in some detail, the concepts of risk, uncertainty and ignorance, and in particular we offer a taxonomy of the ways in which surprise and ignorance can occur, especially with respect to environmental issues.

In Part V we turn to economic modelling, which reflects the conceptual analysis developed in Parts II, III and IV. In Chapter 8 we develop upon Chapter 6, and derive a framework for modelling long-run economy-environment interaction, in terms of the conceptual elements of economic theory and the three types of time irreversibility already mentioned. In Chapter 9 we introduce neo-Austrian capital theory. In particular, we stress the similarities and differences between this approach and the corresponding elementary neoclassical model. In Chapter 10 we further develop the neo-Austrian approach, and combine it with the use of rolling myopic plans for decision making. Chapter 11 further extends the neo-Austrian model to embody resource use, pollution production and abatement, and predictable technical progress of known techniques. From this a long-run simulation model is derived, and the results of this simulation are discussed in detail.

In Part VI we seek to draw some lessons from the earlier discussion and analysis. In Chapter 12 we note some implications for policy formulation and modelling of the explicit recognition of the emergence of novelty in economic systems. In particular we note that with this conceptualization the problem of pollution becomes more difficult to plan for, and to model, than the problem of resource depletion. We also discuss the role and the importance of interdisciplinary work for economics in general, and for our understanding of the recursive relationships between economic activity and the natural environment in particular. We stress the implications of the need for such an interdisciplinary approach, in both teaching and research.

Part II

Evolution

2 The Concept of Evolution

2.1 Introduction

Modern humankind wishes to predict in order to influence developments. Prediction has always to do with the future. When we analyse in the following the possibilities and limits of prediction it is useful to reflect the notion of the future. A precise scientific definition of the 'future' might be: 'Any time which is later than now'. However, by making this definition, we move our problem to that of the definition of 'time', which is by no means easy (see Part III, in particular Section 4.2).

Therefore, instead of trying to analyze the abstract notion of the 'future', we shall concentrate on the more concrete notion of 'future events', as reflected in our everyday lives. Every day we ask ourselves the questions:

1. What is going to happen?

2. What shall we do?

These have in common that they both concern future events; i.e. events which have not yet occurred. These questions are different because the attitudes they are based on are different. The question 'what is going to happen?' is theoretical, and reflects a contemplative and passive attitude; the question 'what shall we do?' is practical or ethical, and reflects an attitude of activity and intervention[1].

Of course, in everyday life these questions, and their corresponding attitudes, are interrelated. The answer to the first question provides a basis for answering the second question. For example, if a farmer 'knows' what the weather pattern will be like during the growing season, then he can 'know' what will be the 'best' course of action regarding planting, weed control, harvesting, etc.

---

[1] It is interesting to note that the German construction for reference to future events, i.e. the future tense, uses the modal verb 'werden', the literal sense of which is 'to become, to grow'. On the other hand, the English future tense uses the verb 'to will', which, what native English speakers often forget, means 'to desire, to aim to bring about'. Clearly, the German future tense is based upon the first question, 'what is going to happen?', while the English future tense derives from the second question, 'what can we do?'.

On the other hand, in the course of time interventions taken on the basis of answers to the second question, 'what can we do?', may alter the circumstances in such a way that the answer to the first question, 'what is going to happen?', will itself be changed. For example, in many parts of the world, hilly countryside can only be cultivated in the long-run by contour ploughing. If the farmer chooses *not* to use contour ploughing, then the result will be soil loss and, eventually, the loss of the option of cultivation at all.

In earlier times, most predictions about future events were experientially based (e.g. the weather lore of farmers). However, over the past two hundred years the rise of western science has given experiential regularities some conceptual underpinnings, often expressed as 'Laws of Nature' (e.g. Newton's laws of motion, the laws of thermodynamics, etc.). This has been immensely important in extending the range of prediction possible. We feel it has also been a source of misapprehension regarding the potential for knowledge about the future, as such theory allows prediction outside the range of experienced events. This may lead to the mistaken notion that with sufficient theory, anything and everything may be predicted. Why this notion is mistaken is the major topic of the rest of this chapter, Chapters 3-5 and Chapter 7.

The development of modern science characterised above has led to a total identification of the epistemological statuses of past and future events, e.g. as in Classical Mechanics. That this identification is erroneous can be seen by our everyday experience of the past and the future.

The statuses of the past and the future in our everyday life is well reflected by the nature of our diaries. Diaries seem to be of two distinct sorts, though both may be kept by one individual. First, the diary may take its 'classic' or reflective form, as a discourse upon, and interpretation of, the events of the day which have occurred. The classic diary is therefore 'backward' looking; it has reference to the past. The second, more modern, form of the diary is that of the 'appointments book', which details planned events for the future. This form is clearly 'forward' looking; it has reference to the future.

That we can keep diaries that are referring both to the past and to the future, and indeed that we may keep both diaries in a single volume, is indicative that our subjective imaginings of the future are similar to our subjective remembering and imaginings of the past. Thus the subjective statuses of the past and the future are often not dissimilar, in that both may seemingly be 'known'. Indeed, it is this sense of familiarity with the future that allows us to live our everyday lives at ease with the world, rather than in constant trepidation over the unknown.

However, we also recognise that often our imaginings of the future are not realised. Appointments may not be kept, planes may crash, crops may fail. Although we can predict or plan for some, perhaps many, events and have reasonable expectations about many others, we often experience surprises. In contrast to this modern science tries to eliminate surprise in order to influence and to control developments.

Predictions are applied to systems of all levels of scale, from microeconomics to the global ecosystem. If such predictions are successful they allow to control the corresponding systems. However, to achieve control about a particular system one needs to know the following about a system:

(a) The initial conditions and boundary conditions of the system.

(b) The laws governing the development of the system.

(c) That the system does not exhibit novelty.

If these three conditions hold, then predictability is possible, at least in principle. Then, by the manipulation of the initial conditions and the boundary conditions of the system, the development of the system may be controlled.

Many branches of conventional science tend to conceive of their objects of study as timeless; they therefore tend to represent their findings, in 'eternal' laws, such as the Laws of Classical Mechanics. The application of such kinds of science easily leads to the belief that future events are predictable. This predictability would have even been complete for that ideal scientist, LAPLACE's demon [PRIGOGINE and STENGERS 1984].

In contrast to this scientific approach, our remarks on the future in everyday life lead us to start from the assumption that the processes, and their relationships, which science examines are:

(a) unknown to us in many respects; i.e. we are ignorant of them, or of certain aspects of them, and

(b) these processes are intrinsically characterised by the complete or partial emergence of novelty over the course of time.

This leads us to ask the question of predictability in a new way; to answer this question demands the formulation of new concepts. One key notion for our approach is 'evolution'.

It is known that the objects of study in biology at any period of time are the result of an evolutionary process. We shall try to show that this is also true for other sciences, in particular for economics, and even for physics.

Our task in this chapter, and Chapter 4, is to develop a general framework for conceptualizing evolution. We shall proceed in such a manner that biology, physics and economics can be contained within it. In this way we also intend to contribute to the furthering of interdisciplinary research between these three disciplines. For example, physics, biology and economics are all of vital importance for environmental analysis, where the simultaneous and interacting evolution of physical, biological and economic systems is involved.

Evolution is a very encompassing concept, and is used in many different contexts. For example, one speaks of physical, biological, social, political and economic evolution. Key concepts for a definition of evolution in biology are mutation, heredity and selection, while in systems theory one employs the concepts of self-evolution, self-sustained development, and self-reference. For our conceptual framework it is useful to begin with the broadest possible starting point, for otherwise there is the danger that evolution is seen in too narrow a sense. Such a narrow conceptualization risks the exclusion of important aspects of evolutionary processes.

In our view the key characteristics of evolution are (1) change, and (2) time; we consider them also to suffice as elements for the following starting point:

Evolution is the process of the changing of something over time.

In a strict sense this is not a definition but a tautology. It simply gives information as to how we use the word 'evolution'. This we do purposely so as not to exclude any processes from our consideration. This approach is in line with HEIDEGGER's [1927/1979] insight that fundamental notions con only be explained in a circular way. Complementary to this approach is WITTGENSTEIN's [1922/1969] method. He would have qualified our definiton as 'nonsense'. Instead he would have asked how ne could use the notions of evolution in different contexts. It is precisely in the spirit of WITTGENSTEIN that, throughout this and the next chapter, we seek to illustrate the concept of evolution in biology, physics and economics, rather than seeking a definition of the concept of evolution in a close analytical way.

Our aim in this chapter is to specify and operationalize this conceptualization of evolution. To develop our conceptual framework we use concepts originally formulated in biology. In particular, we shall use the notions of genotypic and phenotypic evolution. In our generalization, by 'genotype' we mean the 'potentialities' of a system, and by 'phenotype' we mean the 'realization' of these potentialities. In this sense our concepts are not *derived* from biology; rather, they had their first expression, as a special case, in the biological literature. Thus, when we use the terms genotype and phenotype, we are *not* making analogies with biology. We are, rather extending the usage of these terms in what we feel is a natural manner. (For a discussion of the use of analogy, and its problems, see Chapter 12, Sections 4.1 and 4.2).

It will turn out that the evolutionary process, as we understand it, always takes place, albeit with different velocities. The evolution of our present physical laws and fundamental constants took place a long time ago and within a very short period of time (see Section 2.4). The biological evolution of species lasts millions or thousands of years and proceeds continually (see Section 2.3). The evolution of social and of economic institutions takes place in hundreds of years, decades, or even shorter periods. The contemporary evolution of techniques, and of world politics in 1989, show that social evolution may even have a much faster pace (see Chapter 3).

We are interested in particular in those changes in the course of time which are related to the emergence of novelty, because it is the latter which restricts the area of validity of predictability.

The degree of predictability varies in different areas of science (see Section 2.2). Clearly, there are unpredictable processes in physics (see Chapter 5); but in comparison with economic processes, the degree of predictability is very high. This difference can be explained by the emergence of novelty during very short time periods in economics (e.g. invention, and the spontaneous behaviour of people).

Before proceeding briefly to indicate the contents of this chapter, we wish to acknowledge that there is a considerable, and growing, literature in economics which uses, to a greater or lesser extent, evolutionary ideas drawn from biology. Examples of such work include MARSHALL [1890], VEBLEN [1902], ALCHIAN [1950], PENROSE [1952], CYERT and MARCH [1963], HIRSHLEIFER [1977], SCHELLING [1978], BOULDING [1981], NELSON and WINTER [1982], MATTHEWS [1984], NORGAARD [1984], WITT [1980, 1987] and CLARK and JUMA [1987].

In Section 2.2 we distinguish between two types of processes in time: predictable and unpredictable processes. While it turns out that the former may be of an 'equifinal' nature, the latter are not.

Section 2.3 is pivotal to this chapter, in that in biology the concepts of evolution, particularly the notions of phenotype and genotype, have been originally developed and applied. Here is laid the conceptual foundations for our evolutionary framework.

In Section 2.4 we apply these evolutionary concepts to physics.

We discuss the hierarchy of concepts in natural and social science in Section 2.5. In particular we stress the inevitability of the emergence of novelty in a world of only partial and incomplete knowledge.

Section 2.6 offers some general conclusions.

(Part II draws on material which we originally developed in FABER and PROOPS [1991a]).

2.2 Predictability and the Evolutionary Process

To allow us to proceed to our conceptual analysis of evolution we distinguish between two types of processes in time. We call these 'Predictable' and 'Unpredictable' processes. Before discussing these processes it is appropriate to note that actual processes lie on a continuum with regard to their degree of predictability. That is to say, certain processes are predictable with great certitude, while others are entirely unpredictable; many processes fall into neither of these categories, because we are ignorant of them, or of their structures. However, for our purposes it is convenient to employ the above rough categories.

2.2.1 Predictable Processes in Physics, Biology and Economics

We shall illustrate predictable processes with five examples, from physics, biology and economics. We have ordered them according to their degree of predictability.

(i)   Consider a ball falling on to a pavement. Using the laws of classical mechanics one can predict with great exactitude the movement over time of the ball. After a certain amount of time the ball will come to rest, and a mechanical equilibrium will be established.

(ii)   The dynamics of the launching of an Earth satellite offer a different type of predictable mechanical process. The satellite initially follows a path determined by the rocket propelling it, but it eventually achieves a stable and predictable orbit. In contradistinction to example (i), in this case the predicted equilibrium outcome achieved is dynamic rather than static.

(iii) An example from thermodynamics is the case of an ice cube exposed in a warm room. Depending on its volume and the temperature, it will melt in a predictable way and be converted into a puddle of water and atmospheric moisture. If the room is sealed, an equilibrium will be established between the liquid and gaseous water. However, in terms of the molecules that constitute the water, predictability in an exact sense is impossible. The description of the behaviour of the water molecules at thermodynamic equilibrium can be at best stochastic.

(iv)   The life-cycle of an organism is generally predictable. The life of a chicken begins as a fertilized egg, continues as a chick developing within the eggshell, progresses to the newly hatched chick, and thence the mature chicken, the old chicken, and the dead chicken. In this example, while the general pattern of the process is well known, the detailed development of a particular chicken will be impossible to predict with any accuracy.

(v)   For an economic example of a predictable process, we can consider a simple market which is initially not at equilibrium; that is, the price of the commodity does not equate supply with demand. Assuming that market mechanisms exist to allow adjustment of supply and demand, using price signals, we would expect that eventually a market equilibrium would be established. The exact time path of the adjustment would, of course, depend on the exact nature of the supply and demand functions and the adjustment process involved.

From these five illustrations we conclude that a predictable process, as we will understand it, is one whose time-path can be described deterministically or stochastically.

An important further characteristic of many predictable processes is that they are 'equifinal'. We call a process equifinal, if, given certain boundary conditions, the predictable outcome is independent of the initial conditions governing the process. For example, if a small ball is placed anywhere on the inner surface of a large bowl, then under gravity the ball will eventually settle at the unique base of the bowl. We see that the final position of the ball is predictable, and is also independent of the initial position of the ball. It is therefore clear that any equifinal process whose dynamic behaviour is known is predictable, though, of course, not all predictable systems are equifinal.

2.2.2 Predictability and Ignorance

Beyond the dichotomy between predictable and unpredictable processes, we have already introduced the notion of processes of which we are (a) completely or (b) partially ignorant. Of course, as long as we remain in ignorance of (a) whole processes, or (b) certain aspects of known processes, these processes, or these aspects of processes, remain outside our dichotomy concerning predictability

Ignorance is an essential constituent of living. All scientific endeavours are made because there exists ignorance concerning many aspects of the world. If we have reason to assume that this ignorance is reducible then we can make efforts to reduce it by study, i.e. by observation, applying scientific methods, etc. In this way it may become possible to predict processes, or aspects of processes, which in former times were unpredictable. However, it is often the case that our ignorance is irreducible. Then, essential traits of processes cannot be predicted, even when we know a great deal about them. An illustration is the weather. We recognize that we cannot exactly predict the weather, though it is in principle predictable, as it is governed by (very complex) deterministic laws. This inability to predict can largely be attributed to the weather being extremely dependent on the initial conditions for its determination, and our inability to determine these boundary conditions sufficiently accurately. (This problem is discussed further in Chapter 5, with the problem of dynamic 'chaos').

The notion of ignorance is relevant because it reminds us, on the one hand, of the limits to predictability which lie in the human structure of cognition. But on the other hand, there are also limits to predictability which lie in the nature of certain processes themselves[2]. It is to such processes that we turn in the next section.

2.2.3 Unpredictable Processes

We now give three examples of processes which are in principle unpredictable; i.e. independent of our state of knowledge or ignorance. These illustrations are taken from physics, biology and economics.

(i)   The first example we use may surprise the reader somewhat, but it illustrates an important point to which we wish to return later. There is a growing literature suggesting that what we now regard as Universal Physical Constants (e.g. the gravitational constant G, Planck's constant h, etc.) were far from constant in the first few microseconds after the Big Bang which brought the universe into being. At the time of the Big Bang it seems that these constants could have ended up with values different from those they finally assumed. Modern theory therefore suggests that the whole nature of the universe was, in principle, unpredictable at the time of the Big Bang [HAWKING 1988] (for more details see Section 2.4).

---

[2] Both types of ignorance will be analysed extensively in Chapter 7.

(ii)   The whole history of the evolution of species demonstrates unpredictability. Surely no reasonably intelligent dinosaur would have expected that this very successful and long-established group of species would not only be extinguished, but replaced by mammals.

(iii)   The modern world we inhabit is largely the product of cumulated human inventiveness. By its very nature, inventiveness is unpredictable, for correctly to predict the nature of an invention is equivalent to making that invention.

(iv)   Another important sphere of creative activity, involving the emergence of unpredictable novelty, is artistic endeavour, in music, literature, etc. For instance, the move from representational art to non-representational methods in the early twentieth century was certainly note foreseen, though ex post it can be understood.

2.2.4 Predictability and Ex Ante Theory

As noted above, to speak of 'predictable' and 'unpredictable' processes is to make a rough categorization. When speaking of 'predictability' in the following, we will often mean '*in principle* predictable'. By this we mean that it is possible to get to know the dynamics of a system, which allows one to make some predictions concerning future developments. It is also useful to note that when we say that a process is 'predictable in broad terms', this only means that we can say at least something about its behaviour, be it that it is equifinal, unstable, chaotic, stochastic, etc. In the case of processes which are predictable in broad terms, there may remain areas of ignorance. This implies that whenever we are able to conceive an ex ante theory about an empirical subject we are able to obtain 'predictable' results, at least in 'broad terms'. In this sense, this part of the book deals with the question: 'In which cases can one hope to develop ex ante theories?'

It is obvious from the above considerations that the concepts of predictability and unpredictability are difficult to define. It was for this reason that we have been using the terms 'predictability in principle' and 'predictability in broad terms'. However, we hope that the above examples give the reader an idea of what we mean by these terms. Once one accepts these notions, it is useful to relate them to other important concepts.

The first such concept is 'novelty'. Let us consider the class of all processes which are 'unpredictable in principle'. Events generated by this class of processes we term 'novel events', or simply 'novelty'[3]. We shall therefore speak of the 'emergence of novelty' from in principle unpredictable processes.

Wherever an area of study is in an essential way subject to the emergence of novelty, an ex ante theory cannot be developed. To give a simple illustration, it is not possible to conceive a theory on the behaviour of lions as long as lions do not exist.

2.3 Conceptual Elements of Biological Evolution

In this section we shall draw upon some well developed concepts from biology; in particular we shall use the notions of phenotype and genotype employed in the Darwinian framework of the evolution of species. We shall relate these evolutionary concepts to the notions of predictable and unpredictable processes, as developed in Section 2.2. In particular we shall contrast predictable and equifinal processes with unpredictable processes.

As the concepts of phenotype and genotype are central to all our discussions below, we first define these terms as they are generally used in biology.

An organism has a certain appearance, capabilities, characteristics, etc. The appearance that it presents to the world is known as its phenotype. The phenotype displayed by an organism results from the interplay of two factors. The first factor is the potential inherited from its parents; i.e. its genetic make-up, or genotype. The second factor is the environment of the organism; for example, organisms that are otherwise identical (e.g. identical twins) will grow to different sizes and exhibit differing capabilities if they are subjected to widely differing nutritional regimes.

It is generally accepted, in biological systems, that the genotype affects the phenotype directly, but there is no such direct influence of phenotype on genotype. For example, a chance mutation may cause the genotype to alter, such that the phenotype becomes, for example, longer-necked. Further, this characteristic of being longer-necked may be inherited by that creature's offspring. On the other hand, an animal might, through its feeding habits, stretch its neck, thus altering its phenotype. This alteration will not influence its genotype and therefore this will not be a heritable characteristic.

---

[3] This notion of novelty will be broadened in Chapter 7.

From the above discussion it is clear that the genotype reflects the 'potentialities' of the organism. The phenotype represents the 'realization' of these potentialities, in so far as is permitted by the environment of this organism. In all the discussion that follows we shall be concerned with how the potentialities of biological, physical and economic systems evolve, and also how the realizations of these potentialities evolve.

To clarify the concepts of potentiality and genotype, it is helpful to draw on the discussion of novelty at the end of the preceding section. In terms of novelty, we may say that the potentialities at a certain point in time comprise all possible future events, through the interaction with the environment, with the exception of novelty. Hence a change in the potentialities of a system, i.e. a change in its genotype, is equivalent to the occurrence of novelty.

As a convenient short-hand, and to reflect our desire to discover a fundamental conceptualization of evolution, when we refer to 'realizations' we shall use the term 'phenotype', and when referring to 'potentialities' we shall use 'genotype'.

2.3.1 Organism, Species and Biological System

At this stage it will be useful to clarify what is meant by 'organism', 'species' and 'biological system'.

An *organism* is the basic unit of independent life, whether plant or animal, that contributes to reproduction.

A *species* is the set of all organisms whose genotypes are so similar that they allow interbreeding (e.g. horses, dogs, primroses, etc.).

A *biological system* consists of an interacting set of species, each species being made up of distinct but genetically similar organisms. For example, the flora and fauna which coexist in and on an area of wetland would constitute a biological system.

The phenotype as described above refers to an individual organism. As organisms, of their various species, interact with each other in large and heterogeneous biological systems, it is useful to consider an overall description of such a biological system. Such a description would be a listing of the phenotypes of all the organisms within the biological system in terms of the species represented and their relative abundances. We term this description a 'macro-phenotype'.

Similarly, the genetic potential of a biological system of organisms could be listed to give that system's 'macro-genotype'. This list comprises all genotypic information of all organisms of the corresponding system, and is independent of the relative frequencies of the organisms.

The advantage of descriptions of biological systems in terms of macro-phenotype and macro-genotype is that it gives explicit recognition to the fact that the evolutionary process deals with systems rather than with individual organisms, as is more fully discussed in Sections 2.3.4 and 2.3.5 below.

There has been a long-running debate in evolutionary biology as to whether the unit of evolution is best conceived as being the individual organism, the species, or the entire heterogeneous system [LEVINS and LEWONTIN 1985].

We have noted above the usefulness of describing systems in terms of the macro-phenotype and macro-genotype. It is clear from our discussion that an individual organism can only exhibit phenotypic evolution, but not genotypic evolution, because for the latter at least two successive organisms have to exist in order to exhibit genotypic change. In contrast, a species can exhibit not only phenotypic but also genotypic evolution. The genotypic evolution of a species, however, is influenced by that of other species. It is therefore not possible to study the evolution of one species in isolation. For this reason it is useful to consider the biological system as our unit of evolution.

2.3.2 Phenotypic Evolution: Predictable Equifinal Processes

Macro-phenotypic evolution relates to the relationships between, and the relative abundances of, a number of species in mutual interaction in a given environment, where the genetic make-up, or macro-genotype, of the mixture of species is taken to be given. For example, the process of ecosystem succession subsequent to some traumatic event may lead to systematic changes over time of relative species (macro-phenotype) abundance. For instance, a major fire in an area of woodland will destroy the majority of the vegetation. In the years subsequent to the fire there will first be rapid growth of small plants; later the fast-growing trees will become established, and their shade will reduce the growth of the already established low-growing plants. Ultimately, slower growing but bigger and more robust trees will themselves shade out the faster growing trees. It is clear that in such circumstances the proportions of the species, i.e.

macro-phenotypes, will change radically, but systematically and predictably, over time. It is in this sense that we consider phenotypic evolution to be a predictable process.

One might illustrate the concept of phenotypic evolution by using a simple two-phenotype model, with the dynamics of their interaction shown on a phase diagram. In Fig. 2.1 is plotted the relative abundances of two biological species, as they vary over time. For example, phenotype 1 may be a herbivore and phenotype 2 its foodplant. The arrows indicate the direction of the evolutionary process from any particular starting point along the corresponding phase path. It is clear that an unique, stable equilibrium exists at point A. In the terminology of Section 2.2, we could say that the process described is predictable and equifinal.

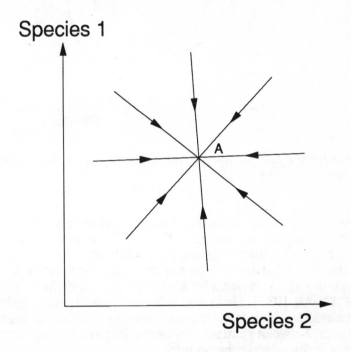

Fig. 2.1. A stable phenotypic equilibrium with two species.

Fig. 2.2 shows a common alternative relationship between two phenotypes. Phenotype 1 in this case is a carnivorous predator and phenotype 2 is its prey animal [CLARK 1976]. Here we see the long-run outcome is a limit-cycle, so that the observed abundances over time in the long-run of these phenotypes will be out-of-phase oscillations over time, as shown in Fig. 2.3.

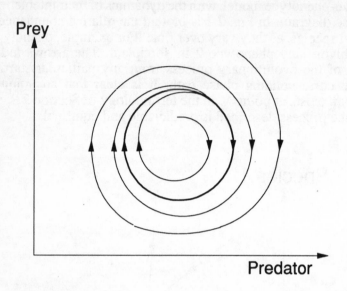

Fig. 2.2. A limit-cycle phenotypic equilibrium with a two species predator-prey system.

The reader will, of course, recognize that in a biological system with many species and organisms, the nature of the equilibria, and the details of the adjustment dynamics, may be extremely complicated. For example, recent work has suggested that the dynamics of some ecosystems may be 'chaotic', as the dynamics are dominated by a 'strange attractor' [MAY and OSTER 1976; BELTRAMI 1987]. However, even such complicated systems will exhibit behaviour which is systematic and reproducible, at least in their broad outlines, between similar ecosystems. It is in this sense that we may say that it is predictable in 'broad terms'.

Phenotypic evolution may also occur when the system is disturbed, for example by an alteration in climate or some other change in the environment. Another source of disturbance leading to phenotypic evolution, that has been well documented, is the introduction into a biological system of a new genotype, with its corresponding phenotype [CROSBY 1986]. Although the disturbance may be of an unpredictable nature, be it because of ignorance or novelty, the consequences of this disturbance may be predictable. The effect will be to shift the equilibrium

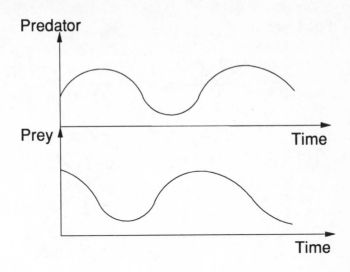

Fig. 2.3. Species population oscillations in a predator-prey model.

of the ecosystem, leading to a process of adjustment from the old equilibrium to the new one. For example, the European rat was unknown in many Pacific and Atlantic island ecosystems until the arrival of European explorers and traders. The rat was introduced accidentally from the European ships, so these ecosystems received a new phenotype. These rats rapidly established themselves on these islands and proved to be fierce competitors for resources with the indigenous fauna. Over a period of decades they became important, even dominant, components of the island ecosystems. Eventually, new equilibria were established, where the existing macro-phenotype was changed both in species represented, and markedly different in relative species abundances, compared with the situation prior to the introduction of rats.

This type of process is illustrated in Fig. 2.4, where a particular herbivore is partially, or even completely, replaced by a new one which has been introduced into the ecosystem. Here the term 'herbivore' is used to represent an entire system of various types of herbivores. The introduction of the new phenotype markedly alters the characteristics of this system, and hence causes the equilibrium to shift.

From the above discussion we see that phenotypic evolution involves alterations to the relative abundances of species, but no alteration to the underlying potentialities of these species, as embodied in their genotypes. Therefore, such evolution does not involve the emergence of novelty, as the species are taken as given. Further, phenotypic evolution is susceptible

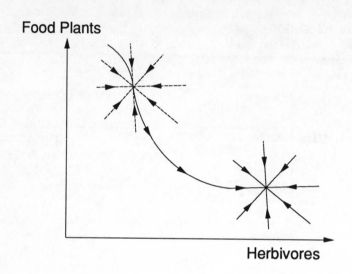

Fig. 2.4. A shifted phenotypic equilibrium.

to description, in principle, in terms of dynamic models which give rise to well-specified, and predictable, outcomes. In particular, these outcomes are equilibria, which indicates that phenotypic evolution exhibits predictability. If the equilibrium is unique, the system is also equifinal.

2.3.3 Genotypic Evolution: Unpredictable Processes

Let us recall the meaning of the term genotype. For an organism the genotype is the underlying description of its potential for development, in interaction with its environment. In organisms the genotype is embodied in the genetic material, which mainly resides in the nuclei of the organism's cells.

Changes to the genotype of an organism will be inherited by its progeny, and this new genotype may give rise to a new phenotype. In organisms, alterations to genotypes typically occur through the effects of chemicals or ionising radiation (e.g. gamma rays, X-rays, ultraviolet light, etc.) on the reproductive organs. As we shall discuss below, changes to the genotype for economic systems correspond to, for example, changing available techniques of production.

Genotypic evolution may be defined as the alteration of the genotypic description of an organism and its progeny over time. For example, the chance impact of a cosmic ray upon an animal's genetic material may alter that genotype so that the animal's progeny have, say, a slightly longer neck. The first-generation progeny may, in turn, produce second-generation progeny which are also longer-necked.

It is well understood that random alteration to the genetic material of organisms only rarely produces mutations which 'improve' the capabilities of that organism's progeny. Therefore the process of changing the genotype is usually extremely slow, although there have been occasional cases of it being recorded in recent times (e.g. the appearance of melanic [dark coloured] moths in nineteenth century industrial Britain) [KETTLEWELL 1973]. Only long and patient study by palaeontologists has given us a still partial understanding of the genotypes that existed on earth over the past three billion years. Such study has also indicated the relative abundances of the genotypes and how, over very long periods, the appearance of new genotypes led to changes in the relative abundance of the phenotypes.

Unlike phenotypic evolution, genotypic evolution is unpredictable. This unpredictability arises from three sources.

1. The mutating influence (e.g. radiation) cannot be specified beforehand.

2. The effect of the mutating influence on the genetic material cannot be predicted.

3. The influence of this genetic change on the phenotype is also unpredictable.

In economic terminology this means that we are confronted with true uncertainty if genotypic evolution occurs. (We shall return to the concept of uncertainty in Chapters 4 and 7).

2.3.4 Genotypic and Phenotypic Evolution in Biological Systems

It must be stressed again that changes to biological genotypes take place extremely slowly. In contrast, the relative abundance of phenotypes may change relatively rapidly, as discussed in Section 2.3.1. The full scheme of biological evolution is thus seen to be the interplay of extremely slow and unpredictable changes to macro-genotypes with relatively rapid but predictable changes to macro-phenotypes.

It is worth noting that the very different rates of phenotypic and genotypic evolution in biological systems allows the predictable and unpredictable parts of the whole evolutionary process to be distinguished. (As we shall discuss in Chapter 3, in economic evolutionary processes it is usually much more difficult to separate out the predictable from the unpredictable processes).

To illustrate the interaction of genotypic and phenotypic evolution in a biological system, let us imagine an ecosystem composed of a given macro-genotype. We suppose that this system has been left undisturbed sufficiently long for it to achieve an 'equilibrium' state (such 'equilibria' may be stationary, limit cycles or chaotic). Now let us suppose that there is a significant alteration of one of the genotypes in the system, and we further suppose that this new genotype is reflected in improved, but unpredictable, 'competitive effectiveness' of its progeny. The result of this appearance of a new and more competitive phenotype will be a predictable macro-phenotypic evolution, leading to altered relative abundances of these phenotypes, and hence of the embodied genotype. The outcome of the macro-phenotypic evolution will therefore be a changed relative frequency of species genotypes.

The long-run genotypic evolution can be illustrated by reference to the observed evolution of certain predator and prey species [BAKKER 1983]. We begin by considering such an interaction with a given pair of genotypes, and with an equilibrium phenotypic relative abundance. Let us suppose a random genetic mutation causes the prey phenotype to become longer-legged and swifter. Supposing further that the genotype of the predator is unchanged, then the relative abundance of the phenotype will evolve towards a new equilibrium, as shown in Fig. 2.5.

Point A1 represents the equilibrium for the phenotypes of the original genotypes. With the introduction of the new genotype of the prey a new phenotypic equilibrium is established at A2. Phenotypic evolution takes place as the system moves from point A1, which is now no longer an equilibrium, towards A2 along the corresponding phase path.

Any mutation in the predator genotype which increases its swiftness will in turn generate yet a further new equilibrium at A3 so that a further phenotypic evolution would take place, as shown in Fig. 2.6.

This series of mutations of genotypes will lead to successive periods of phenotypic evolution.

Now in biological evolution, genotypic mutations which are 'beneficial' take place at intervals which are long compared with the time taken in phenotypic evolution to re-establish 'equilibrium'. Thus, in the long-run time scale, the observed macro-genotypic evolution can be represented by the locus of the successive macro-phenotypic equilibria, as shown in Fig. 2.7.

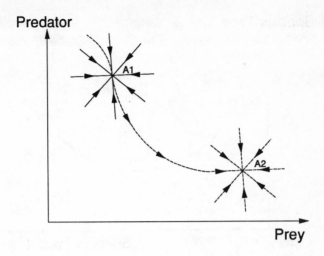

Fig. 2.5. Genotypic evolution of phenotypic abundance for two species (1).

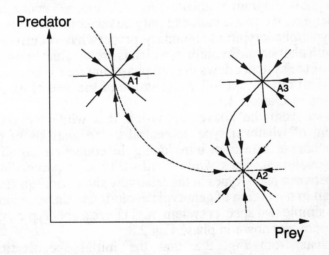

Fig. 2.6. Genotypic evolution of phenotypic abundance for two species (2).

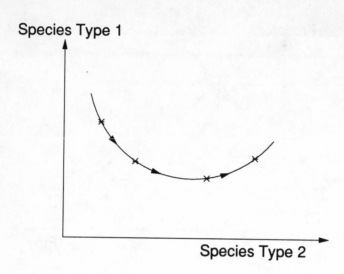

Fig. 2.7. Long-run locus of phenotypic abundances under genotypic evolution.

Fig. 2.7 can itself be interpreted as an evolutionary phase diagram. But unlike the phase diagram in phenotypic evolution, as genotypic evolution is unpredictable, the phase path can only be constructed ex post, i.e. once the genotypic/phenotypic evolutionary process has occurred. This is in contrast with phenotypic evolution, which is predictable; knowledge of the dynamics of the system allows the full phase diagram to be constructed ex ante. We shall return to a fuller discussion of the role of ex post and ex ante analysis in Chapter 3.

It follows from the above discussion that while the notion of an equilibrium, of whatever type, is central to the analysis of phenotypic evolution, there is no way of introducing the concept of equilibrium into genotypic evolution. Thus while equifinality is important in assessing relations between phenotypes in the relatively short-run, equifinality plays no part at all in the notion of genotypic evolution in the very long-run. For example a simple two species system might have a genotypic evolutionary phase diagram, as shown in phase Fig. 2.8.

It is clear from Fig. 2.8 that the initial specification of the macro-genotype leads to a unique evolutionary path. For example, if in an isolated ecosystem (e.g. a large island) the system were in state A initially,

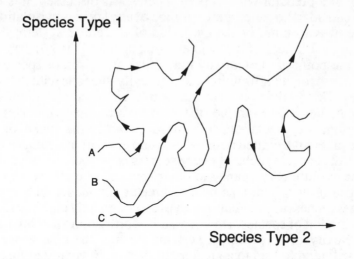

Fig. 2.8. A two species genotypic evolutionary phase diagram.

while other isolated ecosystems were in states B and C, there will be no
reason to expect that long-run genotypic evolution would lead to similar
outcomes.

To illustrate this, consider the cases of Australia and New Zealand, which
were isolated from what is now the Asian landmass approximately forty
million years ago, and from each other shortly thereafter (in geologic
terms). In Australia there has evolved a rich fauna of marsupials, such as
kangaroos and wombats, while in New Zealand the fauna came to be
dominated by flightless birds such as the kiwi and the moa. [KEAST 1981].

From these illustrations we see that the time-path of a process exhibiting
genotypic evolution has no 'end'. We can expect that genotypic evolution
will be a never-ending process. Certainly, there is no particular final state
towards which it tends, unlike the many systems exhibiting predictable
equifinal phenotypic evolution.

2.3.5 Coevolution and Niches

Genotypic evolution is sometimes described in terms of being 'selected'
by interaction with the environment. The environment can be viewed as a
'filter' of the corresponding phenotypes. However, every species, and
indeed every organism, is part of the environment of each organism in a

biological system. As described in Section 3.3, where successive genotypic evolution of a predator with its prey species was discussed, it is less than useful to consider the genotypic evolution of any species in isolation. Much more useful is to think of the evolution of the entire system; that is, to consider 'coevolution' of many interacting species [THOMPSON 1982].

From the point of view of any individual organism, or species, only a limited amount of the full environment actually interacts with the organism or species. This limited range of interacting environment is known as the species' 'niche'. For example, the niche of the honeybee comprises a limited range of vegetation and airspace, while the niche of the fox comprises a relative limited range of land and the flora and fauna it contains.

In coevolution, the niche of every species is periodically disturbed by a genotypic evolutionary change to other species. Sometimes a niche may be enlarged or enriched, leading to a greater abundance of a species. At other times niches may be reduced, or even completely eliminated, leading to the extinction of species. However, it is worth noting that an increase in the complexity of a biological system, through the emergence of new species, will tend to lead to a greater number and diversity of niches. This will open up possibilities for further genotypic evolution. This is clear when we recognise that any new organism that evolves can act, for example, as both a prey (or forage) species for external predation, and as a host to parasites. Therefore the process of macro-genotypic evolution has the potential to sustain itself, and may lead to ever increasing complexity and diversity, through the continual opening up of new niches.

We shall indicate the importance of the concepts of coevolution and niches for economic evolution in Chapter 3.

We now turn to a discussion of the role of phenotypic and genotypic evolution in physical systems, before we move on to an analysis of evolutionary concepts in economics in Chapter 3.

2.4 Evolution in Physical Systems
2.4.1 Novelty

In our discussion on biological evolution we have stressed that the potentialities of a system, its genotype, interacts with the environment to give a realization of these potentialities, in the phenotype. The systems with which physics is mainly concerned have their potentialities defined by the fundamental constants and laws of nature. The realization of these potentialities is the observed behaviour of that physical system.

We therefore define the genotype for a physical system to be its potentialities; i.e. the fundamental constants and laws of nature. We similarly define the phenotype of a physical system to be the realization of those potentialities; i.e. its observed physical behaviour. As a consequence of this conceptualization, we see that, unlike biological systems, all realised physical systems have the same genotype. That is, different physical phenotypes are not derived from different physical genotypes.

As was discussed under the heading of 'predictable processes' in Section 2.2.1, predictable changes are often exhibited by physical systems. As these changes are in the nature and appearance of the physical world, in its realization, we term such change phenotypic evolution.

To illustrate how the potentialities (the genotype) of the physical world may, through interaction with the environment, give rise to a phenotype and to phenotypic evolution, we present the following simple example.

A ball held a certain distance above a pavement has potential energy because of its position and because of the laws of nature. If the ball is released, the interaction of the ball and the pavement cause it to behave in a certain predictable manner. The system containing the ball and the pavement tends towards a new physical equilibrium. The underlying genotype of this whole process is the laws of nature. As we know the initial conditions, and as there is no genotypic evolution, we can say that the system exhibits predictable phenotypic evolution.

From the above discussion it should be clear that physical systems, like biological systems, may exhibit phenotypic evolution towards an equilibrium state. However, unlike different biological systems, physical systems all share a unique and unchanging genotype, comprising the physical constants and the laws of nature.

We mentioned in Section 2.2.3 that modern thought suggests that the universe was unpredictable in its first few moments, as the physical constants attained their present values. One could say, therefore, that even physical systems have experienced one period of genotypic evolution, albeit for a vanishingly short length of time. Even if this theory should be falsified, it is important because it introduces an understanding of time and evolution into physics, instead of the still present myth of 'eternal laws of nature'.

2.4.2 Ignorance

One important development in modern physics is the exploration of the theory of chaos, which will be discussed in Chapter 5, Sections 5.4 and 5.5. Consideration of chaotic systems shows us that we cannot escape large areas of ignorance which limit our human possibilities of cognition. This ignorance has the consequence that we meet chaotic structures which are 'novel' for us, in the sense that we are not able to form realistic expectations of them. Here we may speak of the emergence of 'chaotic novelty', to which we return in Chapter 5 and extensively in Chapter 7. Although chaotic behaviour should not be described in terms of genotypic evolution, as there is no change in potentialities, nevertheless it offers features which are similar to genotypic evolution.

2.5 Novelty, Genotypes and Hierarchy

In this chapter we have stressed the difference between the *potentialities* of a system (its genotype), and the *realization* of those potentialities (its phenotype). So far we have discussed biology and physics in these terms, and in the next chapter we shall similarly discuss the phenotypes and genotypes of economic systems.

Now much modern natural science implicitly assumes one can find a physical understanding of biological systems; this has been called the 'reductionist fallacy' by KOESTLER [1967]. Also, it is implicit in much social science that biological explanations are available for human behaviour, including economic behaviour.

If these two assumptions hold, how can there be more than a single genotype, viz. the physical genotype? Further, above we argued that this genotype is presently unchanging, so how can there be any emergence of novelty? One rather brusque reply would be to ask, 'What use is quantum mechanics for understanding biological evolutionary strategies, or for doing macroeconomics?'.

The point here is that there is a hierarchy of knowledge structures which science, including social science, seeks to encompass. At the base we have physical science, now including chemistry, where quantum mechanics is often very useful. As part of the realization (phenotype) of the physical genotype we have complex structures, including biological structures.

Thus in the next layer of the hierarchy we have the biological sciences, where at the scale of macro-organisms, and in terms of long-run evolution, a completely different set of concepts from physical science has been found useful and necessary. A part of the realization of the potentialities of biological systems are human beings.

So the next stage of the hierarchy is social activity, including economics. Here again different types of modelling and different concepts have been formulated, that distinguish social science from the physical and biological sciences.

It is this hierarchical layering, where the concepts and techniques of one layer cannot easily be applied to either the layers above or below, that allows for the conceptualization of independent genotypes and phenotypes in different disciplines.

With regard to novelty, if one took the view that the physical genotype was a complete description of the potentialities of all levels of the hierarchy, and one also assumed that one had unlimited powers of theorising and computation, i.e. there is no ignorance, then one could think of being able to calculate all possible states of the world at all past and future times. In these circumstances there could never be any novelty.

The above is reminiscent of LAPLACE's concept of the computability of the natural world. It is, of course, not presently possible, nor is it remotely in prospect. Indeed, it has been argued that it is, in principle, an impossible notion [PRIGOGINE and STENGERS 1984:Chapters 2, 3].

If one accepts that LAPLACE's dream of computability can only remain a dream, then the notions of ignorance and novelty must be accepted. Things do happen which were unexpected and not predicted. One must accept that human knowledge is limited, and unexpected increases in that knowledge base can occur.

2.6 Conclusions

Understanding the long-run confronts us squarely with the problem of predictability, ignorance and the emergence of novelty. In this chapter we have drawn on concepts from biology to show that precisely the emergence of novelty has been encountered in discussing biological evolution.

We have distinguished between the potentialities of a system, the genotype, and the realization of those potentialities, the phenotype. We noted that the concept of evolution can be applied to both the changes over time of the phenotype and the genotype. The evolution of the phenotype is predictable in principle, albeit subject to the problem of human ignorance, while the evolution of the genotype is not predictable in principle.

We have also suggested that the concept of genotype and phenotype is applicable to physical systems, though the genotype in such systems is unchanging at present.

Finally, we have noted that there is a hierarchy of conceptualization to science, both natural and social. Further, the impossibility of computing all future events means that knowledge of the future is limited, i.e. there is ignorance, and there exists the possibility of the emergence of novelty. (The distinction between knowledge of the past and the future is a theme that will be taken up in detail in Part III).

In the next chapter we shall apply these concepts of evolutionary change to economic systems, and seek to show how economics differs from physics and biology in its conceptual structure and concerns, as dictated by the relative speeds of phenotypic and genotypic evolution that occur in the three disciplines.

3 An Evolutionary Approach to Production and Innovation

3.1 Introduction

In this chapter we apply our evolutionary concepts to economics, in particular to production and innovation. Section 3.2 discusses the application of the concepts of 'genotype' and 'phenotype' to economic systems.

In Section 3.3 we analyse one main area of evolutionary economics, the interaction between invention, innovation and the natural world.

Section 3.4 shows why physics is 'easy' and economics is 'difficult', with biology 'in between', because of the different relationships between genotypic and phenotypic evolution in the three disciplines.

In Section 3.5 the importance of ex post and ex ante considerations for conceptualizing evolution are discussed.

Section 3.6 offers some conclusions for economic analysis.

3.2 Economic Genotypes and Phenotypes

In economics, as in biology and physics, we can conceptualize economies in terms of potentialities and their realizations. The former we will call economic genotypes, and the latter economic phenotypes. Before proceeding, we should point out that in practice often it may not be easy to distinguish between these two categories, for reasons to be discussed below. We also note that we again encounter again the problem of ignorance in this chapter.

We first consider economic genotypes. The notion of the genotype in this broad sense has not, up to now, been defined in economics[1]. Unlike in biology, there is no obvious evidence for an economic genotype. Hence there does not exist an obvious way to recognize changes of an economic genotype i.e. economic mutations. However, if we consider social activity as a macro-phenotype (i.e. an interaction of various social phenomena), we often observe changes that cannot be predicted ex ante. For example, we observe the emergence of new preference orderings, new technologies,

---

[1] NELSON and WINTER [1982:160] use this expression in a very specific way (see also 128-134).

as well as new legal, economic and social institutions. Such processes of change may lead to a complete reorganization of the macro-phenotype, i.e. social activity.

How can these transformations of the macro-phenotype be understood? To this end, we believe it is helpful to suppose there has occurred a change in the potentialities of the social system; i.e. a genotypic change. Although the essential genotype of society is not exhibited by this change, and hence cannot be observed directly, we may highlight those structures which are particularly apt to be considered as candidates for social genotypes.

The elements of an economy which we consider to be suitable candidates for the economic genotype are as follows:

1. Preference orderings of the economic agents (including religious and ethical norms).

2. The technology (i.e. the set of all techniques which are known in that economy).

3. The legal, economic and social institutions.

If we observe changes in any of these three elements we shall speak of genotypic change of the economy. The nature of these elements defines the potentialities of a particular economy, i.e. defines its genotype.

As mentioned above, in Chapter 2 Section 2.3, the phenotype in biology results from the interplay of the genotype and the natural environment. The same holds for the economic phenotype. It can be conceived of as resulting from the interaction of the economic genotype and those aspects of the (natural) environment relevant to the society, such as the endowment of natural resources[2] and ecological conditions. From this it follows that even if the economic genotype is constant, the development of the economic phenotype may alter, because of changes in the environment.

The economic phenotype is a realization of these potentialities. For a market economy it may contain the following elements:

1. The techniques of production employed.

2. The types of capital goods employed, and their amounts.

---

[2] The endowment of resources is determined both by the naturally occurring materials, and by the technology available. Material can only be regarded as a resource if it can be exploited (e.g. before 1940 uranium was not a valuable resource, but simply an available type of material).

3. The types of capital and consumption goods produced.

4. The quantities of these goods, and their prices.

5. The distribution of consumption, income and wealth among the economic agents.

6. The market structure.

From the above definition it is clear that, just as in biology we defined the unit of evolution to be the whole interacting biological system, so for economics we define the unit of evolution to be the entire set of interacting economic agents and their institutions and artefacts. We note that over the course of history, the size and complexity of economic systems, and thus our unit of economic evolution, has tended to increase. For a self-sufficient hunter-gatherer society the unit would be the band, while at the present time the high level of integration of national economies suggests that the unit of evolution should be regarded as the global economy.

We suggest that the great bulk of dynamic economic modelling can be regarded in terms of the evolution of economic phenotypes. For example, comparative international trade theory can be conceptualized as phenotypic evolution. In the classical model, England shifts its production towards cloth, while Portugal shifts its production towards wine. The equilibrium pattern of trade that is eventually established is mainly dependent upon the structure of production, tastes, resources and techniques available. Pursuing this example further, were there to be a disruption to this equilibrium pattern, and this disruption was then removed, the equilibrium pattern would be re-established in due course.

Considering entire societies, some exhibit very slow rates of genotypic change, and hence can be adequately described purely in terms of the phenotype. Hunter-gatherer societies seem to have changed very little over many thousands of years, and peasant agrarian societies also seem to show relatively stable genotypes. This, of course, is in contrast to the rapid rates of genotypic change exhibited by modern industrial socities. From these considerations it follows that the distinction between genotype and phenotype might be useful for the analysis of economic history. Very often the assumption of given constraints to behaviour by economic agents, and a general expectation of optimising by these agents, will give us equilibrium outcomes; i.e. the system will be predictable and equifinal. This tendency in economic analysis is most clearly seen in the struggle by general equilibrium theorists to discover 'reasonable' models of economic activity which give rise to unique and stable equilibria in price-quantity space. In our view, this working through of the dynamics of economic systems, where tastes, techniques and resource availability are taken as fixed, can justifiably be termed economic phenotypic evolution.

Genotypic evolution, by contrast, requires changes in tastes and techniques, as well as in economic institutions. For example, the process of industrialization of the past two hundred years has been one of continually changing economic institutions, changing techniques of production, and a continually expanding list of natural resources which have been put to economic use. For instance, discoveries in physics stimulated the engineering development of nuclear power, which rendered uranium an economic resource, whereas previously it had been regarded as a material of only limited usefulness. The development of microelectronics and the corresponding increase in the economic valuation of germanium (used in transistors) is another example of this process of economic genotypic evolution.

Just as in the biological illustration above, economic genotypic evolution cannot involve the notion of an equilibrium outcome. Unlike the case of biological evolution, however, economic genotypic evolution may take place very rapidly, as is particularly evident in the evolution of the microelectronics industry. Indeed, the rate of change of the genotypic specification (the technical capabilities) in this industry is so rapid that successive changes in specification occur before a new phenotypic equilibrium can be established. The very notion of an equilibrium in such rapidly evolving industries seems to us therefore to be of limited usefulness. The complexity of the phenotypic response to such rapid genotypic evolution is illustrated is Fig. 3.1.

In Fig. 3.1 rapid genotypic change moves the equilibrium of the phenotype from point A to point B, and subsequently to points C and D. The rate of phenotypic evolution towards these successive equilibria is, for economic systems, of the same order as the rate of genotypic evolution. The result is that phenotypic evolution proceeds along the ray towards the stable equilibrium B which passes through point A. However, the genotype changes before equilibrium B is achieved, and the phase path shifts to one converging on C, the new equilibrium. At point b on the original phase path, the old phase path is replaced by a new phase path leading towards the new equilibrium. This new phenotypic evolution is also incomplete, as by the time the system achieves point c, the phenotypic equilibrium has shifted to D.

It is important to note that in Fig. 3.1 the observed trajectory of the system in phase space is a combination of several rays associated with different equilibria, and except for the starting point, no phenotypic equilibrium state is attained, or even very closely approached, as long as genotypic change continues.

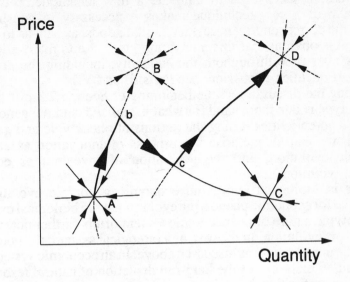

Price

Quantity

Fig. 3.1. Combined genotypic and phenotypic evolution for an economic system.

3.3 The Interaction Between Invention and Innovation

In this Section we shall restrict our analysis to one main area of evolutionary economics, the interaction between invention, innovation and the natural world. To introduce these concepts we first need to define some terms.

The *technology* of an economy, at any moment in time, is the set of techniques which are known, even though not necessarily all of them will be used.

Invention is the addition of a novel technique, which thus expands the technology.

Innovation is the process of introducing a technique of the technology which is not currently being used.

While invention occurs at some point in time (or during a relatively short time period), it takes time to innovate a new technique, because the introduction of a new technique makes it necessary to construct and establish the corresponding necessary capital goods, as well as to train the workers. It is obvious that this innovation gives rise to many adjustment processes over time throughout the economy, including the process of diffusion. (For fuller discussions see Parts III and V.)

Recalling the discussion at the beginning of Section 2.3 of Chapter 2, the phenotype is our short-hand for what is realized, and the genotype for a system's potentialities. Using the notions of phenotypic and genotypic evolution, we can characterise the process of innovation as economic phenotypic evolution, and the generation of invention as economic genotypic evolution.

Just as in biological evolution, economic genotypic evolution is a prerequisite for economic phenotypic evolution. As in biological evolution, the phenotypic nature of the economic system offers further potentialities for genotypic evolution. In the case of a biological system, the potentiality lies in niche exploitation, as discussed above. In an economic system, niche destruction, in the sense of the long-run depletion of natural resources, is an important motivation for seeking an improvement in economic technical potentialities; i.e. in seeking economic genotypic change. This genotypic change leads, in turn, to niche production through the bringing into use of new natural resources.

We may illustrate the interplay of phenotypic and genotypic evolution as follows. Consider a resource using economy which, through the workings of its market system, has established a predictable equilibrium; i.e. relative prices and relative quantities produced are stable and overall output of the economy is growing at a predictable rate. This would be equivalent to the phenotypic equilibrium of an ecosystem, as discussed above in Section 2.3.2 of Chapter 2 (see e.g. Fig. 2.1). If the resources used are steadily depleted by economic activity, then this will initially cause marginal adjustments in relative prices and quantities, and a reduction in the overall rate of growth[3].

The long-run relationships between these elements may be illustrated as in Fig. 3.2. (This figure has already been outlined and discussed in Chapter 1).

This phenotypic evolution can be compared with the phenotypic evolution of an ecosystem subject to, say, a slight but continuing alteration in climate over a long period, such as the general warming in northern latitudes after the last ice age. However, long-run depletion of resources

---

[3] The role of prices for both phenotypic and genotypic evolution has been investigated in much greater detail by SCHMIDTCHEN [1989].

by an economy is likely to initiate a search for new and unpredictable techniques of production, which use less of the diminishing resource (resource-saving invention) or make use of alternative resources (resource-substituting invention). The new techniques give rise to a new and unpredictable genotypic description for the economic system; the new economic genotype in turn produces a new phenotype which must now, through market operations (phenotypic evolution), establish a new, predictable equilibrium economic structure.

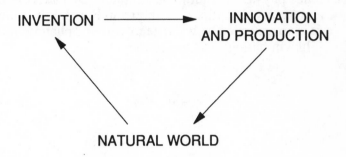

Fig. 3.2. Long-run economy-environment interactions.

While we have restricted our considerations to the production side we could widen them by taking into account the inventions and innovations of economic, social and political institutions.

3.4 Why Physics is Easy, Economics is Difficult and Biology is in Between

The title of this section is certainly provocative to physicists, and also to those familiar with some of the developments in modern physics. Our statement, however, concerns only those parts of the three sciences in which ignorance (i.e. subjective novelty) is not of importance. In this section we therefore restrict our attention to that novelty which occurs because of genotypic evolution. If ignorance is taken into account, all three sciences have similar degrees of difficulty. But in contrast to biology, physics has much larger areas where physicists are able to make clear predictions. Again, compared to economists, biologists are much more able to predict.

We start our discussion by representing physical, biological and economic evolution in a diagrammatic way. In Figs. 3.3 to 3.5, G_i and P_i (i=1,2) denote the genotype and the phenotype, respectively, of population i. G_i^p and P_i^p (i=1,2) denote the perturbed genotype, and its corresponding phenotype.

We recall from Section 2.4 of Chapter 2 that the complete genotypic physical evolution of the universe seems to have occurred in the very first few moments of its beginning i.e. in less than a second [HAWKING 1988]. Thereafter, there was no more genotypic evolution, but only phenotypic evolution. Hence physical evolution is simple to characterise in terms of phenotypic and genotypic notions, as shown in Fig. 3.3. It is important to note that there is no recursion between genotypic and phenotypic evolution in physics, unlike in biology and economics.

$$G_1 \longrightarrow P_1$$

Fig. 3.3. The evolutionary scheme for physical systems.

In the physical world there is no longer genotypic evolution, i.e. no emergence of novelty of potentialities, and physics is only concerned with phenotypic phenomena, in our terminology. This stability of the potentialities of physical systems has allowed physics to deal only with predictable processes, enabling physicists and mathematicians to seek and to find numerous simple and elaborated methods of dynamics. This ability to concentrate on problems which have predictable dynamics is, we believe, the major source of the enormous success physics has enjoyed over the past three centuries. It might have been just this feature of physics that led PLANCK to comment to KEYNES that he gave up the study of economics in favour of physics because he found the former too difficult! In our terminology, this is so since in physics there are many areas in which there is little scope for the emergence of novelty, as there is little ignorance, and no genotypic change.

We now turn to evolution in biology. As we see in Fig. 3.4, the interaction between genotypic and phenotypic processes is much richer than in physics. It may be useful for the reader to explain this diagram in some detail. We see that the representation consists of three phases.

Phase 1 The genotype and phenotype of a biological population at an equilibrium; here the genotype and phenotype are recursively maintaining each other through the reproductive process.

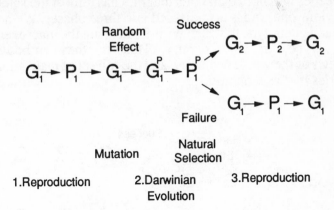

Fig. 3.4. The evolutionary scheme for biological systems.

Phase 2 This illustrates Darwinian Evolution; this consists of two parts, Mutation and Natural Selection. In the first part, Mutation is initiated by a random effect which perturbs genotype G_1 to G_1^P, which in turn produces a corresponding new phenotype, P_1^P. In the second part, Natural Selection, the environment acts as a filter for the new phenotype P_1^P. If this new phenotype is successful in its environment then the new genotype, G_1^P, becomes established, and as it is no longer provisional we rename it G_2. If the new phenotype is unsuccessful in its environment, it is eliminated and the original genotype, G_1, remains.

Phase 3 This is a further reproductive phase. If the perturbed phenotype, P_1^P, is unsuccessful then the reproduction is still of the old phenotype and genotype, as for Phase 1. If the mutation is successful, there will be a period of reproduction where the potentialities of the new genotype, G_2, are being realized in the new phenotype of the biological population, P_2. This will consist of altering species abundances, and therefore constitutes a period of phenotypic evolution.

Supposing the mutation is successful, once a new phenotypic equilibrium is established in Phase 3, one could say that genotypic evolution has occurred.

Finally, we turn to evolution in economics, which we represent in Fig. 3.5. The reader will notice that this diagram has almost the same structure as the previous one, and is also divided into three phases. We note that the genotype and phenotype to which we refer here are the macrogenotype and macrophenotype for an economy. That is, they embody the full potentialities of the whole economy, and the full set of realisations of those potentialities by the economy.

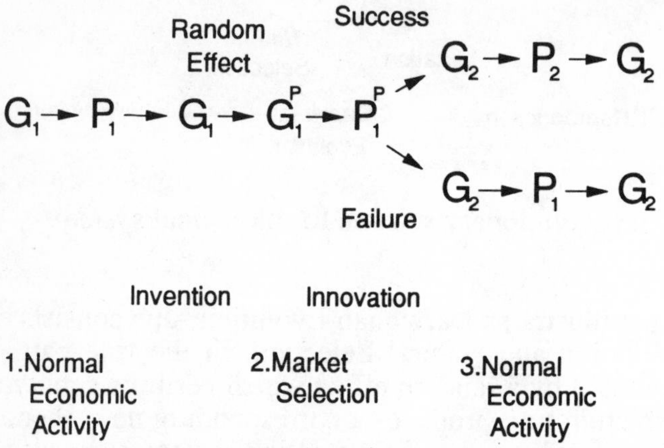

$$\text{Random} \quad \overset{\text{Success}}{} $$

$$G_1 \rightarrow P_1 \rightarrow G_1 \rightarrow G_1^P \rightarrow P_1^P \nearrow \overset{G_2 \rightarrow P_2 \rightarrow G_2}{}$$

$$\searrow G_2 \rightarrow P_1 \rightarrow G_2$$

Random Effect — Success — Failure

Invention   Innovation

| 1.Normal Economic Activity | 2.Market Selection | 3.Normal Economic Activity |

Fig. 3.5. The evolutionary scheme for economic systems.

Phase 1 Here the economy can be described as exhibiting 'Normal Economic Activity'; for ease of illustration, this may be supposed to be a stationary or steady state. The potentialities (i.e. knowledge base) of the economy are being realized in productive economic activity, and this production in turn allows the maintenance of the knowledge base. Therefore, as in the biological case, the genotype and phenotype are in a recursive, self-maintaining relationship.

Phase 2 At the beginning of this phase an invention changes the genotype of the economy; the market conditions will act as a filter for whether this invention will be realized.

Phase 3 However, unlike the biological case, this increase in the potentialities of the system is often retained. Thus G_1 is maintained, as a subset of G_2. Here we recall that this can be the case because we are referring to the macrogenotype and macrophenotype. So the realisation of an economy may not alter, even though the potentialities *do* alter. It may be possible for a new invention to be retained in the knowledge base, but not affect the rest of the economy.[4]

In a biological population, if natural selection rejects the mutation, the mutation disappears from the macro-genotype of that biological population, as the only host for the mutation is the genetic material of the phenotype of that organism[5].

However, in an economy knowledge is not necessarily restricted to any individual or group. It can be stored and made available to a wide range of economic actors. For this reason it is much more difficult to assert that an invention is rejected by the economic evolutionary process than to assert that a biological mutation has been rejected by the biological evolutionary process.

If the market judges the invention to be successful at any subsequent time, the invention will be innovated, leading to a minor or major restructuring of the economy. That is, economic phenotypic evolution takes place. The new economic genotype, G_2, and the new phenotype P_2, become established as the new economic phenotypic equilibrium of the economy. If the invention is unsuccessful, then the original phenotype, P_1, remains in force. However, as the new invention is a permanent addition to the technology of the economy (the economic genotype), it is the new genotype, G_2, which is maintained. We note once more that unlike in biological systems, G_1 often remains as part of the corresponding economic genotype, even if it is not used any more.

The above discussion has shown one major reason why economics is conceptually more complex than biology. A second reason has been mentioned already in Sections 2.3.3 and 2.3.4 of Chapter 2, where we noted that successful genotypic changes in biology occur relatively infrequently. Biological genotypic evolution can be regarded as movements between successive phenotypic equilibria. For economies, on the other hand, it is obvious that in modern times scientific and technical knowledge has been increasing rapidly, and at an accelerating rate. This has led to a tremendous amount of economic genotypic change, which takes place at a rate

---

[4] We are grateful for a reviewer of the first edition of this book [KLEPPER 1992] pointing out the lack of clarity of the original discussion of this point.

[5] It is possible, however, that a genetic mutation may occur to a biological genotype that has no immediate effect on the phenotype. In this case there can be no operation of the selection mechanism upon that alteration, until it is perhaps revealed by the effect of another, later, genetic mutation.

comparable to market adjustments (phenotypic change). Therefore economic genotypic evolution cannot be regarded as movements between successive phenotypic equilibria.

We now offer a third reason for why economics is conceptually more difficult than biology. As we pointed out at the beginning of Section 2.3 of Chapter 2, in biology the phenotype cannot affect the genotype. In contrast to this, in economies the phenotype not only maintains the genotype (its potentialities, i.e. the knowledge base), it also generates it, through research and development activities. That is, the phenotype does affect the genotype in economics.

In summary, while we see great similarities between the evolutionary processes exhibited in the biological world and in economies, we consider economics to be conceptually more difficult than biology for the following three reasons:

1. In economies, 'unsuccessful' additions to the genotype can be preserved.

2. In economies, genotypic evolution often takes place at a similar rate to, and sometimes even at a faster rate than, phenotypic evolution.

3. In economies, the phenotype can effect the genotype.

3.5 The Importance of Ex Post and Ex Ante Considerations

Considering again Fig. 3.2, where the interaction of invention, innovation and the natural world is illustrated, it will be clear to the reader that historical experience supports this conceptualization. For example, we may return to the example discussed in Chapter 1.

Industrialization in eighteenth and nineteenth century Europe can be understood, ex post, in terms of the substitution in industrial processes of relatively abundant fossil fuels for the rapidly depleting sources of wood. The rising price of charcoal in the eighteenth century led to intensive research into finding a technique of smelting iron using coal as fuel rather than charcoal. The key invention was the transformation of coal to coke, which is nearly pure carbon and can act as a good substitute for charcoal in iron-smelting. This invention dramatically reduced the price of iron and led to enormous changes in the structure of everyday life. An economic phenotypic evolution of great proportions was initiated by this economic genotypic change.

With the massive expansion in iron making went an equally massive expansion in coal mining. Just as early iron making encountered natural limitations when the genotype demanded the use of charcoal, so coal mining encountered limitations when the genotype demanded the use of solely human and animal labour. The genotypic change that occurred as a result of further search for invention, to counter the flooding of deep coal mines, was the introduction of steam engines driving water pumps.

Ex post this analysis of the invention, innovation and natural world relationships is clear. Phenotypic evolution depleted the natural resource and thereby stimulated a search for a new genotype. With the benefit of hindsight the invention of smelting with coke, and of the steam engine, seem both timely and inevitable. Prior to their invention, however, industrialists were far from sanguine about the prospects for the iron and coal industries. This will always be the case prior to a major invention.

The conceptualization of the evolutionary process must recognize the very different statuses of the past and the future. The concept of novelty is an ex ante concept, and by its nature novelty can only occur in the future, and by the nature of the future it cannot be known in detail. Further, if the perspective of the future is sufficiently long, even the broadest notions of future novelty that actually comes to pass may be impossible to envisage. Here, uncertainty and unpredictability in its most stark form is encountered. This distinction of the ex ante and ex post in systems which exhibit novelty, and are therefore subject to genotypic evolution, is in marked contrast to a system without the emergence of novelty, where only phenotypic evolution may occur. Here we stress again that phenotypic evolution is often closed and in many cases equifinal, and accessible to prediction, while genotypic evolution is open, not equifinal, and not accessible to prediction.

From the above discussion it will be clear that phenotypic evolution may be considered both ex post and ex ante, while genotypic evolution may properly be understood only ex post. As we have noted above, for biological systems the distinction between phenotypic evolution and genotypic evolution is generally clear because of the enormously different time scales on which these processes operate. However, evolution in economic systems will generally exhibit phenotypic and genotypic evolution, which often operate on similar time scales, making the discrimination between the phenotypic and genotypic evolutionary processes a source of some difficulty in economics.

Of course, we know that different industries have different rates of technological change (i.e. of the occurrence of novelty embodied in new genotypes). This rate is very slow in long-established industries, such as electricity generation by fossil fuel power plants, and steel production. On the other hand, industries such as electronics and aerospace exhibit rapid rates of invention. The evidence even suggests that the rates of invention in these two industries is still increasing.

These observations suggest that conventional economic analysis can be used in those industries which exhibit a low rate of genotypic evolution, but that it is only of limited value for industries with rapid rates of genotypic evolution.

As a further example of the importance of the distinction between genotypic and phenotypic evolution in economics, we turn to environmental economics. We note that there are a multitude of models in resource economics, particularly relating to the depletion of fossil fuels, which seek a market oriented, phenotypic characterization of economic activity in the long-run. Now the complete depletion of fossil fuels with a fixed technology of production (i.e. a fixed genotype) inevitably leads to the collapse of the economy This is dealt with by invoking a more or less arbitrary back-stop technology, which becomes available in the long-run [see e.g. DASGUPTA and HEAL 1979], and leads to a new and unique genotype and thence a new phenotype. As this change is to a technology which is considered to be known ex ante (i.e. predictable), we cannot consider this to be genotypic evolution, as we have discussed above.

This is not to say that speculation about the long-run evolution of economic systems is either impossible or worthless. Discussions of the nature of future inventions (i.e. changes to genotypes) offer, through the construction of scenarios, forecasts about economic development that may be both interesting and valuable. However, we feel it important to stress that predictions based on models of phenotypic evolution (e.g. market dynamics) have a completely different status to models based on notions of possible genotypic evolution (e.g. invention). In addition, we remind the reader that the problems that may arise through ignorance need to be taken into account. We shall examine the possibility that phenotypic processes may be unpredictable because of ignorance in Chapter 5 Section 5.5, and at length in Chapter 7, below.

One reviewer of the first edition of this book [PERRINGS 1992] suggested that: "The intellectual task is to incorporate the dynamics of ecological systems into models of economic behaviour so as to trace the feedbacks that threaten the genotype." While we accept this challenge to ecological economics, we do not agree that by identifying the threats to the geneotype (e.g. pollution) would allow one to identify the nature of the genotypic response. Certainly one would not be able to assess the 'optimal' genotypic evolution in the light of the threat, as might be sought within a traditional neoclassical paradigm.

In summary, the nature of the predictions possible for phenotypic and genotypic evolution are quite different. While for the former, specific and concrete predictions can be made in many cases, this is not possible for the latter. We shall return to the policy implications of this distinction in Chapter 12.

3.6 Conclusions

In this and the preceding chapter we have offered a general and broad conceptualization of evolution. Here we wish to summarise our discussion so far. We began by suggesting that evolution should be regarded as a very general notion. We remind the reader that we conceptualized it as follows: evolution is the process of the changing of something over time.

Biology offers useful insights into this kind of conceptualization of the general nature of evolution, as the notions of genotype (potentialities) and phenotype (realizations) are most clearly delineated in this area. The former allows for the emergence of novelty, while the latter does not. We saw that phenotypic evolution allows for equifinality, and hence for equilibrium solutions, while genotypic evolution does not. This in turn implies that the former allows for prediction, while the latter does not. This further implies that phenotypic evolution may be understood in both ex ante and ex post terms, while genotypic evolution may only be understood ex post. That is, one may forecast phenotypic evolution, but not genotypic evolution.

A summary in the form of a juxtaposition of the characteristics of genotypic and phenotypic evolution is given in Table 3.1.

Table 3.1. Characteristics of genotypic and phenotypic evolution.

Genotypic Evolution	Phenotypic Evolution
Evolution of Potentialities	Evolution of Realization
Emergence of Novelty	No Emergence of Novelty
No Equifinality of Process	Equifinality of Process Possible
No Equilibrium Possible	Equilibrium Possible
Unpredictable Process (in principle)	Predictable Process (in principle)
Modelling Possible Ex Post only	Modelling Possible Ex Ante and Ex Post

In particular, we have seen that economies are characterised by an extremely complicated interaction of genotypic and phenotypic evolutionary processes. Since the rate of genotypic change in the modern global economy is so rapid, it is often not possible to distinguish between the consequences of phenotypic and genotypic changes. Since conventional economics concentrates on the adjustment to equilibrium for given potentialities, it can only be expected to be of limited help for understanding economic evolution.

In summary, predictable, phenotypic economic evolution may be subject to ex ante analysis, allowing sensible predictions of future economic realizations. However, genotypic economic evolution, such as the invention of techniques, or the emergence of new institutions, is by its nature unpredictable and therefore amenable only to ex post analysis.

Since physics is entirely concerned with phenotypic evolution, this explains why this discipline has been so extremely successful, and also why so many other disciplines have tried to emulate its method. As our analysis shows, however, this emulation can be successful only so far as other disciplines are concerned with phenotypic processes.

As we have noted in the introduction, the key characteristics of evolution are change, and time. While we have concentrated on change in Part II, in Part III we bring concepts of time into our analysis explicitly. Therefore, it is to time, and time irreversibility, that we now turn.

Part III

Time

4 Economic Analysis and Concepts of Time Irreversibility

4.1 Introduction

In our discussions in Part II we concentrated upon change. In particular we noted that we can distinguish between two types of change: predictable change (in phenotypic evolution) and unpredictable change (in genotypic evolution). In this chapter, and in Chapters 5, 6 and 8, we turn to considerations of time. (In this chapter we use material originally developed in FABER and PROOPS [1986, 1989]).

In Section 4.2 we consider the problem of time, its asymmetry and its irreversibility.

In Section 4.3 we consider the role of time in economics, and note that to date time has received only limited treatment. In the light of this gap in economic analysis we note that the tendency towards 'closure' in general equilibrium theory, the current dominant economic paradigm, has led economics further away from considerations of time irreversibility.

In Section 4.4 we examine how time has been treated in economic analysis more generally. In particular, we identify three distinct ways in which the different statuses of the past and the future have been recognised.

Section 4.5 discusses how various schools of economic thought have used or embodied concepts of time, and time irreversibility. However, to date no methodology has involved all three types in a formal modelling framework.

In Section 4.6 we relate these concepts of time and time irreversibility to the notions of phenotypic and genotypic evolution, which were developed in Part II.

Section 4.7 contains a summary of the ideas developed in this chapter.

4.2 The Problem of Time Asymmetry and Irreversibility

In Chapters 2 and 3 we explored the concept of evolution. We defined evolution as follows:

Evolution is the process of the changing of something over time.

Now time is a notoriously difficult subject to discuss. As AUGUSTINE [1961:264] noted:

> "What, then, is time? I know well enough what it is, provided that nobody asks me; but if I am asked what it is and try to explain it, I am baffled".

Whereas our concepts of space seem well established, perhaps 'hard-wired' into our brains, time is altogether more elusive. Since ARISTOTLE (or even before) the nature of time has been a source of contention among philosophers, both pure and natural. (For a recent collection of views on time by physicists, mathematicians and philosophers, see FLOOD and LOCKWOOD [1986]).

There is a wide range of views on what 'time' means; there is even one school of thought that time is an illusion. Perhaps our difficulty in understanding time is that time is not a 'thing', but rather the underlying prerequisite for there to be 'things'. To that extent, perhaps all discussions of time must be about 'no thing', and therefore to a greater or lesser degree 'nonsense'. This implies, however, that all discussions about things are about nonsense, because all things can be conceived only in time (cf. KANT [1956]). So perhaps our aim should be to make this nonsense 'time' as sensible and as plausible as possible.

In Part III we shall be considering our understanding of time, as we can apply it to matters of importance to economics of the long-run, especially ecological economics. In particular we shall stress the importance of the 'irreversibility' of time. When discussing 'irreversibility' one needs to be careful, as this term may be given two interpretations. Both relate to our state of knowledge about the world.

The first interpretation is that processes are irreversible because time runs only 'one way', from the past to the future. This interpretation may be better termed the 'asymmetry' of time. The statuses of the past and the future are different, and this difference derives from the fact that the past has already happened, and is known to some extent, while the future is yet to happen, and so is unknown. This we can relate to our ignorance and the possibility of the emergence of novelty, discussed in Part II and to be further discussed in Part IV. The future is unknown because our knowledge is limited and novelty may yet occur. In contrast, our knowledge of the past is, albeit incomplete, more reliable, because any novelty that was to emerge has already occurred.

The second interpretation relates to the 'appearance' of a process. Suppose a film were made of a process, and then run backwards. Would the process still appear 'natural'? If it would, we could say that the process is 'time reversible'. If not, we could say the process is 'time irreversible'. Here, knowledge of the world tells us that certain processes have certain appearances over time. Certain things happen first, then other things happen later. It is, of course, the existence of such irreversible processes that indicates the 'direction' or 'arrow' of time. This point is taken up in more detail in Chapter 5. Let us now consider some examples of reversible and irreversible processes.

1. The orbiting of a planet around a sun.

The film, if run backwards, would appear quite natural. The motion of the planet is regular and repetitive, and is not particularly tending towards any end state. This process is time reversible.

2. The bouncing of a ball without friction.

As for the orbiting planet, the motion is regular and repetitive, with no particular end. This is also a time reversible process.

3. The burning of a lump of coal.

The film of this process would look distinctly odd when run backwards. We simply do not see diffuse energy combining with carbon dioxide and water vapour to give coal and oxygen. This process is clearly time irreversible.

4. The growth of an oak tree.

This is also a process that can only be run one-way on film and still look sensible. Mature oak trees gradually shrinking, until they form only an acorn, are just never observed. This is also a time irreversible process.

5. The production of a consumption good.

The production of goods needs an input of effort. Thus, to manufacture a good generally requires the prior construction of capital equipment. Therefore, the temporal ordering of the process of producing a consumption good would be: produce the appropriate capital equipment, then construct the consumption good. The reverse ordering would be neither possible, nor compatible with the aim of producing the consumption good.

In the light of the above discussion about time irreversibility, what are the implications of considerations of time for economics in general, and for the ecological economics of the long-run in particular?

4.3 Time and Economic Analysis

Economic theory seems to be at an impasse. Many of the urgent practical and theoretical issues faced by economists (environmental degradation, technical innovation, organisational evolution of institutions) fall outside the dominant paradigm of general equilibrium analysis in its traditional form. In particular, these issues require an explicit and coherent treatment of time asymmetry and irreversibility, which the general equilibrium approach does not offer at present. In this chapter, and Chapter 6, we shall attempt to contribute to the clarification of the role which time irreversibility plays in several areas of economic analysis.

Although economists have developed certain dynamic approaches, it is our opinion that some important aspects of time are not within the mainstream of economic research, in contrast to, say, physics. For example, the temporal structure of consumption and production have not been treated as major issues of economic discussion. This is even more the case for the teaching of economics at colleges and universities. The principles and foundations of economics are taught in microeconomic and macroeconomic courses, where dynamics and aspects of time generally are only of secondary importance. The same holds for much of the teaching of general equilibrium analysis.

4.3.1 Closure and Time in Economics: General Equilibrium Theory

Neoclassical general equilibrium theory [cf. e.g. DEBREU 1959] is still widely accepted to be the dominant paradigm in economics. In the course of the last five decades it has won acceptance in more and more areas; for example, in the microfoundations of macroeconomics, capital theory, monetary theory, public finance, international trade, and development theory. Among the reasons for the success of this framework are the following:

(a) In contrast to the experience in other social sciences, general equilibrium theory has given economists a common language and a consistent set of concepts of formal elegance.

(b) It allows the simultaneous solution of the primal and dual problems of how equilibrium quantities and prices can be established in a decentralized economy.

(c) The general equilibrium approach explicitly recognizes the interdependence of the many parts of an economic system, in an internally consistent fashion.

These positive features of the general equilibrium approach, which is the basis of neoclassical economics, have been made possible by defining the boundaries of the corresponding problems in terms of preference orderings, technology, resources, and legal and political institutions. The better defined are the boundaries of the problem, the more tractable is the corresponding model and the more completely characterised is the set of solutions. That is, the nearer is the model to closure, the less ambiguous are the solutions to the model[1]. However, there is a growing awareness of the opportunity cost of this reduction in ambiguity through greater closure. In particular, the move towards greater closure has the following consequences, to be explained in more detail in Section 4.5 below:

(i)   The path-dependence of the boundary conditions of economic systems cannot be properly accommodated; that is to say, economic theory has become divorced from economic history.

(ii)   General equilibrium theory can treat invention and sources of novelty only through the introduction of ad hoc assumptions, as has often been conceded.

(iii)   The approach of general equilibrium theory to problems of resource depletion and environmental degradation has been mainly in terms of 'internalizing externalities'. We believe that the restriction to these aspects of resource and environmental economics is too narrow an approach. It should therefore be widened, as demanded by ecologists (see e.g. EHRLICH [1989], PROOPS [1989], BINSWANGER, FABER and MANSTETTEN [1990]).

In the following sections we attempt to show that all three of these consequences can be attributed to the treatment of time in general equilibrium models.

---

[1] We note that even a very high degree of closure, as exhibited in advanced textbooks in general equilibrium theory [e.g. DEBREU 1959, ARROW and HAHN 1970], does not ensure a well-determined solution set [SONNENSCHEIN 1972, 1973; DEBREU 1974; MANTEL 1974, 1976, 1977].

4.4 Notions of Time
4.4.1 On Concepts of Time in Economic Theory

We now refer to the literature to give examples of how time has been discussed in economics. The notions of statics, comparative statics and dynamics form the triad familiar to every student of economics [see e.g. SAMUELSON 1947]. While the first two of these have clear cut meanings, the last one has many aspects. HICKS [1939/1946:115] states:

"I call ... Economic Dynamics those parts where every quantity must be dated".

HICKS's [1939/1946:126-7] central notions in his dynamic analysis are:

"... the week, the plan, the definite expectations .... by employing them we do a certain amount of violence to the phenomena of the actual world, but not more than necessary, if we are to make any headway in dynamic theory".

SAMUELSON [1947:315] distinguishes between "Dynamic and causal (nonhistorical)" and "Dynamic and historical", a distinction also used by SCHUMPETER [1954:965]:

"It should be pointed out explicitly that, as defined, dynamic theory in itself has nothing to do with historical analysis: its time subscripts do not refer to historical time - the simple model we used as an example tells us nothing about whether that demand-supply configuration obtained in the times of President Washington or of President Roosevelt; and its sequences are theoretical and not historical or, as we may also put it, it uses theoretical and not historical datings." (See also GEORGESCU-ROEGEN [1971:136]).

Further, SAMUELSON [1947:315] notes that:

"... a truly dynamical system may be completely nonhistorical or causal, in the sense that its behaviour depends only upon its initial conditions and the time which has elapsed, the calendar date not entering into the process. For many purposes, it is necessary to work with systems which are both historical and dynamical. The impact of technological change upon the economic system is a case in point. Technological change may be taken as a historical datum, to which the economic system reacts non-instantaneously or in a dynamic fashion."

In analysing dynamic systems SAMUELSON [1947:Part II; see in particular: 260-269] is mainly interested in stability problems. In the literature of modern intertemporal equilibrium theory, essential targets of analysis are the questions:

1. How can the concept of efficiency be extended to the long-run [see CASS 1972]?

2. Can intertemporally efficient development be achieved by the market mechanism [KURZ and STARRETT 1970]?

Finally we mention BOLAND's [1978:240] study of the 'HAYEK Problem':

"... as HAYEK recognised many years ago, how time is treated is an important aspect of any explanation of historical change. It is the main purpose of (BOLAND's, the authors) paper to offer a solution to the 'Hayek Problem': How can we explain the process of change in economics and remain consistent with the principles of (individual) rational decision-making? The present solution proposes a dynamic concept of knowledge in which learning is a real-time (irreversible) process."

We agree with BOLAND that the irreversible process of learning is of great importance to the understanding of economics, but we feel that there are also other concepts of irreversibility to be taken into account.

We note in passing that since the seminal paper by ARROW [1968], there has been a growing awareness of irreversibility in the economic literature, which has treated various aspects of the problem in a rather technical manner; e.g. ARROW and FISCHER [1974], HENRY [1974], NICKELL [1978], CLARK, CLARK and MUNRO [1979], BERNANKE [1983], WODOPIA [1986b], PINDYCK [1988] and HANEMANN [1989]. In some respects the pioneering paper by KOOPMANS [1964], on flexibility of preferences, also belongs to this literature. In spite of this rise in awareness, PINDYCK [1988:969] could still write recently:

"The irreversibility of investment has been neglected since the work of Kenneth ARROW [1968], despite its implications for spending decisions, capacity choice, and the value of the firm."

4.4.2 Six Approaches to Time in Economics

Time in economics has been treated in various ways. In this section we wish to distinguish six approaches to time in economic reasoning, which we now summarise. Thereafter we exemplify this classification with reference to general equilibrium theory, BÖHM-BAWERK based Austrian capital theory, the Post-Keynesian approach, evolutionary economics, and Austrian subjectivism. We begin by considering 'reversible time'.

4.4.2.1 Reversible Time

Here we distinguish three types of the treatment of time in economics.

Approach 1: Static

Events are assumed to occur at one point of time, or in one period of time, i.e. time does not appear as a variable.

Approach 2: Comparative Static

States of the system at two discrete moments are compared.

Approach 3: Reversible Time

Time has the same status as a spatial variable; its direction is not uniquely defined so that the future and the past are treated symmetrically.

We note that no time irreversibility, in either sense, is invoked by these three approaches.

4.4.2.2 Concepts of Time Irreversibility

The 'historical time' to which SAMUELSON refers requires the explicit recognition of the different statuses of the past and the future, the asymmetry of time. Common experience tells us that the past is unambiguous (though not necessarily known in all detail), while the future is ambiguous in many respects. We usually recognize this in economics by referring to 'Risk' and 'Uncertainty' being associated with future states of the world [KNIGHT 1921].

The asymmetrical nature of time has long been recognised in the natural sciences through the 'Two Arrows of Time', to be discussed in more detail in Chapter 5. The First Arrow of Time refers to the tendency over time of natural systems to disorder (under certain circumstances); this notion is summarised in the Second Law of Thermodynamics, the Entropy Law [GEORGESCU-ROEGEN 1971]. The Second Arrow of Time reflects the tendency over time of certain systems towards greater organisation and complexity; this cannot be summarised in a simple thermodynamic law, but the physical principles involved have been explored in detail by PRIGOGINE and his school [see PRIGOGINE and STENGERS 1984]. This subject will also be taken up in greater detail in Chapter 5.

As discussed above, in neoclassical economics the asymmetry of time has not been a central issue, and so has received relatively little attention, with this being mainly in production theory. In particular KOOPMANS' [1951:48-51] axiom that the production process is irreversible, meaning that inputs cannot be produced from outputs, is an explicit recognition of the operation of the Second Law of Thermodynamics in production [see also DEBREU 1959:39-42]. However, the majority of neoclassical theorising and modelling does not deal explicitly with the asymmetry of the past and future, and the irreversibility of processes in time [see STEPHAN 1989:Chapter 2]. In contrast, the time irreversibility of investment processes is a central feature of the evolutionary and Austrian schools of thought, although in our view a detailed analysis of the full implications of time irreversibility for economic analysis has yet to be completed satisfactorily.

A necessary precondition of such a detailed analysis is the description and classification of the types of time irreversibility that can be identified. Towards this end we have tentatively identified three types of time irreversibility which are important in economic analysis (see for a more detailed analysis of risk and uncertainty Chapter 7 below):

Approach 4: Risk - Irreversible Time 1

The future and the past are treated asymmetrically because of asymmetric information structures, i.e. past events may be known and therefore certain. Future events are not known for certain, but can be associated with known objective or subjective probability distributions, based on knowledge of the past. In economics this kind of uncertainty is called 'risk'.

Approach 5: Uncertainty - Irreversible Time 2

The future may contain novelty that is definitely unknowable, i.e. some future events cannot be associated with probability distributions based on knowledge of the past. In economics this kind of uncertainty is called 'uncertainty'.[2]

Approach 6: Teleological Sequence - Irreversible Time 3

Particular goals often require economic developments, or particular temporal sequences of decisions and actions. This phenomenon has two properties:

1. On the primal, technologies and production structures have to be provided in a temporal order.

2. On the dual, this sequence of actions implies a sequence of prices (e.g. a discrete cobweb model defines a price path to its equilibrium which embodies the history of its evolution).

A teleological sequence can be understood as a social kind of irreversibility, as noted in Chapter 1 Section 1.7. We can distinguish three characteristics of this type of irreversibility:

(a)   The time order of the stages of teleological sequence is fixed and hence invariable.

(b)   From (a) it follows that each teleological sequence is fixed and hence invariable.

(c)   Each teleological sequence is characterised by a goal, its 'telos'.

Aspects (a) and (b) of teleological sequence appear also in processes of natural science; they exhibit an order of stages and therefore a direction. However, in contrast to teleological sequence (i.e. social irreversibility), processes in natural science do not have a *chosen* telos. We shall return to this issue in Chapter 5 Section 5.3.

---

[2] In decision theory the differentiation is made between two cases: (a) all states of the world are known, but not all the corresponding probabilities, (b) Not all states of the world are known. Case (a) is dealt with by Bayesian analysis [LEE 1989]. In this book we are particulary interested in case (b), which is also 'radical uncertainty'. For a fuller discussion see Part IV. (We thank Christopher Helle and Charles Perrings for pointing out this distinction.)

4.4.3 Teleological Sequence - Irreversible Time 3

Our notion of teleological sequence has several aspects. We employ the adjective teleological to indicate that economic activities are directed toward a definite end (Greek: telos). This end, however, cannot be attained directly. Hence time has to pass before it is reached. For example, production takes time, as was stressed by MENGER [1871/1950] and in particular by BÖHM-BAWERK [1889/1891] (see SCHUMPETER [1954])[3].

In the production of consumption goods, first raw materials are extracted and intermediates have to be produced before the final product appears. Also, it is not possible to introduce new techniques within one period; rather, it is necessary in the course of several periods to build up corresponding stocks of new capital goods.

All this shows that economic processes have an inertia, whose temporal length depends on the aim to be attained. We accept that such economic inertia may be reversible with a very long time horizon. In general the following holds: the shorter the economic time horizon the more events are irreversible, and the longer the time horizon the more events are reversible. Of course, there are also events which may be completely irreversible, such as the combustion of coal, or the extinction of a species.

A corresponding economic condition is the postulate of the Impossibility of the Land of Cockaigne, which was introduced by KOOPMANS [1951:50-51]. This says that it is impossible to produce a good without an input. The relationship between the two postulates, of Irreversibility and the Impossibility of the Land of Cockaigne, is discussed by WITTMANN [1968:39-42]. KOOPMANS [1951] has represented both postulates within a linear technology, but DEBREU [1959:39-42] has also employed the Axiom of Irreversibility in a nonlinear formulation of a general equilibrium model.

However, it is our impression that while irreversibility has begun to be accepted as an axiom, the physical meaning of such irreversibility has yet to be 'internalized' in the conceptualization of most economists. This lacuna has been recognized by SAMUELSON [1983:36]:

"In theoretical economics there is no 'irreversibility' concept, which is one reason why GEORGESCU-ROEGEN [1971] is critical of conventional economics."

---

[3] For a modern survey of the Austrian School see NEGISHI [1989:Chapter 8].

One might object that 'the Irreversibility of Production' and 'the Impossibility of the Land of Cockaigne' are so obvious from a purely economic point of view, that it is not necessary to study physics or to undertake interdisciplinary work in order to find them. However, we do not consider it pure chance that it was KOOPMANS who introduced these two assumptions into economic analysis, for he had studied physics and had even written his first publication in that field. We believe his educational background gave him a particular outlook when studying production problems, which was a prerequisite for his seminal work in economics.

Up to now we have only considered the time structure of processes which enable one to reach an end, such as the introduction of a new technique. Similar considerations, however, are also valid for the many cases where one wants to get rid of techniques which have been introduced earlier. For reasons based in social, economic or natural phenomena, it takes time to phase out such techniques. Incidentally, this is the main reason it takes so much time to introduce environmental laws. The inertia of the corresponding political, legal, economic and social processes is considerable, and thus restricts the flexibility of society.

4.5 Time Irreversibility and Economic Theory

In Table 4.1 we indicate which types of time irreversibility we believe are accommodated within each of the five areas mentioned above. These are, neoclassical general equilibrium theory, neo-Austrian capital theory, Austrian subjectivism, the Post-Keynesians and evolutionary economics. In the following we shall explain this representation.

4.5.1 Neoclassical General Equilibrium Theory

It is clear that mainstream neoclassical economics encompasses at least the Static, Comparative Static and Reversible Time approaches. In particular we see the use of intertemporal equilibrium, and many growth models, as all taking the Reversible Time approach. In these models the time variable does not have a uniquely defined direction. Thus LEIJONHUFVUD [1984] wrote:

"By itself, the dating of goods only adds dimensions to the commodity space considered in 'timeless' statics ... Dating brings in future time, but it does not necessarily help in bringing in the passage of time." [p.30]

Table 4.1. The relationship between concepts of time and some economic schools of thought.

	Risk (1)	Uncertainty (2)	Teleological Sequence (3)
General Equilibrium	X	-	-
Austrian Capital Theory	X	-	X
Austrian Subjectivism	X	X	X
Post-Keynesians	X	X	-
Evolutionary Economics	X	X	-

Similarly HICKS [1965:47] noted:

"The more precise capital theory became, the more static it became ...".

Since neoclassical general equilibrium theory is the dominant paradigm in economics, we shall deal with this school of thought extensively. In the early fifties general equilibrium theory was extended to uncertain events [DEBREU 1959:98-102]; i.e. in our terminology to, Approach 4, 'Risk - Irreversible Time 1'. As noted in Section 4.2, we speak of irreversible time because of the asymmetry of time. In this context, it is because of the corresponding asymmetric information situation. For example, a farmer has to decide what kind of vegetable to plant in the spring. The outcome of this endeavour will depend on the weather during the summer. This is illustrated in Table 4.2.

The expected pay-off for A is $P(A)=2+8p$ and for B it is $P(B)=8-4p$. To make this decision the farmer just compares $P(A)$ and $P(B)$. For probability $p<1/2$ the farmer selects B and for $p>1/2$, A is his choice.

"Pure decision theory, formalized as optimization subject to constraints, is essentially timeless. The choice among the foreseen outcomes of alternative actions is a purely logical calculus that does not involve time in any essential way." [LEIJONHUFVUD 1984:27]

Table 4.2. Risk and decision making by a farmer.

Decision in Spring	Weather during Summer		Expected Pay-off
	Sunny (p)	Rainy (1-p)	
A	10	2	2 + 8p
B	4	8	8 - 4p

[The probability for 'Sunny' is denoted by p, and for 'Rainy' by (1-p)].

Obviously 'Risk - Irreversible Time 1' is the easiest kind of irreversibility to cope with, since the range of possible outcomes and the probability distributions over these events are known. From the latter it follows that this approach is also a closed one: nothing completely unknown can happen[4]. Hence 'Uncertainty - Irreversible Time 2' is not taken care of.

In most publications on investment decisions up to the middle of the seventies it was assumed that these decisions are reversible, i.e. there exist markets for used capital goods (cf. however our remarks at the end of Section 4.4.1). Thus 'Teleological Sequence - Irreversible Time 3' was also excluded.

It is our belief that this reduction in scope regarding time irreversibilities, with the consequences mentioned above, is closely related to the methodological requirements of neoclassical general equilibrium theory. These imply that relationships between exogenous and endogenous variables can be found. This in turn implies that the generative mechanism of this system (i.e. the behaviour of agents) has to be clearly defined (normally expected utility and profit maximisation), and to take place against a background of clearly and fully defined boundaries. In 'real' time, however, in most cases changes in behaviour and boundaries occur in unpredictable ways and can therefore not be known in advance, and in particular not in the long-run (i.e. genotypic evolution takes place). In

---

[4] We remind the reader that this includes the possibility that probability distributions are not known a priori, but that they may be estimated optimally by the economic agents; thus learning is possible. This fact has important implications for economic policy concerning the efficiency of fiscal and monetary instruments.

contrast to the subjects of the natural sciences, these permanent changes in the course of time are characteristic of real social and economic systems. We therefore argue for a stronger consideration of these changes in economic theory, although we know that this is a very difficult task.

This concern has, of course, already been discussed in Chapter 3, where the difficulty of treating evolving economies over time was discussed. There we noted that real economies exhibit unpredictable genotypic change, as well as predictable phenotypic change. In this terminology one might say that the neoclassical paradigm deals only with phenotypic change. We shall return to a more detailed discussion of the relationships between the two types of evolution and the three types of time irreversibility in Section 5.6, below.

We now return to the three consequences of closure in neoclassical general equilibrium models; these we labelled (i) to (iii), and they are listed at the end of Section 4.3.1.

Consequence (i) was that economic theory has become divorced from economic history. As was described in Section 4.3.1, a closed system allows a determinate solution, under fairly restrictive conditions. Regarding this we may note:

"But getting rid of analytically troublesome open characteristics implies at the same time the exclusion from formal treatment of historical phenomena: the emergence of and adaptation to new forms of system behaviour and information concerning feed-back between economy and environment. To put it another way, closed system analysis is couched in terms of logical time rather than historical time" [O'CONNOR 1985:14].

Recently SOLOW [1985:329] has persuasively argued for a major effort to take history into consideration in economic analysis.

"In this scheme of things, the end product of economic analysis is likely to be a collection of models contingent on society's circumstances - on the historical context, you might say - and not a single monolithic model for all reasons."

The difficulties with such a "monolithic model" are described by SOLOW [1985:330] as follows:

"My impression is that the best and brightest in the profession proceed as if economics is the physics of society. There is a single universally valid model of the world. It only needs to be applied. You can drop a modern economist from a time machine - a helicopter, may be, like the one that drops the money - at any time, in any place, along with his or her personal computer, he or she could set up in business without even bothering to ask what time and which place".

SOLOW [1985:331] therefore concludes:

"One will have to recognize that the validity of the economic model may depend on the social context. What is here today may be gone tomorrow, or, if not tomorrow, then in ten or twenty years' time".

If one pursues this approach, history and economic analysis must be reconciled.

Consequence (ii) was that invention and novelty could be treated only poorly within the neoclassical paradigm. Invention and sources of novelty in general equilibrium theory are not dealt with endogenously, but exogenously B[cf. WITT 1987]. In particular it is assumed in general that all production processes are known in advance. This again excludes historical time.

Consequence (iii) was that matters of ecological importance are often ignored in the neoclassical paradigm. A principle aim of this book is to argue that problems of resource depletion and environmental degradation should be analysed in a wider context. In particular, insights from the natural sciences should be employed. This in turn will lead to explicit consideration of time and irreversibility in economic analysis [GEORGESCU-ROEGEN 1971; FABER, NIEMES and STEPHAN 1987]. This theme is taken up in Chapter 5.

4.5.2 Neo-Austrian Capital Theory

The resurrection of neo-Austrian capital theory in the seventies grew out of the dissatisfaction with these restrictions regarding time irreversibilities [BERNHOLZ 1971; HICKS 1970, 1973a, 1973b; VON WEIZSÄCKER 1971; for a survey see FABER 1986b]. In particular it is explicitly taken into account that production takes time (see Section 4.4.3. of Chapter 4 above).

In the production of consumption goods, first raw materials are extracted and intermediates have to be produced before the final product appears. Also, it is generally not possible to introduce new techniques within one period; instead it is necessary to build up the stocks of the new capital goods for these new techniques over the course of several periods. In particular with 'Teleological Sequence - Time Irreversibility 3', it is explicitly taken into account that production takes time.

The concepts of superiority and roundaboutness (to be discussed in detail in Chapter 9) were newly defined to analyse the time structure of production and consumption, as well as the innovation of new techniques.

We note further that neo-Austrian capital theory does not neglect history in so far that its analysis starts with a given composition of capital goods, which imply certain temporal restrictions. These are strongest at the beginning of the economic time horizon. Of course, this also holds for neoclassical capital theory with heterogeneous goods (see e.g. the seminal paper by HAHN [1966]. For a general treatment see BLISS [1975] and BURMEISTER [1980]).

To illustrate this, consider the highway system which has been developed in the United States during the twentieth century. There has been tremendous investment in capital goods such as streets, bridges, tunnels and control systems. The same holds true for the corresponding automobile industry. In contrast to this, the development of the railway system has been neglected. It would take decades to build it up to a similar degree, since it would take much time to expand the stock of railway capital goods and to acquire the necessary know-how. The substitution possibilities between traffic on the streets and on rails are therefore rather limited in the United States.

To sum up, in building up large amounts of capital goods and in generating the corresponding technical knowledge, irreversibility is created, which can be weakened or changed only in the very long run.

For these reasons the neo-Austrian approach is particularly appropriate for analysing environmental and resource problems, because the time structure of ecological processes and of mining are at the focus of the analysis (see Chapter 8 Section 8.5 below). But since neo-Austrian capital theory adopted the same methodological principles as general equilibrium analysis, it is only able to deal with time irreversibilities 1 (risk) and 3 (teleological sequence), and not with uncertainty - time irreversibility 2.

4.5.3 The Post-Keynesians

Post-Keynesian economics is relatively new, and still defining itself. However, like neo-Austrian capital theory and evolutionary economics, discussed below, it arose out of a dissatisfaction with the current dominant neoclassical paradigm. Unlike neo-Austrian capital theorists, the Post-Keynesians do not have a readily established 'tool-kit' of techniques. Unlike the Austrian subjectivists and the evolutionary economists, they lack a clearly defined conceptualization of economic processes. However, if one thing can be said to typify Post-Keynesian concerns, it is the role of uncertainty and market failure. To this extent they seek to encompass time irreversibility 1 (risk) and time irreversibility 2 (uncertainty). To our knowledge they have not yet sought to encompass time irreversibility 3 (teleological sequence).

4.5.4 Austrian Subjectivism

This school of thought has roots that reach back to before the establishment of the neoclassical paradigm [MENGER 1871/1950]. Austrian subjectivists oppose the prediction oriented formal rigour of general equilibrium theory and neo-Austrian capital theory, so they are not compelled to define exact boundary conditions [PELLENGAHR 1986b]. Instead, Austrian subjectivists follow a rather more verbal approach, not directed at prediction, which can therefore encompass all three types of irreversibility, if only in a loose fashion.

Austrian subjectivists focus centrally on the information dissemination function of the market process and the correction of error triggered thereby (time irreversibility 1). However, the real world for them is an open-ended world of radical uncertainty, where the entrepreneurial discovery of novelty is a driving force (time irreversibility 2). Within this world view, subjectivists have traditionally stressed teleological sequence (time irreversibility 3), describing the order of production processes in terms of a structure of higher and lower order goods [cf. MENGER 1871/1950].

4.5.5 Evolutionary Economics

There is some similarity between evolutionary economics [NELSON and WINTER 1982] and Austrian subjectivism [cf. WITT 1989], and even some common ancestry. Just as for Austrian subjectivism, evolutionary economics centrally involves learning and adaptation (time irreversibility 1) and, even more centrally, the emergence of novelty (time irreversibility 2). However, the focus is here on the finding of empirical regularities in learning and adaptation, an endeavour whose neglect by all other approaches evolutionary economists particularly criticise. There is little mention of the consequences of teleological sequence (time irreversibility 3). However, it is our opinion that this neglect is not an inherent characteristic of evolutionary economics, but rather a sort of blank area, which is due to the fact that evolutionary economics is still in its infancy.

We shall return to these five schools of thought in Chapter 6, where we attempt a more detailed discussion of their conceptual structure, particularly with regard to their treatment of time irreversibility.

4.6 Evolution and Time Irreversibility

In Part II we developed notions of phenotypic and genotypic evolution. The former we defined to be the evolution of the realization of a system's potentialities. The latter is the evolution of the system's potentialities themselves. We noted that phenotypic evolution is, in principle, predictable. On the other hand, genotypic evolution allows for the emergence of novelty, so it is in principle unpredictable.

We now wish to relate these two concepts of evolution to the three types of time irreversibility we have developed in this chapter. We proceed by considering each type of time irreversibility in turn.

Time irreversibility 1 (risk) is exhibited by processes which have asymmetric information available regarding their past and future behaviour. However, we are here supposing that all possible future states can be enumerated, and probabilities associated with each possible outcome. Thus processes exhibiting this type of time irreversibility are, at least stochastically, predictable.

Time irreversibility 2 (uncertainty) is more difficult to deal with, in two ways. First, even if we can specify all possible future states of the world, there are at least some outcomes with which we cannot associate probabilities. Second, we may not be able even to specify all possible future states of the world. That is, our ignorance may relate not only to probabilities of events, but even to the nature of the events themselves. Clearly a process which exhibits this type of uncertainty about its future is unpredictable.

Time irreversibility 3 (teleological sequence) is, in some ways, the most difficult to classify. The reason for this is that this type of time irreversibility relies upon the notion of an end, or telos. This telos must lie in the mind of an individual, or be agreed by a group of individuals. If the telos is known, then for a given technology the process is largely predictable. For example, to build a house with current technology one first digs the foundations, pours concrete, constructs the wall, builds the roof, etc. However, it may be that the nature of the telos is not known. As the Austrian subjectivists stress, all human agents have free will, and may decide on goals which are novel, and therefore unpredictable [KIRZNER 1982]. Thus we conclude that processes exhibiting time irreversibility 3 are predictable if the telos is known, but they are unpredictable if the telos is unknown.

This relationship of predictability/unpredictability with the three concepts of time irreversibility is shown in Table 4.3.

We see that risk and teleological sequence, with a known telos, are predictable, and therefore should be part of phenotypic evolution. We see this is so as, in both cases, the process involves only the realization of a system. Its potentialities are unchanged.

Concerning uncertainty and teleological sequence with an unknown telos, here there is the emergence of novelty over time, so the potentialities of the system are evolving. The emergence of these new potentialities must therefore correspond to genotypic evolution.

Table 4.3. The relationship between predictability and time irreversibility.

Type of Irreversibility	Predictable	Unpredictable
Risk	X	-
Uncertainty	-	X
Teleological Sequence (known telos)	X	-
Teleological Sequence (unknown telos)	-	X

4.7 Conclusions

We feel that a potentially fruitful research programme is to attempt explicitly to synthesize the three types of time irreversibility in one approach which does not neglect formal methods. We recognize that such a programme would require a major effort. However, such a synthesis has a parallel in current natural sciences, particularly with regard to concepts in classical thermodynamics, evolution, and far-from-equilibrium systems. For this reason, in Chapter 5 we shall examine how different concepts of time irreversibility are being unified in natural science, and detail some of the techniques used for this purpose.

5 Time in the Natural Sciences: Some Lessons for Economics

5.1 Introduction

In Chapter 4 we discussed the problem of the 'irreversibility of time'; that is, the asymmetry of time, and the irreversibility of the 'appearance' of many processes in time. We also defined three types of time irreversibility, and applied them to various schools of economic thought.

Later, in Chapter 6, we shall return to the analysis of schools of economic thought, so as to set the scene for the analysis of the treatment of time irreversibility in long-run models of economy-environment interactions, to be discussed extensively in Part V.

However, before we proceed to further analysis of economic conceptualizations, and economic models, we consider it timely to assess how the problem of time irreversibility has been encountered in natural science, particularly physical science. We consider this to be useful for two reasons. First, several concepts first introduced in natural science will prove useful for conceptualization in ecological economics. Second, we feel that the way natural science has treated time irreversibility has lessons to offer economics.

In Section 5.2 we therefore review how recent work in far-from-equilibrium thermodynamics and non-linear dynamics has led quite naturally to models involving time irreversibility.

This leads us on to a discussion in Section 5.3 of the 'Two Arrows of Time', and we note how these are related to the time irreversibilities discussed in Chapter 4.

The mathematical techniques necessary for these developments are reviewed in Section 5.4, where it is noted that these techniques are being used more and more by economists.

The relationship between one of these techniques (chaos) and the emergence of novelty is dealt with in Section 5.5.

In Section 5.6 we state our conclusions and note some prospects for a synthesis.

Before proceeding we wish to note that economists have a long tradition of employing concepts from the physical sciences [MIROWSKI 1984; PROOPS 1985]. However, it is well known that there are inherent dangers in analogical reasoning. To avoid these, it is necessary that researchers fully understand and internalize the physical methods in order to be able to adapt them to the particular needs of the social sciences. We return to a discussion of this problem in Chapter 12.

It is our conviction that economics now needs conceptual reorientation with respect to time irreversibility, not unlike that which has already occurred in natural science. In Section 5.5 we note certain areas that would directly benefit from a research programme directed towards such an end.

(Much of the material in this chapter was originally developed in FABER and PROOPS [1986]).

5.2 Newtonian and Modern Mechanics

Newtonian mechanics has been an extremely successful intellectual construct, allowing the motions of earthly bodies, the orbits of the moon and planets, the tides, etc., all to be interpreted as aspects of the universal law of gravitation and Newton's three laws of motion. Using this approach the interactions of bodies can be written as coupled differential equations in three spatial dimensions and one time variable. In the absence of damping terms (i.e. supposing the mechanical system does not dissipate energy) the solutions to these equations are symmetrical with respect to time; that is, if time is represented by the variable 't', replacing t by -t in the solution equations will still give a solution. For example, the orbits of the planets around the sun are in a particular direction. If time were to be 'run' in the opposite direction the rotation of the planets would appear to be reversed, as we discussed in Chapter 4. However, such a reversal would be quite compatible with Newtonian mechanics. Indeed, for simple mechanical systems the time variable plays the same role as a spatial variable [cf. PRIGOGINE 1980; PRIGOGINE and STENGERS 1984].

The implications of such reversible mechanical time are very strong for the way we see the world. If our world view is that of objects interacting through well defined relationships, then the past and future are not only interchangeable in a formal sense in the equations of motion, but also the concepts of past and future must be closely tied together. The natural conclusion would be to invoke 'LAPLACE's Demon' [PRIGOGINE and STENGERS 1984:75] which, given the instantaneous positions and velocities of all particles in the universe, can infer their past and predict their future with equal facility; time becomes an illusion. Indeed, it has been suggested that the explicit acceptance by JEVONS and WALRAS of Newtonian mechanics as a guide for modelling economic systems has caused general equilibrium analysis also to exhibit time reversibility [MIROWSKI 1984, PROOPS 1985].

Fortunately, modern work in mechanics saves us from this demon's siren call [cf. KADANOFF 1983]. It can be shown that even relatively simple non-linear deterministic models can generate behaviour that is apparently random or 'chaotic'. Only knowledge of the underlying process allows one correctly to assess the past and future behaviour of the system from its present state. Also, certain non-linear dynamical systems may exhibit entirely different types of behaviour over time when their initial conditions are changed by infinitesimal amounts (such sensitive dependence on the initial values is typical of so-called chaotic dynamic systems [GUCKENHEIMER and HOLMES 1983]). We see that modern insights into mechanics indicate that even apparently simple dynamical systems require the recognition that the past and future are asymmetrical when it is accepted that present knowledge about the state of the system is partial or limited in its accuracy. (Some applications of these ideas to economics, and their implications for the notions of time irreversibility, are discussed in Section 5.4).

5.3 The Two Arrows of Time

The problem of time irreversibility in natural science has been approached in two apparently distinct ways, dealing with two apparently opposed aspects of the natural world. The first aspect is the observed tendency of systems towards greater 'mixed-upness'. For example, an ice cube placed in a container of hot water will melt, to give cool water. The initially distinct cold ice and warm water become mixed-up. We never observe cool water separating out of its own accord into cold ice and warm water; the process of mixing is temporally irreversible.

This tendency to mixed-upness, and in particular the tendency of heat to flow from hot bodies to cold bodies rather than vice versa, gave rise in the nineteenth century to the area of study now known as thermodynamics. The tendency of systems to mixed-upness is now known as the Second Law of Thermodynamics, or the Entropy Law.

The term 'entropy' was coined originally as an (inverse) measure of how much mechanical work could be extracted from a heat reservoir at a certain temperature by a machine working in a reversible cycle. A looser but more accessible interpretation of entropy is that it measures the 'mixed-upness' of a system, and the Entropy Law says that an isolated system (one which neither energy nor matter can enter or leave) tends towards a state of maximum entropy. It is the Second Law of Thermodynamics that has been put forward as the First Arrow of Time [LAYZER 1976], as entropy in an isolated system can never decrease but only increase over time, or remain constant after reaching its maximum value.

It has been noted that the Second Law of Thermodynamics has been suggested as an explanation of the asymmetry of time, in particular in the sense that the world is developing in one direction, from order to disorder. However, our experience of time in the world is not restricted to dissipation and 'running-down'. We also observe development, structuring, growth and self-organisation. For example, a tree metabolizes and acts dissipatively in a Second Law manner, but the features of a tree we are most likely to note are its growth and development. On a wider scale, the realm of biological activity exhibits generative and self-organising behaviour, both in the short term of an individual animal's or plant's life cycle, and in the longer term on the scale of biological evolution. This tendency of systems to generate self-organisation in an evolutionary way has been termed the Second Arrow of Time, and it too allows one to distinguish between the past and the future.

Until relatively recently there was a tendency to regard the process of biological evolution as being outside the bounds of explanation with thermodynamics [UBBELOHDE 1947]. Does not the Second Law tell us that isolated systems tend towards homogeneity rather than heterogeneity? Recent work in far-from-equilibrium thermodynamics, particularly by PRIGOGINE [1962] and his co-workers [NICOLIS and PRIGOGINE 1977], has shown that systems open to a flux of energy may spontaneously generate further structuring in a way that cannot be described by conventional equilibrium thermodynamics. For example, when a temperature gradient is applied to a liquid, initially heat is transported through the liquid solely by conduction; i.e. through interaction solely at the microscopic molecular level. As the temperature gradient is increased the system will become a 'dissipative structure', spontaneously generating a completely new ordered mode of behaviour. Macroscopic convection cells will form which allow a much more rapid transport of heat through the system than simple conduction. Such phenomena of self-organisation of far-from-(thermodynamic)-equilibrium systems mean that the First and Second Arrows of Time need no longer be seen as separate. Instead, the First Arrow shows time irreversibility for systems that are close to thermodynamic equilibrium, while the Second Arrow is operational for systems which are far from equilibrium. The application of the concept of self-organising, dissipative structures to economies has been explored by FEHL [1983] and PROOPS [1983].

Both the First and Second Arrows of Time can be related to the three types of time irreversibility discussed in Chapter 4. The First Arrow represents the tendency of isolated natural systems to go from a present known state to a future state which is not known with certainty, but about which certain general statements can be made, particularly with respect to increasing entropy. In this respect the First Arrow reflects time irreversibility 1 (risk). However, the First Arrow also has a teleological aspect in that higher levels of system entropy can only be attained by first passing through lower levels of entropy. In this sense the First Arrow also reflects properties of time irreversibility 3 (teleological sequence); viz. (a) time order, and (b) direction (cf. Chapter 4, Section 4.4.2.2). Moreover, we wish to emphasise that the First Arrow clearly reflects properties of the phenotypic evolution of systems.

The Second Arrow of Time illustrates the tendency of certain open natural systems to exhibit the emergence of structure and behaviour which is novel in a chaotic sense. It can therefore be said to reflect time irreversibility 2 (uncertainty). The Second Arrow also has properties (a) and (b) of teleological sequence, in that complex systems emerge from simpler components. We summarise these relationships in Table 5.1.

Table 5.1.   The relationship between the Arrows of Time and types of time irreversibility.

Types of Time Irreversibility	First Arrow	Second Arrow
Risk	X	-
Uncertainty	-	X
Aspects (a) and (b) of Teleological Sequence	X	X

It is important to note that a unified modern thermodynamics, a thermodynamics that includes both the First and the Second Arrow of Time, encompasses all three types of time irreversibility within a single coherent conceptual framework. In the next section we shall turn to the mathematical techniques conducive to bringing about such a unified approach.

5.4 Bifurcation and Chaos in Economic Systems
5.4.1 Dynamics of Non-Linear Systems

In the previous section the seminal work of PRIGOGINE and his co-workers was discussed, in particular the concepts of self-organisation and emergence were outlined. The analysis of systems displaying such behaviour obviously involves the examination of dynamic systems; in particular it requires considering systems which behave in a non-linear fashion. Such systems may be represented by difference equations or differential equations, and the details of their behaviour have been explored by, inter alia, NICOLIS and PRIGOGINE [1977], LI and YORKE [1975], COLLET and ECKMANN [1980], YORKE and YORKE [1981], and GUCKENHEIMER and HOLMES [1983].

Such systems are found often to have unusual properties (compared to linear systems), as mentioned in Section 5.3. In particular they may exhibit 'bifurcation' and 'chaos'. (An excellent popular discussion of modern theories of bifurcation and chaos is GLEICK [1988]; a clear exposition of the mathematics of such systems is BELTRAMI [1987]). Bifurcation may occur when the behaviour of a stable equilibrium for a dynamic system is sensitive to changes in the parameters of the system. In particular, many non-linear, low-order deterministic systems display the behaviour shown in Fig. 5.1.

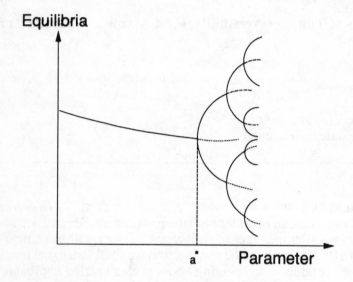

Fig. 5.1. The emergence of chaos through bifurcation.

Here the adjustment of the parameter has only a slight and gradual effect upon the equilibrium until the parameter reaches the value a*. At this value the original equilibrium exhibits a threefold splitting. The original equilibrium becomes unstable, and two new stable equilibria appear and begin to diverge as the parameter increases. As the parameter continues to increase the two stable paths may further bifurcate, in a cascading process. This can lead eventually to certain ranges of the parameter values where there are an infinite number of stable equilibria available. It is apparent that the dynamics of a system with parameters in a range where there are cascading bifurcations will be extremely complicated. Indeed, it can be shown that the dynamics may be so complex that such 'chaotic' behaviour may be indistinguishable from a random walk by the usual methods of spectral analysis [BROCK 1986].

Deterministic systems which exhibit 'chaos' have dynamic behaviour that is extremely dependent on the initial conditions chosen. Indeed, one characteristic of such systems is that two starting points which are arbitrarily close will eventually give rise to dynamics which would be judged uncorrelated by the usual statistical methods. Further, as any point in the dynamics of the system acts as the initial point for the subsequent dynamics, accurate calculation of the dynamics is impossible for more than a few time periods unless infinite accuracy of calculation is allowed. Thus although such dynamic systems are in principle deterministic, as no stochastic elements are invoked, for all practical purposes of calculation and prediction they generate stochastic behaviour.

This problem of the practical indeterminacy of some non-linear dynamical systems was recognised by POINCARÉ as long ago as the late nineteenth century, while investigating the 'many-body' problem of classical mechanics (i.e. the dynamics of many bodies interacting through gravitational attraction). This problem has also been explored in the context of statistical mechanics [cf. PRIGOGINE 1980]. Recently, great advances in the mathematical representation of such systems have been made. In particular, some continuous variable systems, represented by coupled, non-linear differential equations, have been shown to exhibit chaos [cf. GUCKENHEIMER and HOLMES 1983].

Relating chaotic dynamic systems to our conceptualization of predictability, we see that chaotic systems are in principle predictable. However, because of the structure of our human cognition, i.e. our subjective ignorance (see Chapter 2 Section 2.2.2), their detailed behaviour cannot be predicted in reality.

5.4.2 Non-Linear Dynamics in Natural Science and Economics

Apart from the study of dissipative structures, non-linear dynamics have also been used to help understanding of specific physical systems, particularly fluid turbulence [YORKE and YORKE 1981] and weather patterns [NICOLIS and NICOLIS 1984]; they have also been used to explore dynamic models in biology and ecology [MAY and OSTER 1976]. Most important for the purposes of this chapter, non-linear dynamics have been used in economic theory in such disparate areas as growth models [DAY 1982], classical (Malthusian) population models [DAY 1983], cobweb models of supply and demand [JENSEN and URBAN ♠ 1984], macro-models [STUTZER 1980], regional models [ALLEN and SANGLIER 1981, WHITE 1985], and overlapping generation models [BENHABIB and DAY 1980, 1981, 1982; GRANDMONT 1985]. Also, econometric techniques for identifying the existence of economic 'chaos', as opposed to the usual stochastic variation, have been suggested by CHEN [1984] and BROCK [1986]. For an excellent review of the implications of chaos theory for economics, see BAUMOL and BENHABIB [1989].

The implications of these findings for economics are, we believe, profound. As ALLEN and SANGLIER [1981] have noted, an economic system at a bifurcation point is not causally determinate in the usual sense. Which of the available stable equilibria will be observed will depend on the precise nature of the boundary conditions of the system, and these may need to be specified with infinite precision if random influences are to be excluded. For example, it cannot be excluded that the wing beats of a butterfly in Beijing may influence the weather conditions in Berlin. Thus the recognition of bifurcations in economic models:

"... introduce[s] the concept of 'memory' or 'history' into the 'explanation' of the state of the system, as well as an 'uncertainty' or 'choice' as to its future evolution ..." [ibid:167].

It is interesting to note that bifurcating behaviour has been established in a stochastic dynamic model by ARTHUR [1984, 1989]. He has used a modified 'Polya Urn' model to explore the effects of returns to scale on market share by competing techniques, and also of regional agglomeration of industrial activity. The simple Polya urn initially contains only two different coloured 'balls', say one red and one white. These are randomly sampled, and if a red ball is picked, it is replaced and a further red ball is added to the urn. If a white ball is sampled then it is replaced, and a further white ball is added to the urn. It can be shown that if this process is repeated indefinitely the ratio of red to white balls approaches constancy. However, the value it approaches is (ex ante) a uniformly distributed random variable in the interval [0,1].

The Polya urn model can be modified to allow for 'returns to scale', by allowing the number of balls of the sampled type placed in the urn to be a function of the proportions of the balls already in the urn. If this function exhibits diminishing returns to scale then the proportions tend to 1/2 for both colours. On the other hand, if the function has increasing returns to scale, eventually one colour comes to dominate completely, though it can be either colour. So this model exhibits a bifurcation as it passes from diminishing to increasing returns to scale. ARTHUR [1989] has used variations of this model to attempt to account for the way some production techniques come to dominate others, even though the dominating technique may be less efficient in the long-run than one of the techniques abandoned in its favour.

For example, ARTHUR [1984] suggests that for road transport, the internal combustion engine came to dominate the steam engine through a series of historical 'accidents', even though the steam engine has a greater potential (economic) efficiency. In these models again the nature of the future is decided by exogenous and apparently minor events and factors.

The appearance of chaos in economic models is important as it allows indeterminacy in the 'future' to be generated by the internal dynamics of the model, rather than by invoking external stochastic influences. Indeed, it is not difficult to conceive of a completely deterministic model where the 'chaotic' behaviour of one variable may influence the future evolution of another variable by controlling its tendency towards bifurcation. In this case a qualitative change in the behaviour of the model could take place unpredictably, but completely deterministically!

Economic systems are, in our terminology, phenotypic systems and therefore in principle predictable. But if we model such systems by employing the theory of chaos, we see that our knowledge is limited; i.e. we are ignorant. The explicit recognition of this fact makes it possible to incorporate 'ignorance' more fully into the science of economics than has hitherto been possible. This incorporation will allow the recognition not only of novelty in a genotypic sense, but also of chaotic novelty.

Whether chaos and bifurcation are actually important effects in real economies is still an open question; however, theory indicates that these two types of behaviour may be influential. This is most promising for our research, for it is apparent that bifurcation and chaos are intimately linked to notions of time irreversibility. For an observer, a system exhibiting deterministic chaos will appear very similar to a stochastic system, and therefore will exhibit time irreversibility 1. Also, a system which bifurcates may show globally discontinuous and often unexpected changes in its behaviour, while still being dynamically deterministic, and may therefore be associated with time irreversibility 2.

5.5 Bifurcation and the Emergence of Novelty

In our view there are two main things chaos theory offers to economics.

1. A view of 'unexplained variation' in economic variables as deterministic rather than stochastic.

2. A conceptual framework for the appearance of chaotic novelty from deterministic systems because of the structure of human cognition (i.e. ignorance).

Regarding 'unexplained variation', it has long been recognised in economics that a proportion of the variation in observed variables cannot be attributed to the variation in other variables. Hence if the variable y is to be 'explained' in terms of other variables A, B, C, etc., then it would normally be accepted that there is a residuum of unexplained variation, u. Thus the ith observation on this relationship might be written:

$$y_i = f(A_i, B_i, C_i, ...) + u_i.$$

Non-linear dynamics and chaos theory now suggest that at least some of this residual variation, u_i, may be attributed to the existence of chaos in dynamic economic systems.

Regarding the appearance of subjective novelty, the bifurcation properties and sensitivity to initial conditions of chaotic systems strongly suggests that, as discussed in Chapter 2, LAPLACE's notion of a computable world, and a computable future, is unachievable, even in principle.

In particular, it shows that even if one can specify the structure of a model ex ante, it may not be possible to specify its dynamic properties ex ante. Instead, these properties may only emerge from simulations with particular parameter values. That is, the properties of a deterministic system may only be comprehensible ex post. Thus even relatively simple deterministic systems may give rise to ex ante subjective novelty. These considerations enrich our distinction between ex post and ex ante analysis developed above, in Chapter 3 Section 3.5.

5.6 Conclusions and Prospects for a Synthesis

In Chapter 4 we noted that the tendency of modern general equilibrium theory towards ever greater closure in model building and conceptual framework has led to a divorce between economic theorising and the dynamics of economic activity and change in reality. In particular, the irreversibility of time has fallen victim of this trend to closure.

The problem of how explicitly to recognize time irreversibility is not unique to economics. Natural science has also been forced to confront this problem, and has been singularly successful in this, first through the formulation of the entropy concept for near (thermodynamic) equilibrium systems, and more recently through developments in the study of far-from-(thermodynamic)-equilibrium systems.

This recent work has required two types of advance; the first concerns a change in the conceptual framework with respect to time, with the overthrow of the Newtonian mechanical paradigm and the recognition that these two tendencies, towards degradation, and towards greater organisation over time, reflect two aspects of the same phenomenon.

The second, and related, development has been the formulation of mathematical techniques for examining non-linear dynamic systems. We feel that economics now needs to follow the lead set by natural science (as it has done so often before), by both embracing a wider conceptual framework which treats time irreversibility as a fundamental requirement in modelling, and also further exploring the applicability of non-linear dynamics to economic analysis.

We noted in Chapter 4 that while neoclassical general equilibrium theory can encompass time irreversibility 1 (risk), it cannot cope with time irreversibility 2 (uncertainty) and it should make use of the work which has been done on time irreversibility 3 (teleological sequence). We also noted that time irreversibility 2 is treated by evolutionary economics and time irreversibility 3 is treated by neo-Austrian capital theory, while Austrian subjectivism and the Post-Keynesians utilize all three types of time irreversibility, though without formal modelling. We feel there now exists the opportunity for a formal synthesis of these various approaches. Areas of economic analysis which we feel would benefit from such a research programme include:

1. The microfoundations of macroeconomics.

2. The relationships between resource depletion and environmental degradation, the price mechanism, and technical progress.

Concerning area 1, the most popular current approach to the microfoundations of macroeconomics is through stochastic, intertemporal general equilibrium models, with expectations being established 'rationally' [MUTH 1961]. A rational expectation is such that the subjective expectation of economic variables formed by an economic actor is identical with the mathematical expectation based on all currently available information. When time irreversibility 2 (i.e. the emergence of novelty) is recognised, it is clear that unforeseen and unforeseeable changes make the assumption of stable models and stable expectations less tenable. In particular the possibility of bifurcating behaviour may, if unrecognised by economic actors, lead to unstable, non-convergent outcomes, while if recognised as an 'unpredictable' possibility, it might induce behaviour which is optimising but apparently 'non-rational' in the short-run. (The role of 'rules of thumb' in the face of uncertainty has been explored by HEINER [1983].)

With regard to area 2, we note that the physical world acts as a constraint upon economic activity, while technical progress is the mechanism by which such physical constraints are eased or transformed. (These ideas are more fully discussed in Chapter 8). In particular, the intertemporal physical constraints imposed by considerations of resource depletion and environmental degradation are manifestations of the First Arrow of Time (i.e. irreversibilities 1 and 3), while technical progress reflects the generation of novelty and therefore invokes time irreversibility 2.

6 Time, Conceptual Structures and Economic Schools of Thought

6.1 Introduction

In Chapter 4 we began our discussion of time in economic analysis, and commented that so far economics had little success in coping with time in its full 'historical' sense. In Chapter 5 we showed that concepts of time irreversibility had already been encountered in natural science, and we suggested ways that lessons for social science could be learnt from this encounter. Our aim in this chapter is to examine various schools of economic thought, in terms of various conceptual elements, and to show how notions of time and time irreversibility fit into this framework.

In Section 6.2 we define a number of conceptual elements which we find useful in describing and categorising various schools of economic thought.

We apply these conceptual elements to a range of schools of thought in Section 6.3. These are the neoclassical approach, neo-Austrian capital theory, the Post-Keynesians, evolutionary economics, and the Austrian subjectivist school. In each case we also note how concepts of time, and time irreversibility, are involved in the various schools of thought.[1]

In Section 6.4 is discussed the problem of operationalizing the conceptual structures of Section 6.3.

Section 6.5 draws some conclusions from the preceding analysis.

(In this chapter we draw on material initially developed in FABER and PROOPS [1989]).

6.2 Conceptual Structures and Economic Schools of Thought
6.2.1 Conceptual Elements for Economic Theorising

We wish first to identify eight conceptual elements in economics for use as 'building blocks' in characterising various economic schools of thought. These are:

---

[1] It has been suggested by two reviewers of the first edition that other economic schools of thought could also be described and assessed in a similar fashion, e.g. Marxian economics. While welcoming this suggestion, we restrict our analysis to the schools mentioned.

A. Objectives

The objectives can be individual or collective.

B. Theories of the World

Any decision-making individual or organisation uses, explicitly or implicitly, theories about features of the world relevant to their objectives.

C. Boundary Conditions

This constitutes:

C1 Physically determined limits in term of the state of the environment and resources.

C2 Socially determined limits in terms of the political system, the economic system (e.g. market, planned, etc.), the legal framework, economic institutions, market structure, preferences, technology.

C3 Economically determined limits, such as the stocks of intermediate factors and capital goods, and prices if a price guided economy is given.

There are great differences in how each of these limits can be changed over time. In addition, in general it takes a longer time to alter physical (C1) and social (C2) than economic limits (C3). The possibility for adjustment and the duration of the adjustment paths strongly depends on the time irreversibilities discussed in Chapter 4. Of course, there exist interrelationships between the three kinds of limits; e.g. an increase in the stock of capital goods (C3) will in general decrease the amounts of resources in the environment (C1).

D. Procedural Rationality

Following SIMON [1967] we distinguish between 'substantive rationality' and 'procedural rationality'. Substantive rationality requires that the economic actor has a well-defined objective and a set of boundary conditions; the process of choice corresponds to achieving a global optimum. In contrast, procedural rationality is much weaker; it suggests only that the choice process is undertaken systematically, for example by using 'rules of thumb'.

E. Computational Capacity

Again following SIMON [1972], it is necessary to recognize that even well-defined objectives, boundary conditions and procedural rationality may give rise to problems for which optimising solutions make great computational demands. The capacity of an economic agent to solve such problems will be limited and may therefore be a binding constraint upon decision making[2].

F. Decision

On the basis of his state of knowledge, as embodied in the elements Objectives (A), Theories of the World (B), Boundary Conditions (C), Procedural Rationality (D) and Computational Capacity (E), the economic agent reaches a decision.

G. Implementation

The reaching of a decision leads to its implementation[3].

H. Coordination

The implementations by the economic agents give rise to a coordination process, e.g. coordination through markets.

Each of the conceptual elements A to H has various aspects of time associated with it. In the following our main concern will be to examine how the exact involvement of time in these elements varies between economic schools of thought.

6.3 Typifying Economic Schools of Thought

In this section we shall sketch, without demand of completeness, how various economic schools of thought deal with these conceptual elements. The schools of thought to be examined have differing emphases; they therefore have both different combinations of these elements and also give

---

[2] Because of its importance we have not subsumed Computational Capacity (E) under Boundary Conditions (C), but listed it separately.

[3] Not implementing a new production process may be the result of a decision if the currently used process is optimal.

differing interpretations to the elements used. In particular, for some schools of thought, Boundary Conditions (C) reflect either strictly economic limits (C3), while for others it invokes economic (C3) and social limits (C2).

We shall concern ourselves with typifications concerning short- and medium-run models. We turn to a discussion of these relationships in the long-run, particularly with respect to resource depletion and environmental degradation, in Chapter 8.

Rather than pointing out weaknesses, we shall try to show the strengths of each approach. This evaluation will give us hints as to how the different schools of thought may contribute to an encompassing conceptual structure for economic analysis. In particular, by exploring the role time plays in the conceptual elements, and their interrelationships, as utilized by the various schools of thought, we aim to show that time, and in particular time irreversibility, plays an essential role in a wider conceptual structure.

6.3.1 The Neoclassical Approach

With regard to the neoclassical approach in economics, we wish to distinguish between the explicitly 'equilibrium' models, and the disequilibrium models. In the former, adjustment to equilibrium is taken to be sufficiently rapid, so that only descriptions of the equilibrium state are important; in the latter non-equilibrium activity is important.

Equilibrium models of a static, comparative static, temporary, intertemporal and also a stochastic nature have the general conceptual structure shown in Fig. 6.1.

The meaning of the first three arrows in Fig. 6.1 are straightforward. These indicate that the Boundary Conditions (C3) of the problem influence how the outcome of the Objective (A) can lead to a decision. The last arrow indicates that the Implementation (G) leads to a change in economic characteristics for the Boundary Conditions (C3), such as the stocks of intermediate factors and of capital goods.

The element Theories of the World (B) is not an issue, except in Rational Expectations models, where it is taken as given.

It is generally assumed in this case that Procedural Rationality (D) is identical with Substantive Rationality. The meaning of the term 'rationality', as generally used in neoclassical economics, is identical with SIMON's notion of Substantive Rationality, mentioned above.

Computational Capacity (E) has not been an issue; it is assumed always to be sufficient to solve the optimization problems that arise. As to the issue of Coordination (H), traditional equilibrium theorists usually resort to the idea of a fictional 'auctioneer'.

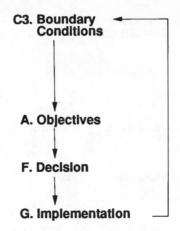

Fig. 6.1. The conceptual structure of Equilibrium Neoclassical Models.

Only those equilibrium models with stochastic elements invoke the asymmetry of time; they then exhibit Time Irreversibility 1 (Risk).

In general, for 'equilibrium' models the steady state attained is independent of the path taken towards it, while for 'disequilibrium' models the steady state attained will, in general, depend upon the path taken [see e.g. FISHER 1981]. For 'equilibrium' models the problem of market coordination becomes the tatônnement process through the auctioneer; in contrast to this, for 'disequilibrium' models coordination is an important issue.

Disequilibrium models can be represented by Fig. 6.2.

Disequilibrium models may also be stochastic and therefore exhibit Time Irreversibility 1 (Risk).

More interestingly, the time structure of the non-equilibrium trading will generally generate a 'ratchet' effect on prices. In this sense it exhibits Time Irreversibility 3 (Teleological Sequence). For example, a SAMUELSON-HICKS trade-cycle model can define a path towards its steady state that embodies the 'history' of the path in its evolution. That is, starting from given initial (boundary) conditions, the adjustment mechanism generates a path from the 'past' to the 'future'. In the terms used in Part II, the neoclassical approach allows for only predictable, phenotypic change. For equilibrium models this is even equifinal.

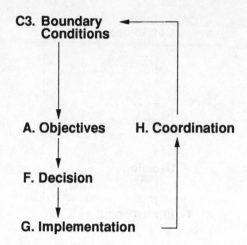

Fig. 6.2. The conceptual structure of Disequilibrium Neoclassical Models.

6.3.2 Neo-Austrian Capital Theory

The structuring of the conceptual elements is the same as for equilibrium models in neoclassical analysis (Fig. 6.1). However, the focus of neo-Austrian capital theory is on Implementation (G). In particular, concentration is given to the process of accumulation of a stock of heterogeneous capital goods to allow the production of consumption goods and the innovation of techniques.

The process of production and thence accumulation of capital goods also exhibits a 'ratchet' effect. For example, the production of consumption goods requires the previous production of capital goods. This implies that Implementation (G) invokes Time Irreversibility 3 (Teleological Sequence). This approach also allows only for phenotypic evolution.

6.3.3 The Post-Keynesians

The Post-Keynesian literature is very diverse in its concerns. Boundary Conditions are seen in terms of both economic (C3) and legal, institutional and market structures (C2). The Objectives (A) are more of a collective than of an individual nature, and do not seem to us a central issue for this

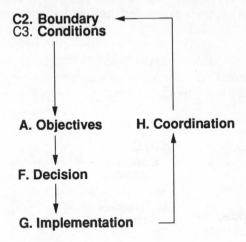

Fig. 6.3. The conceptual structure of the Post-Keynesian School.

school of thought. Generally, the problem of optimization is not in the forefront of the analysis, hence the issues of Procedural Rationality (D) versus Substantive Rationality, and of Computational Capacity (E) are little addressed. However, Decision (F) and Implementation (G) are involved by Post-Keynesians; the issues approached with these elements concern, inter alia, savings, investment, and wages. The central Post-Keynesian concerns are unemployment and relative factor rewards, which are an outcome of the market Coordination (H) process.

The Coordination problem is seen as involving aspects of both Risk (Time Irreversibility 1) and, in a less well-defined way, Uncertainty (Time Irreversibility 2). Thus genotypic and phenotypic evolution are addressed by the Post-Keynesians.

6.3.4 Evolutionary Economics

Evolutionary economics is centrally concerned with the process of learning and adaptation; thus the process of formulation and revision of Theories of the World (B) is an important issue. Another area of major concern is Coordination (H) of market processes. Evolutionary economics does not make the assumption that the decision process is Substantively Rational; instead Procedural Rationality (D) is given prominence, particularly with regard to the role of 'rules of thumb'. Boundary Conditions (C) are seen in terms of both economic (C3) and social limits (C2). Computational Capacity (E) is often seen as limited, and hence appears as an issue here.

Evolutionary economics is still a young discipline and consequently diverse in its concerns and its procedures (see NELSON and WINTER [1982], WITT and PERSKE [1982], CROSS [1983], WITT [1987]). It should be noted, therefore, that formal models in this area up to now generally involve only some of the conceptual elements shown below in Fig. 6.4.

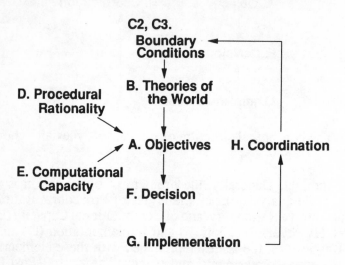

Fig. 6.4. The conceptual structure of Evolutionary Economics.

Risk (Time Irreversibility 1) is frequently explicitly recognised in the Boundary Conditions (C2, C3). Uncertainty (Time Irreversibility 2) of the Boundary Conditions is also often invoked; in particular the emergence of novelty through invention and innovation are frequently discussed. In the human capital approach the process of learning has been regarded as akin to capital accumulation; this indicates that the learning process exhibits Time Irreversibility 3 (Teleological Sequence). Evolutionary economics thus addresses both phenotypic and genotypic evolution.

6.3.5 The Austrian Subjectivist School

In terms of the conceptual elements involved, these are similar to those of evolutionary economics. However, while the evolutionary school uses many of the methods and techniques of neoclassical economics, Austrian subjectivism rejects formal modelling in favour of a more verbal mode of discourse. Moreover, it has distinguished itself strictly from both the neoclassical and Post-Keynesian schools, particularly through its emphasis on the role of the individual decision maker in the face of radical uncertainty and ignorance. With this perspective Austrian Subjectivism emphasises the role of surprise and novelty, and hence genotypic change, in economic life. (For a fuller discussion see KIRZNER [1973, 1982], O'DRISCOLL and RIZZO [1984], DOLAN [1976], PELLENGAHR [1986a, 1986b], WITT [1989]).

Because the Austrian subjectivists employ a rather verbal approach which is not directed at prediction, they are able to encompass all three types of Time Irreversibility, although only in a loose fashion [e.g. SHACKLE 1972].

6.4 Conceptualization and Operationalization

While the neoclassical approach offers methods for the production of operational results in terms of 'logical time', aspects of 'historical' time are only considered to a relatively small extent. This implies that important economic and social questions cannot be dealt with in "... a single monolithic model for all reasons" [SOLOW 1985:330]. The converse holds for Austrian subjectivists, who have an all-encompassing view of real time; however they can offer only few operational results.

We do not feel that this apparent trade-off between operationalism and the comprehensive involvement of time irreversibility is necessary. Indeed, the recent emergence of evolutionary economics raises hopes that it may be possible that some of the powerful formal methods of neoclassical economics can be used to address the wider issues encompassed by Austrian subjectivism. To this end we shall consider once again the eight conceptual elements presented in Diagram 6.4.

Indeed, it is obvious that this diagram implies a certain real-time structure. The Objectives (A), the Theories of the World (B), the Boundary Conditions (C), Procedural Rationality (D) and Computational Capacity (E) will create, within some period of time, a Decision (F). This in due course will give rise to Implementation (G) in another period, and thereafter to a process of Coordination (H), which in turn affects the Boundary Conditions (C); thus a new decision becomes required, and in turn must be implemented, etc. As the rate of change of many economic aspects of the Boundary Conditions (C1) are likely to be reasonably rapid in reality, and as the Computational Capacity (E) is often restricted, it is unlikely that any Procedurally Rational decision process will also be Substantively Rational (i.e. optimizing).

6.5 Conclusions

We recognize the considerable ambiguity in the presentation contained in this chapter. This is because of the encompassing way we have formulated our conceptual elements. Thus, for example, Boundary Conditions (C) contains many aspects, including not only various physical factors, but also political, legal, social, and economic factors.

Further, our typifications of several economic schools has been in terms of those generalities which we see as relevant to the purpose of this part of the book, viz. the role of time in economic analysis. We recognize that such typifications may invite severe criticism from the adherents of the various schools.

Finally, we have not differentiated in an operational way between short-, medium- and long-run considerations. Similarly, our three types of Time Irreversibility are broadly drawn in such a manner that they can be applied in many ways.

These areas of ambiguity clearly demand further work, both for further clarification of the issues involved, and for making substantive progress in addressing these issues. To this end we note the following problems to be confronted.

1. The role and importance of uncertainty and the emergence of novelty need to be explicitly recognised in economic analysis, particularly in long-run studies, such as those concerning resource use and the environment.

2. Recognition must be given to the role of the natural environment in providing both limits to economic activity, and simultaneously a stimulus to invention and economic development. We feel that this requires the economics profession to become much more open to the work of natural scientists; interdisciplinary work is vital here. We shall return to this in Chapter 12.

3. So far, there have been two major types of response to uncertainty and the emergence of novelty by the economics profession. The first has been to neglect these issues, and concentrate on rigorous modelling involving only certainty or risk (the neoclassical school). The second has been to embrace them so whole-heartedly that modelling and formal

representation are seen as impossible (Austrian Subjectivism). As an alternative, we urge that a step-by-step approach to these issues be adopted, as is being pursued by some evolutionary economists [NELSON and WINTER 1982; WITT and PERSKE 1982; CROSS 1983; WITT 1987], with formal modelling being used in particular problem areas. However we also urge that the modelling concentrate, as a first priority, on providing insights; insights should not be sacrificed for the sake of mathematical formalization.

Our analysis of evolution, time and schools of economic thought may now be associated more directly with our concern to understand long-run economy-environment interactions. Such an understanding will need to take an evolutionary approach, carefully distinguishing between phenotypic evolution and genotypic evolution, as well as taking ignorance into account. Further, the time irreversibility of such interactions will need to be conceptualized explicitly. To this end, in Part V we first present a conceptual outline of such modelling, and then a mathematical approach, based on neo-Austrian capital theory, which seeks to embody concepts of evolution and time in a formal framework.

Before we proceed with this task, we turn to one notion which we have often used in the previous chapters: this is the notion of 'ignorance'. We consider ignorance to be a central key to the understanding of humankind and its actions. We consider it to be of particular importance for dealing with environmental problems. It seems to us to be appropriate to analyse this concept in a philosophical and scientific context, just at the stage where we are going to start to deal extensively with formal modelling. Although ignorance can hardly be incorporated into formal modelling, the examination of ignorance is essential for modellers. This is so because reflection on the notion of ignorance makes one aware what modelling can achieve, and what it cannot.

Part IV

Ignorance

7 An Anatomy of Surprise and Ignorance

7.1 Introduction

In Chapters 2 to 6 we have attempted to lay out a new and, we hope, conceptually coherent approach to long-run economy-environment interactions. In particular, concepts of evolution and time have been developed in this endeavour. One issue we mentioned several times in those chapters is that of 'ignorance'. It is to this topic that we now turn for a detailed discussion. This chapter therefore offers an analysis of surprise and ignorance in an evolutionary context. (This chapter draws upon material originally developed in FABER, MANSTETTEN and PROOPS [1992b].)

The stimulus for such an analysis springs from considerations about environmental issues. Concerning these issues, however, it seems to us questionable if it is at all feasible to develop "a general tool for the operationalization of ignorance" [FUNTOWICZ and RAVETZ 1990:7]; this holds particularly for the area of environmental problems. In contrast to this endeavour, we feel that the first task has to be to recognise the whole range of our ignorance. These considerations supplement our previous brief remarks on ignorance above (see Sections 2.2.2 and 2.4.2).

In order truly to understand our ignorance we cannot confine ourselves to the field of environmental questions; rather we attempt to develop a general taxonomy of ignorance and surprise. This will lead us to a high level of abstraction, well beyond any particular problems. Hence the following considerations are widely philosophical, and seemingly far away from environmental issues. However, we feel that a deepened understanding of ignorance will be helpful in gaining a new attitude towards environmental problems; an attitude of openness and flexibility instead of an attitude of control and inflexibility.

From the origins of modern science the problem of knowledge and ignorance has long been recognised, especially by KANT. He asked the fundamental questions of philosophy [KANT 1956:677 B833, our translation]:

"What can I know? What shall I do? What may I hope?"

Especially important for scientists in general, and ecologically orientated scientists in particular, is the question: "What can I know?". The answer to this question is the basis for the questions: 'What can we control? What possibilities of action do we have? What can we do?'. In the search for control of the natural world and protection against environmental damage we usually concentrate on these latter questions. These questions are a driving force of modern humankind [BINSWANGER, FABER and MANSTETTEN 1990]. Conversely, the question "What can I know?" has all too often been ignored by modern science. HAYEK [1972:33, our translation] pointed out:

> "Perhaps it is only natural that the circumstances which limit our factual knowledge and the limits which thereby result for the application of our theoretical knowledge are rather unnoticed in the exuberance, which has been brought about by the successful progress of science. However, it is high time that we took our ignorance more seriously."

The extent to which it is necessary to follow HAYEK's advice can be seen by considering the usual attempt to solve environmental problems. When we meet such problems we are initially ignorant as to how to solve them. Our almost invariable assumption, however, is that this ignorance can, by learning and by scientific exploration, be reduced or even completely eliminated. The outcome of this process is to turn what was initially a problem, through scientific and technological endeavour, into a solution. The presupposition for this approach is that human knowledge can be increased without limit in any given area, giving us a better and better understanding of how the world works. This increase in our understanding will therefore cause us to face fewer and fewer 'surprises' as our science develops.

By their nature, environmental problems are often global and long-run. As such, very often they involve the emergence of unpredictable events (novelty). There is, also, the possibility that they involve dynamic systems which exhibit infinite sensitivity to their boundary conditions [i.e. 'chaotic' systems (see Chapter 5)]. This implies that the simple sequence of problem → science → technique → solution is not necessarily valid. On the contrary, we experience that our increasing knowledge may even impede the investigation for solutions. As SMITHSON [1989:3] states:

> "We are in the midst of an ignorance explosion in the well known sense that even specialists are inundated with information pertinent to their own fields. Likewise, the sheer number of specializations has mushroomed, as has the complexity of most of them".

We assert therefore that the simple structure of problem/solution, based on the faith that knowledge in any area can be increased without limit, and surprise be correspondingly reduced, cannot be valid for science in general. In particular, we believe it to be untrue for problems of long-run economy-environment interactions. Therefore, in this chapter we take an approach which concentrates on 'unknowledge' and surprise, rather than on knowledge and fulfilled expectations. An improved understanding of ignorance and surprise may offer the basis for a more appropriate attitude towards environmental issues. There has already been considerable research about ignorance:

> "The last 40 years, however, and especially the last two decades, have seen a flurry of new perspectives on uncertainty and ignorance whose magnitude arguably eclipses anything since the decade of 1660 which saw the emergence of modern probability theory" [SMITHSON 1988:3][1].

Also, a stimulating taxonomy of some aspects of ignorance in the area of society has been given by SMITHSON [1988:9]. While in this chapter we develop a new taxonomy of surprise and ignorance, this includes no criticism concerning attempts like those made by, inter alia, FUNTOWICZ and RAVETZ [1991], PERRINGS [1991], RAVETZ [1986] and SMITHSON [1989]. However, the emphasis of our endeavour is different from these authors.

In our taxonomy of ignorance and surprise we shall give special emphasis to aspects of time and evolution. Therefore our classification is of special interest for evolutionary problems (in a wide sense), of which environmental questions are particular cases.

Sections 7.2 and 7.3 deal with surprise and ignorance. In Section 7.4 we begin to analyze 'ignorance' systematically. Ignorance is first decomposed into 'closed' ignorance and 'open' ignorance. Open ignorance is further subdivided into 'reducible' ignorance (Section 7.5) and 'irreducible' ignorance (Section 7.6). Reducible ignorance can be understood either as 'personal' ignorance (Section 7.5.1) or as 'common' ignorance (Section 7.5.2). Irreducible ignorance has either a phenomenological (Section 7.6.1) or an epistemological source (Section 7.6.2). Phenomenological sources of certain ignorance spring from genotypic change (Section 7.6.1.1) or from the chaotic behaviour of certain dynamic systems (Section 7.6.1.2). Epistemological ignorance is discussed in Section 7.6.2. It is subdivided into three further categories: 'hermeneutic' ignorance (Section 7.6.2.1), 'axiomatic' ignorance (Section 7.6.2.2), and 'logical' ignorance (Section 7.6.2.3). Following the discussion of 'pure' ignorance and 'uncertain' ignorance in Section 7.7, an overview of all sources of surprise and ignorance is given in Section 7.8. In Section 7.9 we discuss the role of science in seeking to reduce uncertain ignorance to risk. In particular, we discuss the 'acts of faith' necessary in physical, social, and biological science. In Section 7.10 we draw conclusions from our findings for the

---

[1] A detailed bibliography on ignorance and related subjects is to be found at the end of SMITHSON's [1988] monograph.

study of environmental issues. In Section 7.11 we note that philosophers have often demanded an attitude of openness because human beings are inherently ignorant. In Section 7.12 we draw some conclusions of our analysis of surprise and ignorance for the importance of human freedom and will.

7.2 The Notion of Surprise

When we consider the future, when we think and speak about it, we can do this only 'ex ante'; i.e. we regard certain events to be possible, to occur certainly, to be improbable or to be impossible. We cannot experience the future directly; strictly speaking, we cannot experience the future at all. However we can, in the present, imagine aspects of the future as the future presence of certain events which we expect to come into being. This implies that only when the time of the occurrence of the expected events has come about are we in a position to compare the presently occurring events with our past expectations.

The paradoxical tension between present and future exists because, as long as we speak about the future, it is not present to our experience, while as soon as it is present to our experience, it is no longer the future but the present[2]. We see that the 'future' exists in the form of expectations only ex ante, but can be experienced only ex post, as the present or the past.

We find in everyday life that while many of our expectations are later fulfilled, the future present in our imaginings and expectations ex ante is never completely identical with what happens ex post. This difference is an essential aspect of human life.

In particular we find that, in the case where we have been totally ignorant about certain important future events, we experience ex post that the present in which these events actually occur is very different from the future present which we expected ex ante to come into being. This difference between ex ante expectations and ex post experience can be termed surprise. Surprise in this sense refers to the expectations and knowledge of a human subject. Thus, a decisive characteristic of surprise is that surprise is always experienced in the transition between ex ante and ex post (cf. Section 2.1 above and also the following).

In our everyday lives, in our scientific endeavours, and in our attempts to control our social and natural environment, we are continually being surprised. We climb into our brand new car, turn the ignition key, and it

---

[2] For a detailed consideration of such paradoxes, cf. AUGUSTINE [1961:Chapter 11].

refuses to start. We examine a set of data for which economic theory and earlier empirical analysis suggests certain relationships will hold between the variables, but our t-statistics are all insignificant.

Of course, not all surprises are unpleasant ones. We meet a stranger, and develop a deep and long-lasting relationship; our economic data might indicate the existence of a hitherto unsuspected relationship between variables; we discover material which has superconducting characteristics.

The experience of surprise may be accompanied by joy, suffering or indifference. The more one clings to one's expectations and intentions, the more surprise is accompanied by disappointments and emotional disturbances.

However, if one is aware of one's ignorance and of the possibility of surprising, novel events, then one is much less disappointed and disturbed; then surprise may be even a source of joy and happiness. Of course, this implies a certain passivity concerning the corresponding future events, which is very much in contrast to the attitude of modern man, what we have called elsewhere the 'Faustian attitude' [BINSWANGER, FABER and MANSTETTEN 1990]. For this kind of passivity implies also the readiness to encounter surprising events. In the Faustian world one cares and plans a great deal about the future, however, one is not 'ready' for surprise.

Of course, human beings attempt to protect themselves against unwanted surprises. There are various institutions to achieve this. In former times the extended family was such an institution. If one member of the family had an accident and was handicapped, it was supported by the others. In modern times it is possible to insure oneself financially against almost all kinds of events which are contrary to our intentions, wishes and hopes. But one can insure oneself only against those events which lie within the horizon of our expectations (technically expressed: for which objective, or at least subjective, probability distributions exist); i.e. the events, although uncertain and therefore surprising, are known in a subjective probabilistic sense.

7.3 Surprise: Categories and Examples

Regarding how we may be surprised, economists often follow KNIGHT [1921] in distinguishing between 'risk' and 'uncertainty', as mentioned above in Section 4.4.2.2. To this classification we wish to add the third category, 'ignorance', which in the literature, particularly of conventional economics, is not given the attention we feel it deserves. The main focus of our analysis in this chapter will be on this category of ignorance.

We can illustrate the distinction between these three categories (risk, uncertainty and ignorance) with an example of horse racing; in addition we will give an example from the field of environmental problems.

A keen follower of horse racing may frequently visit the track to bet on the outcome of the horse races. Such an individual will, when placing the bet on any race, have two factors in mind. First, what the expected possible outcomes could be: any horse in the race could win. Second, associated with each possible outcome is a subjective probability of that outcome actually occurring. It is this subjective assessment of probabilities, perhaps aided by close study of the racing form of each horse, that determines how the individual will bet. Here the individual can specify all of the anticipated outcomes, and associate a probability of occurrence with each of them. This is what an economist means by 'risk'.

To illustrate the meaning of 'uncertainty', we might suppose that our keen follower of racing form need not also be a student of weather and its forecasting. Such an individual may accept that, from time to time, inclement weather may cause the racing to be abandoned altogether. Thus the outcome 'no racing' may be recognised, but not have associated with it a subjective probability.

Thus we see that our visitor to the race course might be surprised in two ways. First, the horse that wins may not be the one expected by that individual. Second, the race may not take place at all because the weather does not permit it, even though this was recognised as a possible outcome.

However, a visit to a race course might produce an even greater degree of surprise than either of the two above cases. The individual might arrive at the race course after an absence of a few months, to find the course has been redeveloped as a shopping mall. This outcome was one which had never even occurred to our racegoer, let alone been an outcome with which a probability had been associated. SHACKLE termed such an outcome as an "unexpected event" [SHACKLE 1955:57] and characterized it as follows:

"What actually happens can have altogether escaped his (the individual's, the authors) survey of possibilities, so that the degree of potential surprise he assigned to it was neither zero nor greater than zero, but was non-existent, a sheer blank" [SHACKLE 1955:58].

This inability even to specify all possible future outcomes we term 'ignorance'.

For environmental issues we illustrate risk, uncertainty and ignorance with our second example. Let us suppose we begin to use chlorofluorocarbons in refrigeration and manufacturing techniques. In this case, risk consists in the expected effects of this innovation, including possible side effects, where these expectations are based on experiments.

Uncertainty may spring from several sources. Thus the possibility may be recognised that alternative technologies may be invented and innovated (such as freeze drying or radiation techniques); further legislation/taxation may change in an unforeseeable way the conditions of the market for refrigerators. Such possibilities may be seen, but not be associated with subjective probabilities. If these possibilities occur, they already will offer surprise to a great extent.

But the highest degree of surprise will be achieved, when we discover to our horror that the ozone layer has developed a 'hole', and that this effect was caused as an unforeseeable side effect of our innovation of the use of chlorofluorocarbons in refrigeration. This consequence was completely outside the range of possibilities when we surveyed the possible consequences of our innovation. Until the moment the ozone hole was recognized as an effect of the use of chlorofluorocarbons, we had been in a state of ignorance.

It may be worthwhile for clarification to point out how the concept of ignorance used in the literature differs from ours. To this end we refer to an illustration given by KATZNER [1986:61].

"Now let a question be asked of such a kind that the individual is in ignorance of the possible answer that might be given to it. For example the question might be, 'What kind of personal computers will be available for purchase two years from now?' One cannot have knowledge of answers to this question because there is no way of knowing what the future will bring. The set of possible outcomes (answers) cannot be known ...".

For this kind of literature it is typical that at least the area in which ignorance may occur is within the range of knowledge of the individual. Thus, in KATZNER's example, although one is ignorant about the set of possible outcomes, one knows for sure that the outcomes will be personal computers. This kind of confinement is to be found in almost all of the literature on ignorance. We admit that this kind of approach is helpful and therefore we will employ it ourselves. In addition to this approach, however, one focus of our attention lies on that kinds of ignorance which does not pertain to a particular area of occurrences. Such kinds of ignorance are of particular importance for environmental problems, because the complexity in ecological systems is so encompassing that the drawing of any boundaries, or separation of distinct areas, would avoid the recognition of the true scope of our ignorance.

7.4 Closed Ignorance and Open Ignorance

That we experience surprise is a reflection of our ignorance about the world; were we not in some ways ignorant, surprise would be impossible. In this section we therefore turn our attention to ignorance, and how it might be analysed and classified.

Here it may be worth giving a diagrammatic representation of the classification thus far, as shown in Fig. 7.1.

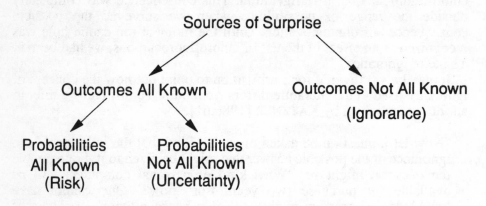

Fig. 7.1. Sources of surprise.

From Fig. 7.1 we note the crucial distinction between risk/uncertainty and ignorance, as we define them, is that the former pair are applied only in situations where all possible future outcomes can be specified, while the latter is applied where possible outcomes may not all be recognised prior to their occurrence[3], or where even the area of possible outcomes may not be known in advance. Before we proceed we wish to distinguish between two main kinds of ignorance.

(1) We are often not aware of our ignorance, and therefore we feel no need for learning or research. We call this kind of ignorance 'closed ignorance'. Closed ignorance may either spring from the unawareness of unexpected events, or from false knowledge[4] or false judgements.

---

[3] Cf. the example of the personal computer given above by KATZNER [1986].

[4] Construed in the same sense as one speaks of a 'false friend': something one has every reason to think is knowledge, but which turns out not to be so.

The condition of closed ignorance characterises precisely the typical victim of the Socratic 'elenchus' (the Socratic mode of eliciting truth by short question and answer), as described in PLATO's earlier dialogues (e.g. Meno). Indeed, the Socratic elenchus is supposed to serve precisely the purpose of converting someone from the condition of closed ignorance to that of open ignorance.

As long as an individual remains in a state of closed ignorance s/he is unable to recognise that state; only if some event forces the experience of surprise, or if another person is able to make the individual aware of its state, can the individual experience, ex post, the previous state of closed ignorance. However, very often individuals (e.g. politicians, scientists, etc.), social groups, or even whole societies, suppress the possibility of surprise and are not open to criticism. Thus they remain unaware of their state of closed ignorance.

It is important to note that very many social phenomena of ignorance occur in the area of closed ignorance; such ignorance may even be created by social processes. That is the reason why SMITHSON [1989:216-263] studies this matter so extensively.

Closed ignorance, particularly in the form of pretended knowledge, is a great barrier to human cognition and insight, as well as to the solution of environmental problems. Thus closed ignorance concerning environmental issues means that we either neglect the problems themselves, or do not take notice of intuitive insights, experience, information, models and methods of solution which are available within society. An example of closed ignorance is the reaction of the Trojan society against CASSANDRA. Another prominent example of closed ignorance within the tradition of Western science is the attitude of Aristotelian scientists towards GALILEO in the 17th century. As a last illustration of closed ignorance we mention the attitude of many scientists, engineers and politicians towards the risks of nuclear power before the accidents at Seven Mile Island and Chernobyl.

(2) If individuals (group, societies) become aware of their previous state of closed ignorance (forced by drastic events, or guided by a changed attitude), they reach a state of 'open ignorance'. In this state one will become attentive, e.g. of events and information, etc., which one had neglected earlier. Only in a state of open ignorance is one able to experience surprise to its full extent, and to react to it adequately. Of course, in a state of open ignorance one will try to understand surprising events by learning and research. However, one is not only aware that one may generate new surprises by research and learning, but knows that one remains, in spite of one's increased knowledge, essentially in a state of ignorance. This is in line with the general tenet: 'The more I know, the more I knows I don't know'.

Concerning environmental issues, a considerable shift from closed to open ignorance can be recognised in some present societies. Some decades ago, few were ready to acknowledge such problems; the environmental movement in some societies has forced this realization upon them. At present we begin to realize that we understand the environmental problems only very incompletely, and that we are, to a great extent, ignorant about their range and their solutions. So perhaps we are now in a position where we gradually begin to turn from closed ignorance to open ignorance, at least concerning some environmental issues.

In Sections 7.5, 7.6 and 7.7 we turn to open ignorance. There we wish to distinguish two further types of ignorance, which we shall call 'reducible' ignorance and 'irreducible' ignorance. We represent this classification in Fig. 7.2.

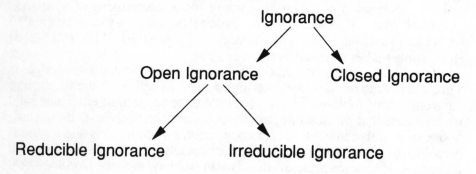

Fig. 7.2. A classification of ignorance.

If our ignorance is such that we cannot even classify it into one or other of these categories, we refer to it as either 'pure' ignorance or 'uncertain' ignorance. We return to this distinction in Section 7.7 below.

7.5 Reducible Ignorance

By reducible ignorance we mean ignorance which may be lessened, or even eliminated. We see reducible ignorance as falling into two further categories. First, ignorance that is personal; that is, the information is available within the society, but not to a particular individual. (Though this should not be taken to imply that one individual could encompass all of a society's knowledge, or even all that of one area, e.g. physics.) Second, there is communal ignorance, where the information is not even available to the society. We represent this classification of reducible ignorance in Fig. 7.3.

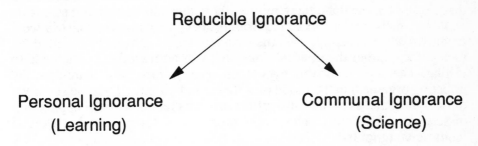

Fig. 7.3. Categories of reducible ignorance.

7.5.1 Personal Ignorance and Learning

One reason we may be surprised at the occurrence of an unanticipated outcome is that we have simply been inefficient in the use of information which is available to us. For example, the racegoer who was amazed to find the race track no longer existed had only himself to blame for not reading the local papers, or speaking to other race track aficionados. In this case the ignorance that existed was avoidable, and with effort it was reducible.

Similarly, persons who suffer lead poisoning from household pipes could have avoided their sickness if they had information about this matter. In this case the responsibility for ignorance may either be attached to the individual, who did not sufficiently strive for knowledge in this area, or to the society (e.g. media, institutions) which did not take sufficient efforts to supply the individuals with the respective information.

This kind of reducible ignorance we term 'personal' ignorance. We can reduce personal ignorance by obtaining information that is already available in the society; i.e. by individual learning.

7.5.2 Communal Ignorance and Science

Although many forms of ignorance that exist in society must be seen as 'closed ignorance', whereas other forms have to be addressed as 'irreducible ignorance', there is still another kind of ignorance, which we shall call 'communal ignorance'. It is related to the 'communal' knowledge of a society.

There are many phenomena in the world which we, as a society, do not understand fully. In the case of some of them we are, more or less, confident that we shall understand them more fully in due course, through scientific exploration. To take an example from history, the causes of malaria were unknown until recently. But the suspicion that it was transmitted by mosquitoes, rather than by 'noxious air', was an hypothesis amenable to testing. The success of this hypothesis lead, in turn, to a search for the infecting organism in the blood of afflicted individuals. Thus the society's initial ignorance as to the cause of malaria was reduced by the application of science. This kind of reducible ignorance of society is what we call 'communal ignorance'.

Communal ignorance is always generated at the edge of the knowledge of a society. As long as we do not know for sure that our ignorance has to be interpreted as irreducible, we are to a certain degree entitled to hope that it will turn out to be reducible. In this sense, ignorance is a stimulus for all scientific endeavours, as long as we can surmise that this ignorance will be found to be communal ignorance. Thus all money spent for scientific research in society is done on the presupposition that there is reducible communal ignorance.

Up to now we have dealt with kinds of ignorance which are already well-known in the literature. We now turn to areas of ignorance which have been studied less.

7.6 Irreducible Ignorance

As well as ignorance which may be reduced by the accumulation and analysis of information, we wish to suggest that certain types of ignorance are in principle irreducible, i.e they cannot be reduced. We wish to distinguish two broad categories of irreducible ignorance. The first of these relates to the phenomena, and the second to the structure of knowledge. We term these 'phenomenological' ignorance and 'epistemological' ignorance[5].

---

[5] Not all ignorance concerning phenomena or epistemological matters can be mapped as phenomenological or epistemological ignorance. Only those kinds of ignorance which are irreducible on the ground of the phenomena or on the ground of science are categorized as phenomenological or epistemological. Fallacy of our senses does not constitute phenomenological ignorance, nor do errors in our scientific approach constitute epistemological ignorance.

These categories of irreducible ignorance can be further subdivided. Phenomenological ignorance may be subdivided into 'genotypic' change (the emergence of novelty; see Chapters 2-3), and 'chaotic' dynamics(see Chapter 5).

Epistemological ignorance may also be divided into finer categories. These are 'hermeneutic' ignorance, 'axiomatic' ignorance, and 'logical' ignorance. We can represent this classification of the types of irreducible ignorance in Fig. 7.4.

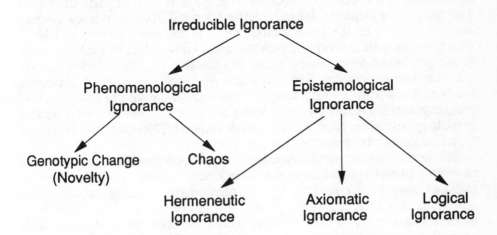

Fig. 7.4. Categories of irreducible ignorance.

7.6.1 Phenomenological Ignorance

We begin by considering the category of phenomenological ignorance, where the nature of the phenomena makes our ignorance about these phenomena irreducible in practice. We begin with the emergence of novelty through genotypic change.

7.6.1.1 The Emergence of Novelty: Genotypic Change

A distinction we find useful for discussing how systems change over time is that between a system's 'potentialities', and its 'realisation'. We developed these notions in Chapters 2 and 3, and we remind the reader that in a biological system the potentialities are given by its genetic material or 'genotype'. These potentialities may be realised to a greater or lesser extent through the development of the, say, organism in interaction with its environment. In biological systems this realisation is known as the 'phenotype'. The realisations of an economic system would be the quantities of goods produced and consumed, the corresponding set of prices, the distribution of income, etc. Hence these descriptions would represent the economic phenotype.

As we discussed in Chapter 3, the potentialities of an economic system are based on human attitudes and structures of social behaviour and structures of production. These potentialities can be recognised from the world view of a society (cf. Sections 6.2, 6.3 and 8.3), in particular from their religion or ideology. It can be further derived from the wishes, desires and preferences of the individuals, from the manners, norms and legal structures, as well as from the technological knowledge. In biology many genotypes can be described by means of genetic codes; but this description has been known for only some decades, while the concept of a genotype has been known for a much longer, time and has proved to have been of great explanatory relevance. In economics we are still in a situation similar to biology before the genetic code was developed. The economic genotype therefore cannot be described precisely.

In a certain sense, our knowledge about economics concerns only the economic phenotype, whereas the economic genotype is itself unknown, and can only be recognised by the phenomena it brings about. This ignorance about the economic genotype is not of much relevance as long as we can assume that the economic genotype does not change. In such cases ignorance does not pose a problem, since for a given set of potentialities the realisation of these potentialities will have a certain dynamics, which generally one could understand from knowledge of the potentialities. That is, we would normally expect to be able to understand the dynamics of the phenotype given knowledge of the genotype. Hence, even if the genotype is unknown, but does not change, there exists the possibility of predicting the phenotype.

Ignorance of such systems may occur when the genotype itself changes; i.e. when the potentialities of the system alter. In biological systems such genotypic evolution is recognised as part of Darwinian evolution and the changes that occur in the system's nature will inevitably generate 'surprise'. Thus the long-run evolution of ecosystems may exhibit the emergence of novelty, and hence be unpredictable. Such evolution of the potentialities of systems is an irreducible source of ignorance.

Regarding environmental issues, these largely result from long-run economy-environment interactions. Now both ecosystems and economies can exhibit the emergence of novelty through genotypic change, so the possibility for the emergence of novel environmental problems (and perhaps solutions) is considerable.

7.6.1.2 Deterministic Dynamics and Chaos

The nature of 'chaos' was discussed in Chapter 5. We recall that the 'classical' concept of deterministic dynamical systems was summarised by LAPLACE who said, in essence: 'Tell me the position and velocity of all the particles in the universe, and I can calculate all future states of the world'. Here the notion is that if a dynamical system is deterministic, it is, at least in principle, calculable for all future states. The assumption LAPLACE made is that if the genotype of a dynamical system is fully specified and also unchanging, then the phenotype can always be completely determined.

Of course, one must recognise that any actual calculation can only be performed using a finite number of arithmetic operations. Therefore the principle of the computability of a phenotype from a completely known genotype requires that the future dynamics of such systems are calculable to any required degree of accuracy. One of the startling findings of recent mathematics, though one can trace the roots of this approach back to POINCARÉ, is that certain dynamical systems do not give better approximations the greater is the degree of arithmetic accuracy used [LORENZ 1963] (an excellent popular discussion is given by GLEICK [1988]). Such systems, known as 'chaotic' systems, have an infinite sensitivity to the initial conditions imposed. The slightest deviation from the intended starting point generates a dynamical outcome which is entirely uncorrelated with the desired outcome (see also Chapter 5).

Such systems are clearly a further source of irreducible ignorance. We may know everything there is to know about the determinants of such a system's behaviour, but still be quite incapable, in principle, of calculating even a 'reasonable' approximation to the system's dynamics. Thus even if a system's potentialities are fully specified and unchanging, it may be in principle impossible to determine the evolution of the realisation of those potentialities. It may be the case that many economy-ecosystems interactions exhibit interrelations so complex that they are, at least in some aspects, chaotic in their dynamics, and hence in principle unpredictable. This is clearly another irreducible source of ignorance regarding environmental issues.

7.6.2 Epistemological Ignorance

Irreducible ignorance need not come only from the phenomena, but may also come from the way we conceive the phenomena. Such ignorance we term 'epistemological' ignorance. We distinguish three kinds of such ignorance: 'hermeneutic' ignorance, 'axiomatic' ignorance, and 'logical' ignorance.

7.6.2.1 Hermeneutic Ignorance

Even if a science is based on mathematical reasoning, it has to use words of the common language as soon as it is applied to phenomena. The general consensus of recent philosophy has been to suggest that it is impossible to construct an ideal language which can escape the ambiguities of common language [cf WITTGENSTEIN 1926/69:63-81; STEGMÜLLER 1969:397-428, 562-568]. So scientists have to accept that, despite their sharpest definitions, they have to use words and notions which are not completely unambiguous. From this it follows that scientific statements also can never be totally clear and unambiguous.

So we remain, in a certain way, ignorant even if we express our surest knowledge, because we cannot do away with the problems of ordinary language. This may be a reason why scientists so often do not understand each other, although their theories seem to be totally clear. Now, hermeneutics is the study of meaning and understanding, in this case as mediated by language. This ignorance, derived from the nature of language and communication, we therefore term hermeneutic ignorance.

7.6.2.2 Axiomatic Ignorance: Falsifiability

All scientific knowledge is based, explicitly or implicitly, on certain basic assumptions, or axioms. The ideal scientist can derive the entire corpus of his knowledge from such an axiomatic system. These axioms are a combination of the distillation of our experience of the world, and also a reflection of our beliefs about the nature of the world. Perhaps in physical science, experience may be the dominating influence, while it seems to us that in much modern economic analysis, the axioms are much more reflections of belief structures.

By their nature the axioms can never be shown, singly or collectively, to be 'true'. However, if the 'theorems' derived from the axioms are at odds with our experience, then the axioms, singly or collectively, may be judged to be 'false'. In that we can never know the truth of our axioms, unless they are shown to be false, we remain ignorant at a very fundamental level of our scientific endeavour.

POPPER [1959] stressed the impossibility of the proof of the truth of an axiomatic science, stressing instead that the most we can hope to achieve is the 'falsification' of our axiomatic assumptions. In addition, it is important to note that there are many statements which can neither be verified nor falsified. For instance ARISTOTLE's axiom that all bodies that move tend to a state of rest contradicts NEWTON's law of inertia. But both axioms can neither be proved nor falsified. Another example is KANT's claim that the statement 'human will is free' as well as the opposite statement, 'human will is determined,' can neither be proved nor falsified. But in contrast to the modern scientific attitude, KANT did not consider it to be meaningless to deal with these kind of statements, because they have such on essential importance.

7.6.2.3 Logical Ignorance: GÖDEL's Theorem

In 1931 GÖDEL proved that any axiomatic system which generates a formal basis for arithmetical operations must allow at least one theorem that, within the proof structure allowed by the axioms, can neither be proved nor disproved. Thus GÖDEL's [1931] theorem shows that even a non-falsified axiomatic system remains a source of ignorance, irrespective of our attempts, or otherwise, at falsification.

Unfortunately, by its nature GÖDEL's theorem gives no indication of what type of theorems may be undecidable in this way. Since 1931 there has been speculation over what thus far unproved theorems in number theory might be undecidable, with FERMAT's Last Theorem being often suggested as one of this type.

From GÖDEL's theorem we therefore now know that even closed logical systems are sources of ignorance, and this ignorance cannot in principle be reduced. That is, even a system of logic is a source of irreducible ignorance. One consequence is that all those sciences which are applied systems of mathematical logic, e.g. physics and economics, contain at least one theorem that cannot be proved.

7.6.2.4 Epistemological Ignorance and Environmental Issues

We wish to suggest that epistemological ignorance presents problems for any analytical science. Problems of language, axiomatisation and the incompleteness of logical systems, have consequences for any discipline using mathematics. Now many environmental issues are approached using mathematical modelling, so even this apparently well-founded method is a potential source of ignorance regarding environmental problems.

7.7 Pure Ignorance and Uncertain Ignorance

Before proceeding to summarise our taxonomy of surprise and ignorance, it is important to point out that this taxonomy is not complete[6]. We further require the distinction between 'pure' ignorance and 'uncertain' ignorance.

7.7.1 Pure Ignorance

We take it to be a self-evident truth that the accumulation and testing of knowledge that informs human activity has a unitary characteristic. The nature of knowledge, and ignorance, that pertains to our scientific work is no different to that relevant to the way we make a cup of coffee, or buy our weekly groceries.

In Western civilizations our response to ignorance is generally the assumption that it is reducible by science. We assume that the scientific method and the abilities of humankind will eventually fill these gaps in our 'knowledge'. However, when we ask ourselves, in everyday life or in science, 'what is going to happen?', we do not know in which area surprises will turn up. Further, we are ignorant of what kind of surprises we will meet. Naturally, in this state we do not know whether our ignorance is reducible or irreducible. From this it follows that the kind of ignorance cannot be specified. If this is the case, we speak of 'pure ignorance'.

This kind of ignorance is an essential element of human life, of which science is only a part. Ignorance in this sense cannot be classified within the taxonomy developed above. This is because pure ignorance is of an indefinite nature, like the future itself. It cannot be limited or constrained to any particular area of knowledge, as it encompasses all areas of life and development. Humankind has developed many styles of coping with and/or reflecting upon pure ignorance. Among these we see ritual behaviour, religion and artistic endeavour.

7.7.2 Uncertain Ignorance

Only when we are in a state where we are able to constrain the question 'what is going to happen', to a particular area of knowledge can we ask

---

[6] We are grateful to Michael HAMMOND for pointing out this lacuna in our classification.

ourselves if our ignorance is of a reducible or irreducible type. Since we then know the possible outcomes (viz. reducible or irreducible ignorance) then in accordance with the literature we denote this 'uncertain' ignorance.

We normally make the act of faith that our uncertain ignorance is reducible (viz. open to learning or scientific discovery). However, this can only be an act of faith. If it transpires that science can reduce our ignorance, then, after the fact, we may classify our ex-ignorance as reducible. Thus we see that the distinction between reducible and irreducible ignorance can only be made ex post. However, it is in principle impossible to classify ignorance as reducible while the ignorance remains. Thus if we feel unwilling to make this act of faith, and if we cannot satisfy ourselves that our ignorance is irreducible, then, until the ignorance is reduced, intellectual honesty should compel us to classify our ignorance as uncertain.

Uncertain ignorance is a doubly uncomfortable state, involving both uncertainty and ignorance. The success of modern science owes much to the circumstance that science promises to convert uncertain ignorance into knowledge.

It seems to us that the normal modern, scientific, response to the recognition of ignorance is initially to assume it is reducible, and further, that it is personal, and accessible to reduction by learning from already available information. When we encounter a new environmental problem we seek the advice of the experts. If the experts are also ignorant on this matter, we turn to a programme of scientific research.

An example of ignorance, which has remained up to now uncertain, is nuclear waste. When society decided to carry through the development of nuclear power it believed that nuclear waste disposal could be dealt with in much the same way as non-nuclear waste. This proved to be untrue. Experts were consulted, and they suggested a scientific research programme be established. We may remain convinced, despite great costs over long periods, that our ignorance is reducible. Another example is nuclear fusion, which has been promised imminently for forty years, and remains still unfeasible.

We are not suggesting that either area is an area of irreducible ignorance. However, as we recognise irreducible ignorance may occur, and as reducible ignorance can only be recognised when it ceases to be ignorance, the possibility of irreducibility must be accepted (though humankind seems to prefer to have faith otherwise).

7.7.3 Conclusions Concerning Pure Ignorance and Uncertain Ignorance

Pure ignorance and uncertain ignorance have in common only that they are not suitable for being included in our taxonomy. But their statuses are completely distinct. If we are confronted with uncertain ignorance, we try to cope with it. First we attempt to classify it as reducible or irreducible ignorance. We expect that sooner or later we will be able to do this. If the ignorance is reducible, then we find this out through its amenability to scientific investigation. Even if our ignorance is for the time being irreducible, we at least hope, and in general even expect, that we will find some method to deal with it. From these considerations we recognise that the state of uncertain ignorance is of a transitional nature; it changes over the course of time. In contrast, pure ignorance is of an unchanging nature over the course of time.

7.8 An Overview of the Sources of Surprise

In this section we summarise our results so far.

Surprise derives from two possible sources. First, when all possible outcomes are known, but where the probabilities of each possible outcome may be known (risk) or may be unknown (uncertainty). Alternatively, we may be in a state of ignorance, where all possible outcomes are not known.

This ignorance may be recognised and included in the world view (open ignorance), or it may be ignored (closed ignorance).

Open ignorance may derive from known sources (reducible ignorance and irreducible ignorance).

Reducible ignorance may be reducible by learning (personal ignorance), or by the application of science (communal ignorance).

Irreducible ignorance may derive from the nature of the world (phenomenological ignorance), or from the nature of reasoning (epistemological ignorance).

Phenomenological ignorance may be because of the appearance of ontological novelty (genotypic change), or from the inherent unpredictability of certain dynamic systems (chaos).

Epistemological ignorance may result from the problems of language (hermeneutic ignorance), the assumptions underlying the reasoning process (axiomatic ignorance), or the incompleteness of the logical system (logical ignorance).

We represent this structure in Fig. 7.5.

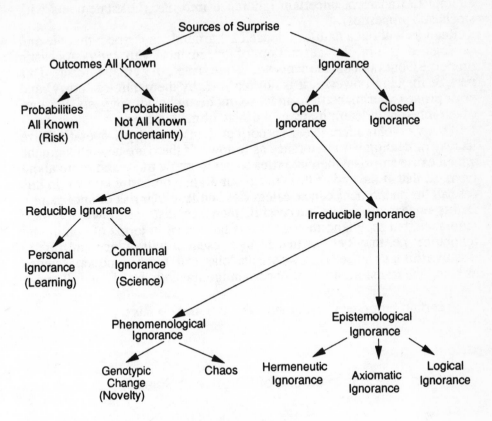

Fig. 7.5. A taxonomy of surprise and ignorance.

7.9 The Nature of Scientific Endeavour

Our view is that the normal 'human condition' is characterised by pure ignorance. We are continually being surprised, and often our surprise derives not from risk or uncertainty, but from ignorance. That is, our surprise is not because things happen to which we attributed low probabilities, or for which we had no probabilities. Rather, our surprise derives from events taking place which were not foreseen as possible.

As we know, classical science has attempted to transform uncertain ignorance into systematically organised knowledge. Modern science has suggested a more modest approach. Science may be considered as the attempt to transform uncertain ignorance into risk (i.e. statements with stochastic properties).

Readers without a natural science background may expect that the aim of science is not the generation of statements with only stochastic properties, but rather statements which are 'true', or perhaps 'false'. This may be the aim; however, it is not feasible, by the nature of 'noisy' and error prone experimentation, and also, modern physics suggests, because of the inherent indeterminacy of the state of matter/energy.

If our view of modern science is correct, then we can try to operationalize its way of dealing with ignorance as follows. If there are new phenomena which cause surprise, then one tries to get to know more and more about them, so that at the end of this endeavour all outcomes are known. In this case all the phenomena can be categorised under either risk or uncertainty. If this endeavour is not successful, then scientists acknowledge their ignorance, but they tend to restrict this ignorance in terms of communal ignorance; i.e. they believe that further research will reduce and finally dissolve this ignorance. Thus we see the 'classical' route of modern science as being the transformation of uncertain ignorance into risk, as follows:

Uncertain Ignorance → Communal Ignorance → Risk

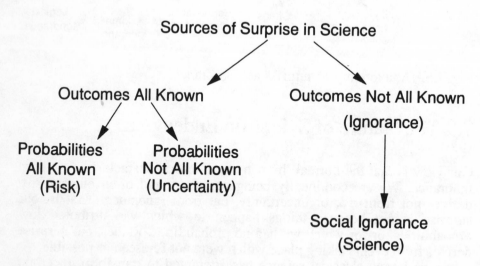

Fig. 7.6. Sources of surprise in science.

Hence, there is no concept of true irreducible ignorance in modern science.

We represent the taxonomy of surprise inherent in science in Fig. 7.6. Implicit within this scientific endeavour is the assumption that the object of scientific study is amenable to this reduction. This assumption cannot be testable, except in so far as it generates 'useful' and, perhaps, 'beautiful', science. Even so, this assumption is an axiom of science; that is, it is an act of faith.

7.9.1 Physical Science

Regarding physical science, little in our experience argues against such faith in the 'reducibility' of uncertain ignorance to risk. However, modern mathematics has shown that what we have termed chaotic phenomenological ignorance is not only possible, but characterizes many important areas [GUCKENHEIMER and HOLMES 1983]. This has demanded the recognition, in the practice of physical science, that knowing more about the nature of a system does not necessarily mean that statements about its behaviour can be reduced to statements which have the status of risk.

7.9.2 Social Science

For economics, and the social sciences generally, the assumption that the systems being studied are amenable to statements with the status of risk seems much more questionable. The systems being studied are social systems, and the elements in these systems are humans whose natural condition is itself the confrontation of uncertain ignorance. It might be the case that over sufficiently short periods, and with sufficiently little 'surprise' affecting the social system being studied, then certain statements on aggregate social behaviour *may* be possible.

However, we view the above assumption that statements on social systems have the status of risk, which underlies social science, as inherently internally contradictory. On the one hand, humans as scientists explicitly recognise their uncertain ignorance through their scientific endeavours. On the other hand, the assumption made by scientists about humans is that there is no uncertain ignorance affecting the behaviour of the social agents whose behaviour they study. This seems to us like wanting to have your cake and eat it!

7.9.3 Biological Science

The leap of faith needed for biological science seems to be somewhere between the relatively modest one of physical science, and the gigantic one of modern social science. For the study of microorganisms and the biochemical subsystems of more complex organisms, the assumption that uncertain ignorance may be transformed into risk is probably generally acceptable. For studies of the behaviour of mammals, the assumption may be as questionable as for social science. For ecological systems, an additional major difficulty in their study is the interaction between the activity of the ecological systems and the human activity, in particular the economic one. (For a more detailed discussion on 'why physics is easy, economics is difficult and biology is in between' see section 3.4 above).

7.10 Surprise, Ignorance and Ecological Issues

We began with KANT's question "What can I know?". Our discussion suggests that one thing we *can* know is, to some extent the nature of our ignorance, even if this is only knowing that we do not even *know* the nature of our ignorance.

How may this knowledge concerning our ignorance inform our behaviour? We have already noted that science is one of several methods of responding to the immanence of our uncertain ignorance. However, in this chapter we have also defined and classified two other types of ignorance; phenomenological irreducible ignorance and epistemological irreducible ignorance. Regarding the former, modern science is itself discovering the limits to which uncertain ignorance may be reduced to risk. The discovery of the existence of chaotic dynamics has forced a somewhat startled recognition of these limits from the scientific community. Modern philosophy and mathematics also shows that there are epistemological constraints on the reduction of ignorance.

How might we respond, both as scientists in general, and as environmental scientists in particular? First, at a basic level, we feel that the nature of uncertain ignorance demands all that we can offer: recognition. We face uncertain ignorance in our ordinary lives, and recognise it at least implicitly. We also face it in our science, and explicit recognition in this sphere is also due.

Regarding epistemological irreducible ignorance, here we know what the very nature of our understanding tells us we *cannot* know everything. The very structure of our rational scientific endeavour imposes limits on the achievements of that endeavour. Here we feel the appropriate response is humility. By this we mean, for example, that the scientific community should be modest concerning their own knowledge and their ability to contribute to the control of the world. Further, scientists should have respect for non-scientific approaches to the world, such as art and religion, as well as common-sense knowledge. Some traits of these ways may be integrated in the so-called 'Second Order Sciences' [FUNTOWICZ and RAVETZ 1990]. Other traits cannot be incorporated into a scientific approach. They remind the scientist of the fact that science is only one way for humans to experience the world (for a fuller discussion see BINSWANGER, FABER and MANSTETTEN [1990], FABER, MANSTETTEN and PROOPS [1992a]).

Finally, phenomenological irreducible ignorance is an area where our recognition of our ignorance may be a key element in altering our behaviour. In a world where the altering potentialities of systems causes changes in those systems which may not, *in principle*, be predicted, our knowledge of that unpredictability may still be useful. If we know that changes in the nature of systems will occur, and we also know that we cannot know the nature of those changes until they occur, then the appropriate response is surely flexibility (for a fuller discussion of these ideas see Chapter 12 below; also FABER, MANSTETTEN and PROOPS [1992a]). For example, a non-flexible measure in the energy sector was the introduction of nuclear plants.

7.11 From Ignorance to Openness

That philosophy involves the study of knowledge is implied by its literal meaning, i.e. 'love of wisdom'. But great philosophers of all periods have recognised that to understand knowledge one has also to understand ignorance. They realised that the region of our possible knowledge is like an island "surrounded by a wide and stormy ocean which is the actual site of semblance and illusion (Schein)." [KANT 1956:B 295, our translation.] This ocean of pretended knowledge is in truth the ocean of our ignorance. In the same vein SOCRATES said that "I know that I know nothing". This led the oracle of Delphi to acknowledge SOCRATES as the wisest of all human beings.

At the end of the middle ages one of the most important philosophers of that period, NICOLAS OF CUSA [1964:Book II, p.93, paragraph 162], postulated an attitude of 'Docta Ignorantia'. This meant the acknowledgment of the circumstance that all human knowledge emerges out of ignorance, and after some time may vanish or be replaced by new types of knowledge. For him, the criteria for true science were adequacy to everyday experience, openness, creativity and flexibility. From this point of view he criticised, already some decades before COPERNICUS, the geocentric world view of the ancient philosophers, with the argument that they lacked the 'Docta Ignorantia', ignorance which is recognised and open to learning and alternative models. In our terms, this reflects their failure to recognise their axiomatic ignorance. As for pure ignorance, 'Docta Ignorantia' includes the faith that human thinking and action springs from a dimension which is greater than human knowledge, and which can be experienced only in humble acknowledgement of our ignorance.

One main intention of KANT's *Critique of Pure Reason* is expressed in the following sentence: "I had to eliminate knowledge to gain room for faith" [KANT 1956:33; B XXX, our translation]. Faith in the sense of KANT does not mean the adherence to any church or confession, but an attitude of openness and confidence towards all matters which lie in the area of our ignorance. KANT's ethics were offered as an attitude which is not only valid for known circumstances and tendencies, but also for the unknown.

The attitude of openness, as described by PLATO, as well as by NICOLAS OF CUSA and KANT, can be seen as the essence of philosophy and knowledge. This attitude allows humans to experience all things as they develop, not as we might prejudge them, but accepting them as they are.

7.12 Freedom and Will

At first sight the conclusions of our anatomy of surprise and ignorance may seem to be negative. Our attempt to give an answer to KANT's first question "What can I know" (i.e of knowledge) has shown that there are inherent narrow limits to human knowledge. This implies that there are limits to purposeful activity, too. Also, the attitude of openness, which was described in the previous section, is not active, but passive: an attitude of openness implies to be prepared and waiting, like the virgins in the New Testament [MATTHEW 25:1-12].

However, this seeming passivity is only one aspect of our conclusions. We remind the reader of KANT's second question "What shall I do". The answer to this question, in the sense of KANT, is in its essence not determined by our knowledge and by our ignorance. KANT's approach refers rather to human freedom, which is essentially not affected by knowledge or unknowledge. Of course, there exist different concepts of freedom in philosophy. For instance, following Greek philosophy human beings are free to act according to the order of the cosmos. Following KANT one may say they are free to act according to the moral law which exists within them. If this or any other kind of freedom is recognised then one can act according to it if one *wants* to do so. That means one has to make a corresponding *decision*; one has to formulate a *will*. This will can then be an orientation for acting in general and for politics in particular. Of course the will cannot be formulated once and for all, but there has always to be a continuous *decision* to keep up the will or to reformulate it. It is important to note that the object of the will may change when there is new information. However, the orientation of the *free will* is unaffected by new information and new concepts. This is so because the orientation is towards the moral law which cannot be changed, not even by new information.

The greater the time horizon, the greater is the ignorance one has to cope with, hence the greater is the significance of the will as a compass for acting. Since environmental problems are of long-run nature, we consider the will to be of utmost importance for their solution.

To clarify the meaning of our concept of will, it is useful to confront it with the concept of wish. For instance, in many western countries, particularly in Germany, there is the wish to have a better environment, to use less polluting industries, to produce less waste etc. Nevertheless, no really drastic policy measures are taken which would lead to corresponding environmental activities. This is so because in society there exists only the desire for environmental protection and not the will. For the latter would require the determination to carry through drastic policy changes, with all its consequences, such as unemployment in certain industries, reduction in growth rates, restrictions in the freedom to move, etc. Thus the main difference between the wish and the will is that the latter implies that people are willing to take into account and to endure all the frictions, the strenuous efforts and sufferings which the wish entails (for more details relating to the global greenhouse effect, see PROOPS, FABER and WAGENHALS [1992:Section 1.4.1]).

Part V

Production and Innovation

8 Economy-Environment Interactions in the Long-Run

8.1 Introduction

In Chapter 7 we discussed, at some length, the concept of ignorance. Now, fore-warned of the limits of our possibilities for understanding, we can turn to modelling. While in Chapter 6 we dealt mainly with short- and medium-run aspects, in this chapter we return to the long-run development of economic activity. The conceptual basis for this long-run analysis was laid in Chapters 2 to 5. We concentrate on the temporal development of the physical limits, i.e. of the Boundary Conditions (C1), defined in Section 6.2.1.

In Section 8.2. we discuss how long-run environmental resource problems have been examined within neoclassical and neo-Austrian frameworks. We discuss how market failures are of particular importance in the long-run and lead to certain time irreversibilities.

The insufficiencies of existing environmental resource models to capture these time irreversibilities lead us to propose a new conceptual framework in Section 8.3. We consider this to be more suitable to examine the historical experience of the relationship between economic activities and the natural environment. It illustrates how production, innovation, physical limits of the environment, and invention interact with each other.

In Section 8.4 we discuss how the conceptual model developed in Section 8.3 might be operationalized, with neo-Austrian capital theory.

The nature and history of neo-Austrian capital theory is summarised in Section 8.5.

In Section 8.6 we offer some concluding remarks.

Chapters 2 to 7 form the conceptual basis of our approach. We introduced the notions of genotype and phenotype from biology, and some general notions on time and irreversibility to formulate an encompassing approach to evolution. We then sought to analyse various schools of economic thought. In this way we were able to explore the similarities and differences between these schools. For example, neoclassical economics was seen to be useful to analyse phenotypic change, while Austrian subjectivism deals mainly with genotypic change. We recall that for economies, genotypic change can correspond to the invention of a new technique, while phenotypic change corresponds to the innovation of a new technique.

The wish to control the economy and the natural environment has given the concept of predictability a central status in modern science and society at large. For this reason, we have examined the conditions for predictability, and made an anatomy of surprise and ignorance. This analysis made us aware of the inherent limits of controlling economy-environment interactions.

We recognise that many of the ideas discussed in Parts 1 to 4 are, in themselves, quite novel, and some may be found challenging. We also realise that the potentialities of these ideas have not been fully realised in our discussion, for reasons of brevity and inspiration. We hope that these ideas can be more fully explored in the future, by ourselves and others.

We feel that while there has been much conceptual work, as well as modelling, in ecological economics, it is rare that there is conceptual work and corresponding modelling within a single volume. However, to exemplify and to explore the weaknesses and stregths of the conceptual work, it is expedient to do both at the same time. In our case, indeed, it was our modelling work which initially inspired our interest in the conceptual foundations of ecological economics. We found that fully to understand the limitations of such modelling, we needed to construct concepts relating to the evolution of systems, and their realisations in time, as well as the constraints of ignorance on our understanding.

When we move from conceptual work to modelling, we immediately constrain the nature and scope of these concepts. This happens in two ways. First, many of our concepts (e.g. genotypic change) concern aspects of the world which are, in principle, difficult to model, at least ex ante. Second, any model must involve a formalism of assumptions regarding technical relations, etc., which will limit the model to being only a special case of the set of models consistent with the underlying conceptualisation. Therefore our modelling endeavour which follows should be seen as only one means of realising, at least partially, the modelling potentialities of our conceptualisation. There is, therefore, a natural and unavoidable tension between the conceptual elements of this book (Parts 1 to 4) and the modelling elements to which we now turn. (We remind the reader that in the prefaces we noted that different readers may wish to approach the material in this book in different ways.)

8.2 Long-Run Resource and Environmental Models

8.2.1 Neoclassical Models with Backstop Technology

A typical neoclassical resource model involves a given resource stock and a given set of techniques, which are either fully known, or at worst risky (Time Irreversibility 1). The operation of the model would indicate how optimal resource depletion leads to relative factor and resource price changes, giving rise to factor substitution through the innovation of new techniques. Price changes under the assumption of perfect futures markets imply that the notion of market Coordination (H) is not an essential issue here. To cope with the possibility of an infinite time horizon it is generally assumed that there is a 'backstop' technology available, which utilizes, at high cost, an unlimited or undepletable resource [see e.g. DASGUPTA and HEAL 1979:175-8]. The conceptual elements in such a model are those already shown in Fig. 6.1, and reproduced in Fig. 8.1. Here, unlike the case obtaining in the short- and medium-run, the focus of Boundary Conditions is upon Physical Limits (C1) rather than Economic Limits (C3).

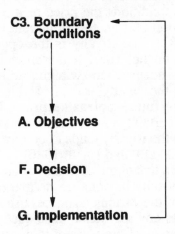

Fig. 8.1. The conceptual structure of neoclassical environmental models.

It is apparent that such neoclassical models are special forms of the intertemporal equilibrium approach and therefore can only exhibit Time Irreversibility 1.

8.2.2 Neo-Austrian Models of Resource Use

The conceptual elements involved are the same as for the neoclassical models above. However, particular attention is paid to Implementation (G). This is because of the emphasis on what HICKS [1965:Chapter 7, 1973b] called the 'traverse'. Once a new technique has been innovated, in response to technical progress and relative prices, there remains the problem of how such a new technique becomes embedded in the wider production process. For example, the innovation of microelectronic components over the past decade has had profound implications in many industries other than electronics. The entire technology of the economy is forced to undergo realignment because of a change of technique in only one sector. This realignment of production because of resource and environmental constraints within an economy reflects Time Irreversibilities 1 and 3 (Risk and Teleological Sequence).

8.2.3 Market Failures in the Long-Run

Using an optimising neoclassical or neo-Austrian approach, one can show that under competitive conditions the price of a resource is equal to its marginal cost of extraction plus an economic rent (royalty), [DASGUPTA and HEAL 1979:167-181]. The royalty is the opportunity cost that the resource is used now and not later. It therefore is an indicator of the substitution costs which occur when switching to another resource. This indicator, in the form of the royalty, is expressed in present values, which is achieved by discounting future spot market prices. Because of Risk (Time Irreversibility 1) and Uncertainty (Time Irreversibility 2), the discount rate is generally so high that the royalty tends to be low. This in turn evokes a high use of resources [EPPLER and LAVE 1980].

It can be further shown that at the optimum of an economy, the price of a commodity should not only be equal to its marginal production costs, including the royalties of the various resources used in its production, but it should also contain its environmental costs [see e.g. FABER, NIEMES and STEPHAN 1987:Chapter 7]. Because of their intertemporally external nature, not only within one country but also between countries, these different cost components are not reflected in competitive market prices[1]. It is well known how difficult it is to enact environmental legislation on a national, and in particular on an international level, to take care of these environmental costs [BROWN and JOHNSON 1982]. Even if this is done, for the same reason as mentioned above, we still encounter the problems connected with a high discount rate. It follows, therefore, that in reality the intertemporal negative external effects are accounted for insufficiently.

---

[1] For a fuller discussion of the determinants of resource royalties and their role in determining long-run economic activity, see FABER and PROOPS [1993].

From these considerations we conclude that the lack of inclusion of intertemporal external effects by markets (concerning resources and environment), cause the actual market prices of goods to be so low that they do not adequately reflect the intertemporal substitution and environmental costs they incur. This, in turn, leads to the Implementation (G) of techniques using high amounts of resources and causing increasing environmental degradation. This, however, implies that the physical Boundary Conditions (C1) are approached quickly. This involves Time Irreversibility 1 (Risk) and Time Irreversibility 3 (Teleological Sequence, in the sense of time order and direction), since the entropy of the Earth increases [see e.g. FABER, NIEMES and STEPHAN 1987:Chapters 3 and 4], and also to Time Irreversibility 2 (Uncertainty). This is because often one does not know the effects of approaching the physical limits. An example of such uncertainty is the current concern about the effect of chlorofluorocarbons on the ozone layer. That is, there is the possibility of potentialities of the economy-environment system changing unpredictably; i.e. there is the possibility of genotypic evolution of this system.

8.3 Conceptual Elements of Long-Run Economic Development

It is apparent that essential aspects of time irreversibility are not captured by simple neoclassical or neo-Austrian environmental resource models. We therefore wish to propose a more encompassing framework, which enables us to relate our conceptual elements to the historical experience of the relationships between economic activity and the natural world. We shall stress in particular the relationships between physical limits, invention, innovation and production. By doing this we wish to recognize more explicitly the asymmetry and irreversibility of time. This analysis will be of a long-run and highly aggregated character. To this end we follow KOOPMANS' [1974:327-8] comment that:

> "In a world of continuing but only dimly foreseeable change in technology and preferences (that means in our terminology in Boundary Conditions (C) and ignorance, the authors), the notion of equilibrium disappears, but that of an adjustment process remains."

We believe that for the analysis of long-run developments one does not need to focus so exclusively upon individual decision making, which is of such central importance for general equilibrium theory. Hence, we shall be concerned with the following conceptual elements only marginally: Objectives (A), Procedural Rationality (D), Computational Capacity (E) and Decision (F).

We retain the other four elements: Theories of the World (B), Boundary Conditions (C), Implementation (G) and Coordination (H). Of central importance are the Boundary Conditions (C); of these we particularly consider their physical aspects, i.e. the environment as a supplier of resources, as a supplier of public goods, and as a recipient and transformer of waste products.

The Implementation (G) of production activities will, in the long-run, lead to the depletion of resources and the generation of pollution. This in turn will cause physical limits to become increasingly binding constraints upon economic activity. First, the price mechanism of the Coordination (H) element will cause substitution of factors of production, in particular of resource use, thereby possibly generating a more rapid rate of innovation of less resource-intensive and of less pollution-intensive techniques.

The more closely the physical limits are approached, the greater will be the pressure on society, via increasing prices, to find new techniques of production. We recognize, of course, that the price mechanism is only one source of invention. Since invention is of extreme importance in the long-run, we retain the element Theories of the World (B) as the means by which inventions are generated.

The interrelationships between the four elements mentioned above, are shown in Fig. 8.2, which we explain in detail below.

We start with the Implementation (G) of the production process, which uses resources and generates pollution. This will directly affect the physical limits (C1) experienced by the economy. As we argued in Section 8.2.3 above, the corresponding intertemporal external effects, because of the use of depletable resources and because of pollution, are not adequately reflected by the Coordination (H), be it a market or a planning agency. This relationship is indicated by the arrows passing from G to C1.

The increasing resource shortages, in turn, will generate relative price changes (arrow from C1 to H). This will lead to the innovation of previously available, but unused techniques (arrow from H to G).

In addition, however, the increased relative prices of resources will lead to research towards inventing new techniques which are resource saving, or allow the substitution of other less costly resources (arrow from H to B). Besides this price induced invention, there will also be considerable non-price induced research, aimed at ameliorating the environmental effects of economic activity (arrow from C1 to B).

The invention of new techniques will allow their innovation in the production process (arrow from B to G).

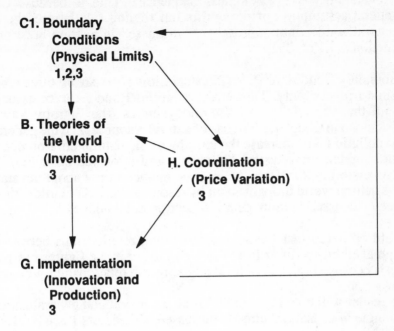

Fig. 8.2. The conceptual structure of long-run economy-environment interactions.

In parentheses we note in Fig. 8.2 those aspects of each element upon which we have focussed attention. We further indicate by the numbers 1, 2 and 3 which types of time irreversibility we consider to be involved in each conceptual element. With regard to these types of time irreversibility in Fig. 8.2 we remark:

(a) Time Irreversibility 2 (Uncertainty) is indicated for Theories of the World (B) (Invention), and reflects the uncertainty about the process of invention. By their nature, inventions cannot be predicted. That is, they are part of economic genotypic evolution.

(b) Implementation (G) (Innovation and Production) is associated with Time Irreversibility 3 (Teleological Sequence), through the assumption of the most general form of capital accumulation and production, as described in Section 8.2.2.

(c) Coordination (H) (Price Variation) is a process which invokes Time Irreversibility 3 (Teleological Sequence). This is because of the general assumption of disequilibrium trading (we here eschew the general equilibrium approach), as discussed in Section 8.2.1 and in Section 6.3.1 of Chapter 6.

(d) Boundary Conditions (C1) (Physical Limits) invoke all three types of Time Irreversibility. Time Irreversibilities 1 and 3 can be associated with the Second Law of Thermodynamics (the Entropy Law), as discussed in Chapter 5. The use of natural resources and the generation of pollution will increase the entropy of the natural environment and thus tighten the physical limits imposed upon the economy. Time Irreversibility 2 reflects the increasing uncertainty about the state of the natural world brought about by resource use and pollution; this has been discussed in more detail in Section 8.2.3 above.

It should be noted that the arrows indicating relationships between the conceptual elements differ from those employed in the figures in Chapter 6. This is because Fig. 8.2 is addressing long-run relationships with regard to production.

The reader will note that Fig. 7.2 is an extension and generalization of the 'triangle of causation' already discussed in Chapters 1 and 3 (cf. Figs. 1.1 and 3.2).

8.4 The Operationalization of the Conceptual Model

Having discussed the conceptual structure of long-run economy-environment interactions, two questions remain:

1. What parts of the conceptual model may be addressed ex ante, and what parts may be addressed only ex post? That is, which parts of the conceptual model reflect phenotypic change, and which parts reflect genotypic change?

2. What is the appropriate mathematical economic formalism for operationalizing the conceptual model represented by Fig. 8.2?

Regarding the first question, the discussion in Section 8.3 has indicated that there are two major sources of uncertainty in the model. These are invention, and the emergence of new economy-environment interactions not previously observed. We must recognize that we cannot, in principle, make sensible predictions on these two matters. We might, of course, speculate about what may occur, and generate scenarios on that basis. However, prediction is not feasible. How we feel these areas of radical uncertainty should be dealt with in a policy framework is a matter to which we shall return in Chapter 12.

Regarding the second question, on operationalizing the conceptual model, we feel a technique is at hand. This is neo-Austrian capital theory, already discussed in Chapter 4 Section 4.5.4 and Chapter 6 Section 6.3.2. We have noted throughout the book so far the importance of invention and innovation in economy-environment interactions. Innovation is the working through of a new technique, and how it impacts on an economy over an extended period. This, of course, models time irreversibility 3 (teleological sequence), where the telos is assumed to be known.

As mentioned in Chapter 4, and as will be discussed in detail in Chapters 9 to 11, neo-Austrian capital theory models innovation naturally and within a straightforward mathematical formalism. Further, the modelling of economy-environment interactions is also accomplished in a natural manner, and has already been applied to studies of water and waste management, as discussed in Section 8.5 below.

A further important element in Fig. 8.2 is the role of coordination through prices. Now in any economic model, prices can arise in two ways.

1. The prices of outputs can be equated to the 'real cost' of necessary inputs, simply by using a basic input as numéraire to evaluate the costs of production.

2. The prices of inputs can be equated to the corresponding 'shadow prices', where these are the extra welfare obtained by consumers when an extra unit of the input is made available.

While 'real costs' of outputs can always be established, the calculation of 'shadow prices' of inputs requires that an optimising framework be used.

Now as discussed in Chapter 6, full optimization in economics, i.e. SIMON's substantive rationality, is not necessarily a useful or true assumption. However, as we are concerned with establishing prices for both outputs and inputs at the same time, we propose to use an optimising approach to decision making.

However, we also recognize that the assumption of full intertemporal optimization would be quite contrary to the acceptance of the possibility of the emergence of novelty. Full intertemporal optimization requires that all possible future states of the world can be known, at least stochastically (or that the decision maker has a subjective probability distribution). If we allow for invention, and the possible emergence of new economy-environment interactions, this is quite implausible.

We therefore limit our assumption of optimization to a finite, and short, time-horizon. As time passes, the horizon stays a fixed but limited time ahead. Thus novelty may begin to influence decision making as soon as it emerges. We term this approach a 'rolling myopic plan', and it is discussed in detail in Chapter 10 Section 10.5.

8.5 Neo-Austrian Capital Theory

Mention has been made of neo-Austrian capital theory in earlier chapters, especially Chapters 4 and 5. However, before we proceed to use this technique in Chapters 9 to 11, it will be useful to give a brief summary of its development.

The dissatisfaction with the way time was treated in capital and growth theory led to the emergence of new areas of research by different schools of thought during the last two decades [see e.g. HAHN 1970:11, BLISS 1976:187, DIXIT 1977:26, FABER 1986b:16-20]. Among these was a renaissance of Austrian Capital Theory. This was an important school of economic thought up to the thirties, but fell into oblivion in the forties. There exist three variants of neo-Austrian Capital Theory, which were started by HICKS [1970], BERNHOLZ [1971] and VON WEIZSÄCKER [1971], respectively. Although the three approaches differ in emphasis, they all have in common that they stress the temporal structure of inputs and outputs.[2]

We shall here concentrate on the first variant, initiated by BERNHOLZ, which has been further developed and applied to resource and environmental problems by members of the Department of Economics in Heidelberg [JAKSCH 1975; FABER 1979, 1985, 1986a; NIEMES 1981; REISS 1981; FABER, NIEMES and STEPHAN 1983, 1987; STEPHAN 1983, 1985, 1987, 1988, 1989; MAIER 1984; WODOPIA 1986a; FABER and WAGENHALS 1988; FABER, STEPHAN and MICHAELIS 1989].

Essential features of this approach are as follows.

1. The concepts of superiority and roundaboutness. Superiority is present in an economy if the possibility exists of increasing the total amount of consumption summed over the whole economic horizon. Roundaboutness is present if there is the possibility of postponing consumption. (For rigorous definitions of these two concepts see

---

[2] The relationship between neo-Austrian capital theory and the approach to capital theory by Austrian Subjectivists (see Chapter 4 Section 4.5.4 and Chapter 6 Section 6.3.5 above) is discussed by PELLENGAHR [1986a, 1986b].

JAKSCH [1975], BERNHOLZ and FABER [1976], BERNHOLZ, FABER and REISS [1978], REISS and FABER [1982]. For an infinite economic time horizon model see STEPHAN [1980, 1983]. For an analysis of the indefinite horizon case see FABER and PROOPS [1991c].)

2. Austrian Capital Theory emphasises the temporal structure of production and consumption: it takes time to convert primary factors first into intermediate goods and then into final goods. In particular, it takes time to build up stocks of capital goods.

3. The interface between the technology of an economy, whose temporal structure is characterised by superiority and roundaboutness, and the time preference of the consumers allows the determination of the sign of 'the' rate of interest and of 'own' rates of interest.

4. The neo-Austrian approach is particularly suited to model SCHUMPETER's notion of the innovation of a new technique, and thus the structural change of an economy. The neo-Austrian analysis is therefore not focussed on semi-stationary, i.e. steady-state, paths but on unbalanced ones, or as HICKS [1973b:81-150] puts it, on the 'traverse' of an economy. The time structure of production, the building up and down of stocks of capital goods are of importance [STEPHAN 1987, 1988, 1989]. These features will be central to the model described in Chapters 9 to 11.

5. Because of their multi-sectoral nature neo-Austrian models can be immediately represented in the familiar input-output form, pioneered by [LEONTIEF 1936]. This representation also allows such models to be summarised in terms of national accounting aggregates. The implicit time structure of neo-Austrian models when allied to the national accounting aggregates, gives valuable insights into the assessment of well-known problems of interpreting such variables as gross-domestic product, particularly in the face of negative environmental externalities [FABER and PROOPS 1991b] and resource use [FABER and PROOPS 1993].

6. As DIXIT [1977:4] noted: "Most of capital theory ... ignores externalities of all kinds." We are interested to take into account external effects not only within one period, but also intertemporally external effects, which originate from long-run environmental degradation and the use of exhaustible resources.

7. The neo-Austrian approach is suited to consider the irreversible nature of environmental and resource processes. To this end FABER, NIEMES and STEPHAN [1987] developed an interdisciplinary approach on the basis of the Entropy Law to analyse long-run effects of environmental problems and of resource extraction. The basic structure of this model will be outlined in Chapter 11.

8.6 Concluding Remarks

The groundwork we presented in Part II, on evolution, and in Part III, on time, has allowed us to reconsider the conceptualization of long-run economy-environment interactions. We have attempted to show that the emergence of novelty, the genotypic evolution of the system, and the need to take account of the Second Law and of Teleological Sequence, mean that simple neoclassical models will not suffice. Neither, on their own, will neo-Austrian models.

However, the neo-Austrian model has the great advantage of dealing with Teleological Sequence through the temporal structure of capital accumulation. We therefore propose to take this as our modelling base. We shall combine this with a rarely used approach to optimization, the 'rolling myopic plan', which is consistent with the assumption of the possible emergence of novelty in the long-run. However, it is important to stress, as we noted at the end of Chapter 6, that mathematical modelling must be tempered with clear conceptualization. We stress, the concepts that must always be held at the front and the back of the mind in long-run economy-environment interactions are evolution and time irreversibility.

We now proceed to a detailed discussion of neo-Austrian capital theory, and its application to modelling long-run economy-environment interactions. Chapters 9 and 10 develop the concepts and some (simple) mathematical methods for the formulation of such models. Chapter 11 reviews the modelling aim we have set ourselves, and then describes a simulation model.

9 Production, Accumulation and Time: A Neo-Austrian Approach

9.1 Introduction

In Chapters 2 to 8 we have discussed at some length the conceptualization of evolution and time as applied to economic activity. In particular, in Chapter 8 we stressed the long-run interaction of the economy and the environment in determining the nature of economic activity, and suggested that natural resource shortages were an important stimulus to the emergence of novelty.

In this chapter we shall concentrate on modelling. In the light of the discussion in the earlier sections, we must therefore concentrate on the predictable, phenotypic, evolution of economies. This does not mean that we omit genotypic change; quite the contrary. However, we have already argued that genotypic change *cannot* be modelled sensibly, at least ex ante.

In particular, we shall derive an approach to modelling production over time which we feel is particularly suitable for modelling long-run economic activity. Because of its lineage, detailed in Chapter 4 Section 4.5.2 and Chapter 8 Section 8.5, this is known as the neo-Austrian approach. Reviews of this method, and its history, are in HICKS [1973a, 1973b] and NEGISHI [1989:Chapter 8]. Much of the theory that is covered in Chapters 9 and 10 derives from FABER [1979]. However, the representation in this book is very different and more easily accessible. In addition, the neo-Austrian approach is further developed, in particular by combining it with the use of rolling myopic plans for decision making.

In Section 9.2, as most readers will not have met this neo-Austrian approach in the form we shall be using, we begin by discussing the well-known neoclassical approach to production.

Section 9.3 introduces the neo-Austrian approach, using the notions of 'Processes' and 'Techniques'. In particular we note that while the neoclassical approach is effectively 'timeless', the neo-Austrian approach not only can reproduce such timeless results, but also allows the study of the temporal structure of capital accumulation for the model economy.

In Section 9.4 the important concepts of 'Superiority' and 'Roundaboutness' of production techniques are introduced.

We then move on, in Section 9.5, to the intertemporal substitution of consumption in the neo-Austrian approach; in particular, we show how the intertemporal production possibility frontier (PPF) can be constructed.

Section 9.6 introduces capital deterioration into the neo-Austrian model, and derives the PPF for this case.

In Chapter 10 we further explore the neo-Austrian model of production. The model is then applied to the case of resource depletion and pollution abatement in Chapter 11.

Unlike the earlier chapters, which were conceptual in nature, in this chapter we deal with material that is technical and fundamentally mathematical. However, we have purposely presented the models so that they can be understood with no other equipment than high-school algebra and a little elementary calculus.

9.2 The Neoclassical Model of Production

For reasons we shall discuss below, we feel the conventional or 'neoclassical' model of production is ill-suited to explore the time structure of production [see GEORGESCU-ROEGEN 1971: Chapter 9; HICKS 1970, 1973a, 1973b, 1976; LEONTIEF 1982; STEPHAN 1989:Chapter 2]. The above statement holds not only for static models of production, but also for dynamic models that use the standard neoclassical production function, e.g. growth models [BURMEISTER and DOBELL 1970:Chapters 9-10}.

Before we go on to examine an alternative formulation of the production process, let us briefly review the 'typical' characteristics of conventional production theory.

The essence of the simple neoclassical model of production, as taught in elementary microeconomics courses, is contained in the following five assumptions, A1 to A5. (For a rigorous statement of the properties of a general production function see BURMEISTER and DOBELL [1970:9-70]).

A1.   There is a single output good (X).

A2.   There are two or more input goods (Y_i) in given amounts.

A3.   The more of any input, with the other inputs fixed, the greater the output.

A4.   For any input, the other inputs fixed, increasing that input increases the output at a decreasing rate.

A5.   Each good is 'necessary' for production; zero inputs generate zero output.

The above five assumptions mean that we can represent output as a function of the inputs:

$$X = f(Y_1, Y_2, Y_3, \ldots, Y_k)$$ (from A1 and A2).

The marginal product of each input is positive, but decreasing:

$$\partial X/\partial Y_i > 0, \quad \partial^2 X/\partial Y_i^2 < 0$$ (from A3 and A4).

Thus for all other inputs constant, the relationship of output to one input is as shown in Fig. 9.1.

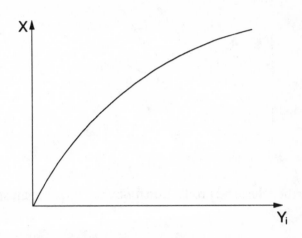

Fig. 9.1. The neoclassical production function: output against one input.

If for any input i, $Y_i = 0$, then $X = 0$ (from A5).

This further implies, if $Y_i = 0$ for all i, then $X = f(0, 0, \ldots, 0) = 0$.

We shall refer to this model of production as the 'standard neoclassical production function'[1].

---

[1] The limits of this approach have often been discussed, and it has therefore been refined and extended in many respects. In addition, alternative approaches have been developed (e.g. DORFMAN, SAMUELSON and SOLOW [1958], BLISS [1975]). Nevertheless, the 'standard neoclassical production function' has been, and is still, widely used in the economic literature, for theoretical analysis, as well as for empirical research and teaching. We believe that this is the case, despite its deficiencies and drawbacks, because it is so simple to understand and to apply both theoretically and empirically. Also, the limits to the applicability of the 'standard neoclassical production function' are difficult to understand thoroughly.

If we restrict our analysis to two input goods (Y_1 and Y_2) then we may sketch this neoclassical production function. It passes through the origin and the Y_1 and Y_2 axes, by A5. It is shaped like a smooth convex 'hill' (with no peak) by A3 and A4. This is shown in Fig. 9.2.

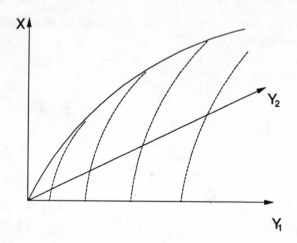

Fig. 9.2. The neoclassical production function: output against both inputs.

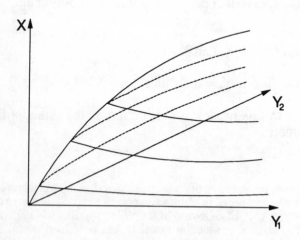

Fig. 9.3. The contours of a neoclassical production function.

We see that the graph of the production function is a surface in 3-space. Any combination of Y_1 and Y_2 (both non-negative) yields a corresponding level of production of the output good.

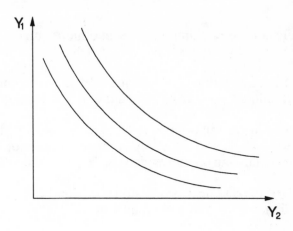

Fig. 9.4. The isoquant map for a neoclassical production function.

Let us now consider the relationship between the two inputs which generate a certain level of output. We can see the sets of such points as the 'contours' of the production surface, as shown in Fig. 9.3.

If Fig. 9.3 were viewed from above, it would lose the X-dimension, and look as in Fig. 9.4.

The family of curves in Fig. 9.4 is simply the set of isoquants, as used in elementary economic theory. It is clear that the positive but diminishing marginal products of the input factors imply that the isoquants are downward sloping and convex to the origin. It is also assumed that the marginal products decrease 'smoothly' (i.e. have no kinks or discontinuities), thus the production surface and the isoquants will both be 'smooth'.

How does the standard neoclassical production function help us to understand the production process?

1. It allows us to make a direct correspondence between a set of inputs and a level of output.

2. It suggests that factors of production may act as substitutes for each other. One may move along an isoquant by decreasing one input while increasing the other.

3. If one makes the assumption that factors are rewarded at their marginal products, then the well-defined first partial-derivatives of output with inputs ensure that such factor rewards are easily established. Hence the distribution of the product between the factors of production can be established.

However, there are certain important economic elements that are not encompassed by this model, such as:

1. We do not have a notion of a 'technique' (i.e. some combination of factors that uniquely generates a certain type and level of output).

2. A commonly used factor of production is capital. However, the conventional production function approach does not contain any implicit understanding of how capital can be produced or accumulated.

3. The standard neoclassical production function contains no implicit dynamics of accumulation and production.

In summary, therefore, the standard neoclassical production function is well-adapted to an analysis of static production systems, where particular attention is given to the allocation and distribution of the product between the factors of production. However, it is very ill-adapted to the analysis of the dynamic process of how a technique may be brought into use, with its corresponding necessary system of capital accumulation (cf. e.g. HAHN [1970], HICKS [1973b]).

Now this book is, above all, dealing with the introduction of novelty, and the effect of this novelty on economic systems over time. It is clear that the standard neoclassical production function approach will be of little service in such an endeavour. We also feel that its extension to two or more sectors [BURMEISTER and DOBELL 1970:Chapters 4, 5 and 9] will be of little help. We therefore now move on to describe an alternative formulation of the production process, the neo-Austrian approach, which does allow the dynamic effects of the introduction of novelty to be treated explicitly.

The essence of this approach is two-fold. First, we use the 'Activity Analysis' approach of KOOPMANS [1951][2], which allows the meaningful

---

[2] It is for this reason that our approach has certain similarities to LEONTIEF models as well as to the one developed by DORFMAN, SAMUELSON and SOLOW [1957]. However, as has already been shown in Chapters 4 and 6 above, and will become more obvious below, they differ in many respects, above all in the spirit in which they are developed.

definition of 'techniques of production'[3]. Second, we have production of capital as an activity, or process, which may then be explicitly embodied in a technique of production.

The capital is produced with only one non-produced factor input, 'labour' (natural resources will be introduced in Chapter 10).

9.3 A Neo-Austrian Model of Production
9.3.1 Production Processes and Techniques

We begin by defining a production process, following KOOPMANS [1951].

Definition: A process is the production of a good, either a consumption good or an intermediate capital good, using a proportional production technology.

For the purpose of comparing this approach with the simple two factor ('capital' and 'labour') production function discussed above, we restrict ourselves here to modelling with only these two factors of production. We now introduce three fixed coefficient production processes.

Process R_1   This uses labour alone to produce the consumption good. In particular, l_1 units of labour can, via this process, produce one unit of the consumption good per unit of time:

l_1 units of labour $\rightarrow$ 1 unit of output

Here the arrow, ' $\rightarrow$ ', indicates a transformation process.

So, if process R_1 uses L_1 units of labour to produce X_1 units of consumption good per unit of time, then:

$L_1/l_1 = X_1$.

Process R_2   This uses labour and (produced) capital to produce the consumption good, i.e.:

l_2 units of labour $\oplus$ k_2 units of capital $\rightarrow$ 1 unit of output.

---

[3] The relationship between the concepts of a neoclassical technique and a neo-Austrian technique is analysed by MAIER [1984:147-154].

Here the symbol '$\oplus$' is used to show that the factors labour and capital are combined in process R_2.

If process R_2 uses L_2 units of labour and K units of capital to produce X_2 units of the consumption good per unit of time, then:

$L_2/l_2 = K/k_2 = X_2$.

Process R_3   This uses labour alone to produce the capital good. i.e.:

l_3 units of labour $\rightarrow$ 1 unit of capital good.

If process R_3 uses L_3 units of labour to produce δK units of capital good per unit of time, then:

$L_3/l_3 = \delta K$.

We are now in a position to define a 'technique of production' [BERNHOLZ and FABER, 1976:349; MAIER 1984:152].

Definition: A Technique of Production is the minimal combination of production processes which allows the production of the consumption good from the non-produced input.

For this model, the only non-produced input is labour. It is clear that the above three processes allow the formulation of two distinct techniques for the production of the consumption good.

Technique T_1   This consists of process R_1 alone, as this process uses the input of only labour, and gives the consumption good as its output.

Technique T_2   This consists of processes R_2 and R_3 in combination. Process R_3 uses only labour to produce the capital good. The produced capital good may then be combined with labour in process R_2, to produce the consumption good. Thus the combination of processes R_2 and R_3 will produce the consumption good, using only non-produced labour as an input.

9.3.2 Time and Production

Looking at technique T_2 a little more closely, we see that time is explicitly embodied in production. Labour must first be used in process R_3 to produce capital. Then, labour and the previously produced capital can be combined in process R_2 to produce the consumption good. If we suppose that process R_3 takes one unit of time to produce the capital good, and process R_2 takes one unit of time to combine labour and capital to produce the consumption good, then to produce the consumption good from labour alone takes two units of time.

9.3.3 'Timeless' Production

To compare this neo-Austrian approach to production with the 'standard neoclassical production function' approach, it is useful to make the neo-Austrian model 'timeless', by ignoring the possibility for capital accumulation. That is, we shall ignore process R_3, and for the moment concentrate only on processes R_1 and R_2. Also, for comparability with the neoclassical approach, we shall suppose there is a certain given labour force (L), which is constant over time, and initial capital stock (K). Our problem is now two-fold:

1. How should we use K and L between processes R_1 and R_2, to produce the greatest total output of the consumption good?

2. What is the greatest output of the consumption good for a certain given K and L?

To answer 1, we have two alternatives. First, it might be more efficient to use scarce labour in process R_1 than to combine it with capital in process R_2. This would imply $L/l_1 > L/l_2$, i.e. $l_2 > l_1$. Second, the converse might hold ($l_1 > l_2$). We shall assume that the latter is the case. That is, labour is more effective at producing output when combined with the capital good.

If it is the case that labour is more productive in process R_2 than in process R_1, we now need to know how much labour we are permitted to use in process R_2. Here, of course, we may be constrained by the availability of capital. We define L_1 to be the labour used in process R_1, and L_2 to be the labour used in process R_2. We know that we use fixed input-output coefficients in the processes, so we require:

$L_2/l_2 = K/k_2$

i.e. $L_2 = Kl_2/k_2$.

Now so long as K is not so large that $L_2 > L$ (i.e. that $Kl_2/k_2 > L$: there is no 'capital saturation'), we are constrained in the use of process R_2 by capital availability. This also seems a sensible assumption, for what purpose would it serve a firm, or society, to accumulate more capital than it could use? We therefore assume that $L_2 \leq L$. Thus, the output generated by R_2 is:

$$X_2 = K/k_2 \ (= L/l_2).$$

Now as $L_2 \leq L$, this means that when (more labour efficient) process R_2 is fully utilized up to its capital constraint, some labour is still left over. The obvious thing to do with this is to use it in process R_1, to generate yet more of the consumption good. The labour we can use in process R_1 is:

$$L_1 = L - L_2.$$

Now: $L_2 = Kl_2/k_2$

so: $L_1 = L - Kl_2/k_2$.

We see that output by process R_1 is given by:

$$X_1 = L_1/l_1 = (L-Kl_2/k_2)/l_1.$$

We can now write the total output of the consumption good as:

$$X = X_1 + X_2$$

$$= K/k_2 + (L-Kl_2/k_2)/l_1$$

i.e. $X = L/l_1 + (K/k_2)(1-l_2/l_1)$ (9.1)

We recall that this relationship holds for there not being excess capital. i.e.:

$$Kl_2/k_2 \leq L.$$

Of course, we also require $L > 0$, $K > 0$.

We are now in a position to sketch the isoquants for this production system. First, we draw in the K and L axes, and the ray $Kl_2/k_2 = L$. This is shown in Fig. 9.5. The shaded area in Fig. 9.5 is the domain where there is excess capital.

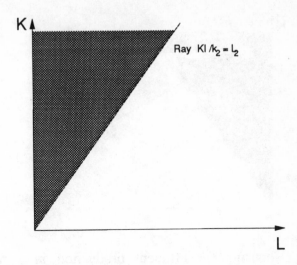

Fig. 9.5. The area of excess capital for a neo-Austrian production model.

Looking now at our 'production function' relating output to capital and labour, in equation (9.1):

$$X = L/l_1 + (K/k_2)(1-l_2/l_1).$$ (9.1)

If we set output at some constant level, X', then we can reorganise this to give:

$$K = (X'-L/l_1)k_2/(1-l_2/l_1)$$

i.e. $K = l_1k_2X'/(l_1-l_2) - k_2L/(l_1-l_2).$ (9.2)

Now if process R_2 is to be worth using, we require $l_1 > l_2$, as discussed above. So equation (9.2) is the equation of a straight line, with a positive intercept and a negative slope. Increasing X' increases the intercept, but leaves the slope unchanged. Thus a family of straight lines is defined, on the unshaded part of the non-negative (K,L) domain, as shown in Fig. 9.6.

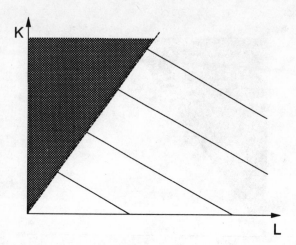

Fig. 9.6. The isoquants for efficient production in a neo-Austrian production model.

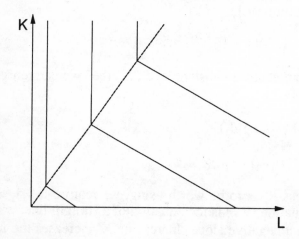

Fig. 9.7. The full isoquant map for a neo-Austrian production model.

These straight lines are clearly isoquants for this production system. Can they be extended into the shaded region? They can, by noting that in the shaded region there is excess capital, so adding extra capital, for a given amount of labour, adds nothing to the level of ouput. Therefore the isoquants are vertical in this area, as shown in Fig. 9.7.

Thus in Fig. 9.7 we have the full isoquant map for a production system embodying production processes R_1 and R_2.

In Fig. 9.2 we sketched the production surface for the neoclassical production function. We can easily construct such a surface for this neo-Austrian production system, as in Fig. 8.8.

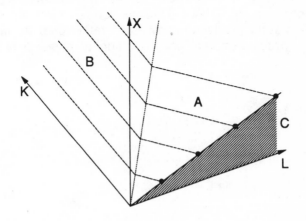

Fig. 9.8. The production surface for a neo-Austrian production model.

We see that the production surface is composed of three adjoining facets. Facet A represents the domain of 'efficient production', with both processes R_1 and R_2 in use. This domain is described by equation (9.1).

$$X = L/l_1 + (K/k_2)(1-l_2/l_1). \tag{9.1}$$

Facet B represents the domain of excess capital; it corresponds to the cross-hatched areas of Figures 9.5 and 9.6. Here only process R_2 is used. This domain is described by:

$$X = L/l_2 \quad \text{for all K in the domain.}$$

Facet C represents the domain of zero capital. Here only process R_1 is used. Output in this domain is described by the equation:

$X = L/l_1$.

The general shape of this surface is reminiscent of the neoclassical production function in Fig. 9.2. The major difference is that this Activity Analysis production surface is composed of facets, while the neoclassical surface is 'smooth'. In particular we see that on facet A, we can regard capital and labour as 'substitutes', as the isoquants are downward sloping. However, unlike the standard neoclassical production function, this has an underlying rationale. The apparent substitutability of capital for labour lies in the ability to substitute process R_1 for process R_2 in the production of the consumption good. Of course, both these two processes use 'fixed coefficient' production processes, so do not themselves allow the substitution of capital for labour. Thus the neo-Austrian approach stresses the substitution of the production processes, rather than the substitution of the factors of production, as does the standard neoclassical production function.

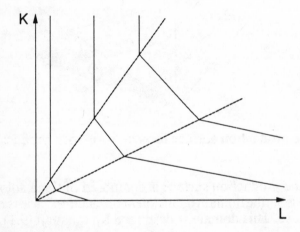

Fig. 9.9. The isoquant map for a neo-Austrian production model with three production processes.

In discussions of the Activity Analysis approach, it is often suggested that the standard neoclassical production function is the 'limiting' case of the Activity Analysis approach, as more and more processes using capital are introduced. This is clearly seen if we examine the isoquants for the case when we have three production processes, two of which use capital. This is illustrated in Fig. 9.9. With four processes, the isoquants may look as in Fig. 9.10.

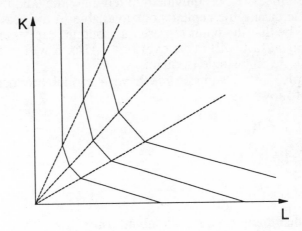

Fig. 9.10. The isoquant map for a neo-Austrian production model with four production processes.

Of course, this argument can be generalized to infinitely many processes. It is clear that as the number of capital-using processes increases, both the isoquants and the production surface, take on a more 'neoclassical' character.

9.3.4 Production in Time

The above construction has been based on the assumption that both capital and labour are available in given amounts. The problem was simply to apportion the labour between processes R_1 and R_2. Therefore, the analysis in the previous section is a 'timeless' approach to production. The real strength of the neo-Austrian approach, compared with "a 'Walrasian' model of growth equilibrium, or 'steady state'" [HICKS 1970:257], is when process R_3 is reintroduced into the analysis, for it is this process that brings time into the model. Process R_3 can be used to generate extra capital, thus moving the production system across the production surface defined by processes R_1 and R_2. Further, process R_3 uses labour, so production of capital today requires that processes R_1 and R_2 have less labour available, and therefore can produce less of the consumption good.

Thus, in terms of the production surface generated by processes R_1 and R_2, operating process R_3 is equivalent to reducing the labour force in that period, but increasing the capital stock available in the next period. The outcome will be that the point representing output, capital and labour on the production surface will move over time. Also, it will certainly not be constrained to lie on a single isoquant.

For example, let us suppose we have a model production system, described as follows:

Process R_1: $l_1 = 10$

Process R_2: $l_2 = 1$; $k_2 = 1$

Process R_3: $l_3 = 5$.

We suppose that there is a constant labour force, $L = 100$.

We start with an initial stock of capital of $K(0) = 10$.

We see that process R_2 combines one unit of labour with each unit of capital, so if all 10 units of capital were to be utilized, this would require 10 units of labour to be used in process R_2. The remaining 90 units of labour could then be used in process R_1. This reassures us that we are not starting with an inefficiently large quantity of capital, so the initial production possibility, using processes R_1 and R_2, lies on facet A of Fig. 9.8.

Now, supposing the capital good does not deteriorate over time (we shall introduce capital deterioration later), we can easily calculate how a certain path of capital accumulation causes the output to move over the production surface.

Suppose we wish to accumulate capital at 10% per annum, starting in period 1. (We treat each time period as one year at present). This means that in period zero, we do not operate process R_3 (i.e. $\delta K(0) = 0$). Instead, we use all the labour ($L = 100$) and capital ($K = 10$) to generate the consumption good using processes R_1 and R_2. We can calculate the resulting output using equation (9.1):

$$X = L/l_1 + (K/k_2)(1-l_2/l_1).\tag{9.1}$$

We can reorganise this, to show the effects of processes R_1 and R_2 on output, in equation (9.3).

$$X = (L/l_1-Kl_2/k_2l_1) + K/k_2.\tag{9.3}$$

       Process R_1 Process R_2

So for period zero we have:

$$X(0) = (100/10 - 10 \times 1/1 \times 10) + 10/1$$

$$= 9 + 10 = 19.$$

Here, the 10 units of capital, combined with 10 units of labour, allow the production of 10 units of output with process R_2. The remaining 90 units of labour allow the production of a further 9 units of output using process R_1.

In period 1 we start to use process R_3, to produce extra capital, δK. We want to generate one extra unit of capital (i.e. 10% of 10 units), so we must use 5 units of labour in process R_3. This leaves 95 units of labour to generate output with processes R_1 and R_2. This gives output:

$$X(1) = (95/10 - 10 \times 1/1 \times 10) + 10/1$$

$$= 8.5 + 10 = 18.5.$$

The drop in output in period 1 is the present cost of producing capital in period 1, and therefore being able, potentially, to produce more output in periods 2, 3, etc.

At the end of period 1 we now have 11 units of capital. If we are to continue to accumulate capital at 10% per annum, we need to produce a further $\delta K = 1.1$ units of capital in period 2. This will require the use of 5.5 units of labour in process R_3, leaving 94.5 units of labour for processes R_1 and R_2. This gives output:

$$X(2) = (94.5/10 - 11 \times 1/10 \times 1) + 11/1$$

$$= 8.35 + 11$$

$$= 19.35.$$

We can continue with such calculations, giving the uses of the processes and their outputs as in Table 9.1.

The time-paths of labour available to processes R_1 and R_2, the capital stock, and the output of the consumption good are shown in Fig. 9.11.

We can also plot these in (X,K,L) space, on the production surface, as shown in Fig. 9.12.

Table 9.1. The time-path for a neo-Austrian production process, with 10% capital accumulation per period

t	L	L_1	L_2	L_1+L_2	L_3	K	X_1	X_2	X	δK
0	100	90.00	10.00	100.00	0.00	10.00	9.00	10.00	19.00	0.00
1	100	85.00	10.00	95.00	5.00	10.00	8.50	10.00	18.50	1.00
2	100	83.50	11.00	94.50	5.50	11.00	8.35	11.00	19.35	1.10
3	100	81.85	12.10	93.95	6.05	12.10	8.18	12.10	20.29	1.21
4	100	80.04	13.31	93.35	6.66	13.31	8.00	13.31	21.31	1.33
5	100	78.04	14.64	92.68	7.32	14.64	7.80	14.64	22.44	1.46
6	100	75.84	16.11	91.95	8.05	16.11	7.58	16.11	23.69	1.61
7	100	73.43	17.72	91.14	8.86	17.72	7.34	17.72	25.06	1.77
8	100	70.77	19.49	90.26	9.74	19.49	7.08	19.49	26.56	1.95
9	100	67.85	21.44	89.28	10.72	21.44	6.78	21.44	28.22	2.14
10	100	64.63	23.58	88.21	11.79	23.58	6.46	23.58	30.04	2.36

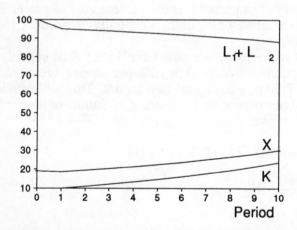

Fig. 9.11. The time-paths of labour, capital and output, for processes R_1 and R_2.

We see that the time-path is traversing a series of isoquants, with capital stock rising, labour (as available to processes R_1 and R_2) decreasing, and output increasing.

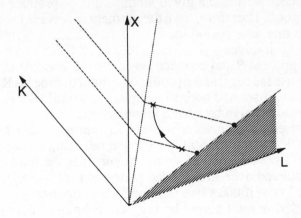

Fig. 9.12. The evolution of production and inputs over the production surface.

Had one not known about process R_3, as in a simple neoclassical growth model, one would still have been able to construct Fig. 9.12, but it would tell us little in itself. To understand why this 'traverse' across the production surface is taking place one needs to know of the existence of process R_3, and that a particular profile of capital accumulation is being pursued. Indeed, to try to understand the traverse without understanding the process of capital accumulation is a little like performing Hamlet without the Prince of Denmark!

Another simile may be appropriate. The movement along the production surface is driven by capital accumulation through process R_3. As this very process is obscured by concentrating on the production surface, the surface can be thought of as rather like Adam Smith's 'veil of money'. To understand the dynamics of capital accumulation (and its long-run consequences for the natural environment), we need to 'draw back' the veil of the production surface, to reveal the underlying capital accumulation process.

9.4 Superiority and Roundaboutness
9.4.1 The 'Superiority' of a Technique

Earlier we noted that our neo-Austrian model involves two techniques of production, with different time profiles.

Technique T_1 involves just process R_1. We suppose that it takes one time period for process R_1 to use a given labour input to produce output of the consumption good. Therefore, from the moment we decide to produce some output it takes one time period for the output to become available.

Technique T_2 involves processes R_2 and R_3. It takes one time period to use labour in process R_3, to produce some capital good. It takes a further time period to use labour and the produced capital in process R_2, to produce the output. Thus, if we had no initial capital, it would take two periods to construct consumption output from labour alone.

Under what circumstances is waiting for output, using technique T_2, preferable to the immediate ability to consume, using technique T_1? As a criterion of relative advantage, we might consider the total consumption that can be achieved over an extended period of time, using techniques T_1 and T_2. As we know it takes two time periods to operate technique T_2, we start by considering total output by the two techniques over two periods. If the two period total produced by technique T_2 is greater than that produced by technique T_1, then we say that technique T_2 is 'superior' to techniqe T_1.

We now seek the condition for technique T_2 to be superior to technique T_1, for a two-period model. To this end we calculate the total outputs, for each technique, for a given labour force in each period, and with no initial capital stock.

(N.B. For simplicity of analysis, here we allow the labour force to vary over time.)

We begin by considering technique T_2. We suppose the labour force available in period 1 is $L(1)$. In period 1 we produce only capital, using process R_3. i.e.:

$$\delta K(1) = L(1)/l_3.$$

So the output of the consumption good in period 1 is zero.

i.e. $X_2(1) = 0.$

In period 2 we have capital stock:

$$\delta K(1) = L(1)/l_3.$$

We suppose we have just sufficient labour available in period 2 to combine with this capital in process R_2, to produce the consumption good.

So output in period 2 is given by:

$$X_2(2) = \delta K(1)/k_2 = L(1)/l_3k_2.$$

We see that the labour needed in period 2, to be combined with the fully utilised capital in process R_2, is:

$$L(2) = l_2X_2(2) = L(1)l_2/l_3k_2.$$

We collate these results in Table 9.2.

We see that over two periods we can produce a total output of $L(1)/l_3k_2$.

Supposing the same labour as above, in periods 1 and 2, were available to technique T_1. What would the output be? This is shown in Table 9.3.

So the total output from technique T_1, over the two periods, is:

$$L(1)/l_1 + L(1)l_2/l_1l_3k_2 = [L(1)/l_1](1+l_2/l_3k_2).$$

We note that as $L(1)$ and the coefficients l_1, l_2, l_3 and k_2 are given exogeneously, this total output is also exogenously determined, in this case.

Table 9.2. Time structure of production with technique T_2.

	Period 1	Period 2
Labour	$L(1)$	$L(1)l_2/l_3k_2$
Capital	0	$L(1)/l_3$
Capital Accumulation	$L(1)/l_3$	0
Output	0	$L(1)/l_3k_2$

Table 9.3. Time structure of production with technique T_1.

	Period 1	Period 2
Labour	$L(1)$	$L(1)l_2/l_3k_2$
Output	$L(1)/l_1$	$L(1)l_2/l_1l_3k_2$

Now if technique T_2 is to be worth using, over two time periods, we should require, as mentioned above, that it produce more over the two periods than technique T_1. That is:

$$L(1)/l_3k_2 > [L(1)/l_1](1+l_2/l_3k_2)$$

i.e. $1 > (l_3k_2+l_2)/l_1$

i.e. $(l_1-l_2)/l_3k_2 > 1.$ (9.4)

We define:

$$S \equiv (l_1-l_2)/l_3k_2.$$ (9.5)

S is known as the 'degree of superiority' of technique T_2 over technique T_1. So $S > 1$ is the condition for technique T_2 to be superior to technique T_1.

9.4.2 Roundaboutness

We might now ask:

"What is the source of this superiority of technique T_2 over technique T_1?"

Clearly, technique T_2 makes a more indirect use of the non-produced input (i.e. labour) than does technique T_1. We might say that technique T_2 is more 'roundabout' than technique T_1; i.e. technique T_2 is a more time consuming way of producing the consumption good than technique T_1. We now seek an unambiguous definition of this term.

The reason for the superiority of technique T_2 over technique T_1 lies in the production of capital in period 1, and its use in period 2. As we saw, this means that consumption in period 1 is lower than it could otherwise be, while consumption in period 2 is higher than it could otherwise be. We recall that using techniques T_1 and T_2 separately gave the patterns of production of the consumption good shown in Table 8.4.

Table 9.4. The patterns of production for techniques T_1 and T_2.

	Period 1	**Period 2**
Technique T_1	$L(1)/l_1$	$L(1)l_2/l_3k_2l_1$
Technique T_2	0	$L(1)/l_3k_2$

Now for superiority of technique T_2 over T_1, we have just seen that the condition is:

$S \equiv (l_1-l_2)/l_3k_2 > 1.$

The coefficients used earlier in this chapter satisfy this criterion. We had:

$l_1 = 10, l_2 = 1, k_2 = 1, l_3 = 5$

i.e. $S = (10 - 1)/(1x5) = 1.8 > 1.$

Using these coefficients, and again setting $L(1)=100$, we get the consumption patterns for the two techniques shown in Table 9.5:

The consumption patterns, derived from the same available amounts of the non-produced factor, labour, are as shown in Fig. 9.13.

Table 9.5. Quantities of production for techniques T_1 and T_2.

	Period 1	Period 2
Technique T_1	10	2
Technique T_2	0	20

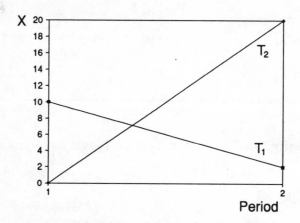

Fig. 9.13. Consumption patterns for techniques T_1 and T_2.

We note that in period 1, consumption derived from technique T_1 is greater than that derived from technique T_2. In period 2, the opposite holds. This allows us to give a general definition of the concept of 'roundaboutness'.

Definition: If two consumption profiles, A and B, are derived from the same non-produced input factors by using two different techniques, and if initially profile A is below profile B, but later profile A is above profile B, then we say profile A was brought about by a more roundabout technique.[4]

---

[4] The Austrian concept of the superiority of roundaboutness was first decomposed into its two components by JAKSCH [1975]; see also FABER [1979]. For generalisations and extensions of these concepts see papers 5 to 11 in FABER [1986a:Part 2].

9.5 Intertemporal Substitution of Consumption in the Neo-Austrian Model

As before, we suppose that two techniques of production are available to us, techniques T_1 and T_2. Further, we suppose that technique T_2 is superior to, and more roundabout than, technique T_1. What 'mix' of techniques T_1 and T_2 should we adopt over time? There are two steps in answering this question, with the first step in two parts..

Step 1a How can we construct the intertemporal substitution possibilities of consumption? i.e. How can we construct the intertemporal Production Possibility Frontier (PPF)?

Step 1b How can we identify the intertemporal constraints on such consumption substitution?

Step 2 How do we chose an 'optimal' pattern of intertemporal consumption from the possibilities defined by steps 1a and 1b?

We now examine each step in turn.

9.5.1 Intertemporal Substitution: Step 1a

We use the three process, two technique, two period model discussed above:

R_1: $L_1(t)/l_1 = X_1(t)$ $\qquad\qquad\qquad$ } $\quad T_1$

R_2: $L_2(t)/l_2 = K(t)/k_2 = X_2(t)$ $\qquad$ }
$\qquad\qquad\qquad\qquad\qquad\qquad\qquad\qquad$ } $\quad T_2$
R_3: $L_3(t)/l_3 = \delta K(t).$ $\qquad\qquad\qquad$ }

Here we assume all capital and labour are always fully utilized. We also assume a constant labour force over time. i.e.:

$L = L_1(t) + L_2(t) + L_3(t).$

Still ignoring capital deterioration, we know that the capital stock must satisfy:

$K(t+1) = K(t) + \delta K(t).$

We can now construct the relationship between first and second period consumption, $X(1)$ and $X(2)$, as follows.

(i) Specify first period capital accumulation, $\delta K(1)$. Now:

$$L_3(t)/l_3 = \delta K(t)$$

so: $L_3(1) = l_3 \delta K(1)$.

(ii) In the first period, we use all capital stock in process R_2, giving:

$$X_2(1) = K(1)/k_2.$$

We assume no capital saturation, so we have:

$$K(t)/k_2 = L_2(t)/l_2 = X_2(t)$$

so: $L_2(1) = l_2 K(1)/k_2$.

(iii) This gives labour force available to work in process R_1 as:

$$
\begin{aligned}
L_1(1) \;&= L - L_2(1) - L_3(1) \\
&= L - l_2 K(1)/k_2 - l_3 \delta K(1).
\end{aligned}
$$

Now: $L_1(t)/l_1 = X_1(t)$

So: $X_1(1) = [L - l_2 K(1)/k_2 - l_3 \delta K(1)]/l_1$.

(iv) Now total output in period 1 is:

$$
\begin{aligned}
X(1) \;&= X_1(1) + X_2(1) \\
&= [L - l_2 K(1)/k_2 - l_3 \delta K(1)]/l_1 + K(1)/k_2
\end{aligned}
$$

i.e. $X(1) = L/l_1 + (K(1)/k_2)(1 - l_2/l_1) - (l_3/l_1)\delta K(1)$. (9.6)

(v) We can use equation (9.6) also in period 2:

$$X(2) = L/l_1 + (K(2)/k_2)(1 - l_2/l_1) - (l_3/l_1)\delta K(2).$$

However, in a two period model, capital accumulation in the second period would never be sensible, as the new capital produced in period 2 could never be used.

So we set:

$$\delta K(2) = 0.$$

Also we know that:

$$K(2) = K(1) + \delta K(1).$$

This gives us:

$$X(2) = L/l_1 + \{(K(1)+\delta K(1))/k_2\}(1-l_2/l_1). \tag{9.7}$$

(vi) Eliminating $\delta K(1)$ between equations (9.6) and (9.7) gives:

$$X(2) = \{L/l_1+(K(1)/k_2)(1-l_2/l_1)\}\{1+(l_1-l_2)/l_3k_2\}$$

$$- \{(l_1-l_2)/l_3k_2\}X(1). \tag{9.8}$$

[We note that if we define:

$$\alpha \equiv L/l_1 + (K(1)/k_2)(1-l_2/l_1)$$

and $S \equiv (l_1-l_2)/l_3k_2$

then we get:

$$X(2) = \alpha(1+S) - SX(1)$$

i.e. $X(1) + X(2)/S = \alpha(1+S)/S$. $\tag{9.9}$]

We can plot equation (8.8) in $(X(1),X(2))$ space, as in Fig. 9.14. It is clear that:

$$\tan \Phi = -dX(1)/dX(2) = -(l_1-l_2)/l_3k_2 \ (\equiv S).$$

Now we saw above that if technique T_2 is superior to technique T_1, then:

$$(l_1-l_2)/l_3k_2 > 1,$$

so: $\tan \Phi > 1$ i.e. $\Phi > 45°$.

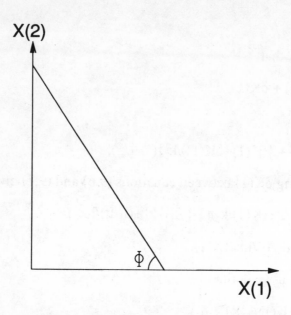

Fig. 9.14. The intertemporal production possibility frontier (PPF) for a
neo-Austrian model.

This implies that if technique T_2 is superior to technique T_1, one unit of
consumption foregone in period 1 will give rise to more than one unit of
extra consumption in period 2. This is clearly another interpretation of the
concept of superiority. Having established the intertemporal PPF, we now
seek the restrictions that apply to it.

9.5.2 Intertemporal Substitution: Step 1b

The line in Fig. 9.14 represents the intertemporal PPF. However, certain
restrictions apply, which eliminate portions of the frontier from
consideration.

First, points on the PPF below and to the right of the 45° line through
the origin represent points where consumption in period 2 is less than in
period 1. This must imply that in this range, less capital or labour is used
in period 2 than in period 1. But we are assuming there is no capital

deterioration, and a constant labour force, so clearly this would be inefficient. Thus the points below and to the right of the PPF must be excluded, as in Fig. 9.15.

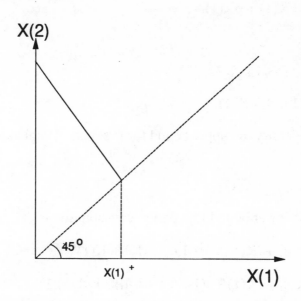

Fig. 9.15. The neo-Austrian model intertemporal PPF, constrained for efficiency.

Where the PPF meets the 45° line, $X(1)$ takes the value $X(1)^+$. This corresponds to zero capital accumulation in period 1. i.e. $\delta K(1) = 0$. Therefore, from equation (9.6) we see that:

$$X(1)^+ = L/l_1 + (K(1)/k_2)(1-l_2/l_1) \ (= \alpha).$$

Another constraint on the PPF is 'capital saturation'. As described above, capital saturation occurs when so much capital has been accumulated that there is insufficient labour available to utilize it fully in process R_2.

i.e. $K(2)/k_2 > L/l_2$

i.e. $K(2) > Lk_2/l_2$.

If we assume that initially there is no capital saturation (i.e. $K(1) < Lk_2/l_2$), then we are able to identify the upper limit for $\delta K(1)$ to ensure that $K(2) \leq Lk_2/l_2$.

Now: $K(2) = K(1) + \delta K(1)$,

so we require:

$K(1) + \delta K(1) \leq Lk_2/l_2$

i.e. $\delta K(1) \leq Lk_2/l_2 - K(1)$.

So we may identify the upper bound for first period capital accumulation as:

$\delta K(1)' = Lk_2/l_2 - K(1)$.

Therefore the lower bound first period consumption is:

$$X(1)' = L/l_1 + (K(1)/k_2)(1-l_2/l_1) - (l_3/l_1)\delta K(1)'$$

$$= L/l_1 + (K(1)/k_2)(1-l_2/l_1) - (l_3/l_1)(Lk_2/l_2-K(1))$$

$$= L[(l_2-l_3k_2)/l_1l_2] + K(1)[(l_3k_2+l_1-l_2)/l_1k_2]. \tag{9.10}$$

Thus the PPF becomes as in Fig. 9.16.

Incidentally, it is possible to choose values of l_1, l_2, k_2, l_3, L and $K(1)$ such that $X(1)' < 0$. In this case, there is no possibility of capital saturation occuring in the second period, so the PPF can extend all the way to the $X(2)$ axis, as in Fig. 9.15.

Having established the intertemporal PPF, we now ask how a particular combination of first and second period consumptions is decided upon.

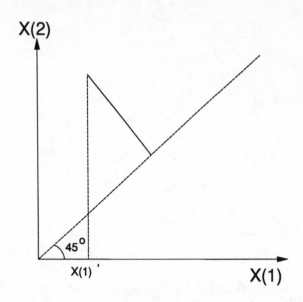

Fig. 9.16. The intertemporal PPF for the neo-Austrian model, constrained for efficiency and for no capital saturation.

9.5.3 Intertemporal Substitution: Step 2

In principle, we could invoke *any* mechanism of choosing a point on the PPF. For example, the choice might be determined by habit, or at random. In line with the conventional approach, here we adopt a simple utility/welfare maximising model. We assume that we can define a preference ordering over $(X(1),X(2))$ space, which allows the construction of 'smooth', convex to the origin, intertemporal indifference curves, as in Fig. 9.17.

The point marked 'M' indicates the $(X(1),X(2))$ combination which gives rise to the highest level of utility/welfare consistent with the PPF. Another possibility is shown in Fig. 9.18.

In Fig. 9.18 we have the solution at the 'capital saturation' corner. This gives rise to the highest possible rate of capital accumulation in period 1, and the highest possible rate of consumption in period 2. An alternative solution is shown in Fig. 9.19

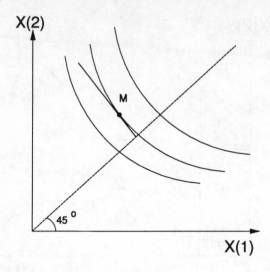

Fig. 9.17. Two-period intertemporal optimization with a neo-Austrian PPF.

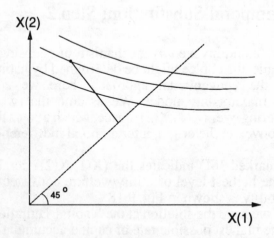

Fig. 9.18. A corner solution with a neo-Austrian PPF.

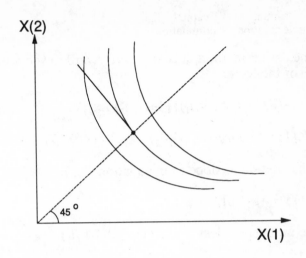

Fig. 9.19. A stationary state corner solution with a neo-Austrian PPF.

Here there is no capital accumulation in period 1, so consumption is the same in the two periods; i.e. there is a stationary state.

We might say that the indifference structure in Fig. 9.18 illustrates 'patience to consume', whilst that in Fig. 9.19 illustrates 'impatience to consume' (see BURMEISTER [1980:27-28]; for a rigorous definition of time preference, i.e. patience and impatience to consume, see KOOPMANS [1960]).

9.6 Introducing Capital Deterioration

A more realistic approach to capital would be to allow that capital physically deteriorates with age, in accordance with the Second Law of Thermodynamics. We therefore assume that, over time, the capital good deteriorates at a proportional rate c ($0 < c < 1$). For example, if $c = 0.1$, then in the absence of capital accumulation, each period the capital stock reduces by 10%.

This implies that the relationship between the capital stock in the two adjacent periods is:

$$K(t+1) = K(t) - cK(t) + \delta K(t).$$

capital   capital
deterioration   accumulation

Following the earlier method, it is straightforward to show that this gives rise to a PPF of the form:

$$X(2)= \{L/l_1+(K(1)/k_2)(1-l_2/l_1)\}\{1+(l_1-l_2)/l_3k_2\}$$

$$- (K(1)c/k_2)(1-l_2/l_1) - \{(l_1-l_2)/l_3k_2\}X(1).(9.11)$$

We see this has the same slope as in equation (9.8):

$$dX(2)/dX(1) = -(l_1-l_2)/l_3k_2.$$

However, the intercept is less, by $(K(1)c/k_2)(1-l_2/l_1)$.

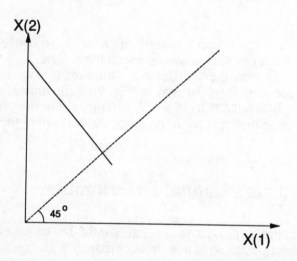

Fig. 9.20. The PPF for a neo-Austrian model with capital deterioration.

When we come to look at the constraints on this function, we notice two things. First, it is now possible for the PPF to extend below the 45° line, because of the deterioration of capital. Zero, or very low, capital accumulation in the first period will give rise to the second period consumption being *less* than the first period consumption. The PPF will therefore be of the form shown in Fig. 9.20.

The second alteration is to the minimum first period consumption. It is straightforward to show that with capital deteriorating at the proportional rate per period, c, this is given by:

$$X(1)' = L[(l_2-l_3k_2)/l_1l_2] + K(1)[(l_3(1-c)k_2+l_1-l_2)/l_1k_2]. \tag{9.12}$$

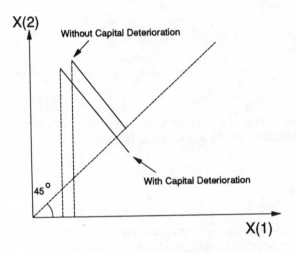

Fig. 9.21. The PPF for a neo-Austrian model with capital deterioration, constrained for no capital saturation.

We note that this is smaller than the corresponding minimum without capital deterioration. The overall effect on the PPF of introducing capital deterioration is therefore as shown in Fig. 9.21.

We note that with impatience to consume, we now have an actual reduction in the capital stock between periods 1 and 2, and also a reduction in consumption between the two periods. This is illustrated in Fig. 9.22.

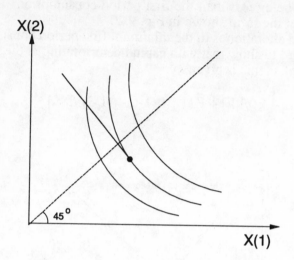

Fig. 9.22. The possible reduction of consumption with capital deterioration in a neo-Austrian model.

9.7 Summary

In this chapter we have developed the neo-Austrian approach to the modelling of production and capital accumulation.

We have attempted to demonstrate how neo-Austrian capital theory differs from the conventional neoclassical approach, and how it offers substantial improvements in the explicit modelling of the temporal structure of capital accumulation. In particular, we have stressed the use of activity analysis as the basic tool, as opposed to the use of the standard production function approach. We have done this for two reasons.

First, activity analysis allows one to represent the production of many different commodities, with the use of many different types of capital. This reflects actual production processes much better than the use of aggregate capital and aggregate output.

Second, The explicit use of capital goods draws attention to the need to produce these capital goods, by the use of other techniques. This production of the capital goods will, of necessity, occur before the capital goods are used. Therefore, the modelling approach itself induces an attention to the time structure of production. In particular, time irreversibility (Teleological Sequence: see Chapter 4) is naturally introduced into the modelling approach.

Although this chapter has contained a considerable amount of detail, the material developed so far is still insufficient to allow the derivation of the simulation model in Chapter 11. In Chapter 10, therefore, we shall further develop the neo-Austrian approach. In particular we shall develop the notions of shadow prices and 'myopic' optimisation, in a neo-Austrian context.

10 The Neo-Austrian Approach: Extensions to the Model

10.1 Introduction

In the previous chapter we introduced neo-Austrian capital theory as a means of modelling phenotypic evolution in economies. In this chapter we extend this model in several ways. However, it should be stressed that we still restrict ourselves to modelling phenotypic change ex ante. Of course, as discussed in earlier chapters, true genotypic change can only meaningfully be modelled ex post. Thus, if invention occurs, one might model its effect *after* its occurrence, but *not* before its occurrence.

In Section 10.2 we show how exact algebraic solutions to the neo-Austrian model can be obtained, and how these can become numerical solutions when a particular functional form is assumed for the welfare function, and when the model parameters are specified.

In Section 10.3 we show how shadow prices of the factor inputs can be calculated and interpreted in the neo-Austrian model.

In Section 10.4 we generalize the model, from two periods to n periods. We note, however, that such models are intrinsically difficult to solve, and also make behavioural assumptions about economic planning which are untenable.

In Section 10.5 we introduce, as an alternative to the full intertemporal plans of Section 10.4, the notion of 'rolling myopic' plans. We show that such plans are both realistic in their assumptions in a world which allows the emergence of novelty, and are also easy to solve analytically.

Section 10.6 shows how the neo-Austrian approach can allow the ex post modelling of the emergence of a new technique, through invention, in the framework of a rolling myopic plan.

10.2 Calculating the Optimal Consumption Pattern

So far in our explorations of the two-period neo-Austrian model we have used diagrammatic solutions only. We now turn to finding an explicit algebraic solution to the model. This will be useful not only because the technique we shall use will also allow the determination of the 'shadow prices' for the model, but also because such a solution forms the basis of the simulations to be discussed in Chapter 11. For ease of presentation we now revert to the two-period model without capital deterioration.

First, we note that we may associate a strictly quasi-concave utility/welfare function with this problem, which has indifference curves as its contours. The problem of finding the optimal intertemporal consumption pattern may then be written as one of constrained maximization. If the utility/welfare function which gives rise to the indifference curves is $W(X(1),X(2))$, then the problem becomes:

Max $W(X(1),X(2))$

$X(1),X(2)$

Subject to:

$X(2) = \{L/l_1+(K(1)/k_2)(1-l_2/l_1)\}\{1+(l_1-l_2)/l_3k_2\} - \{(l_1-l_2)/l_3k_2\}X(1)$

$X(1) \geq L[(l_2-l_3k_2)/l_1l_2] + K(1)[(l_3k_2+l_1-l_2)/l_1k_2]$

$X(1) \leq L/l_1 + (K(1)/k_2)(1-l_2/l_1)$

$X(1), X(2) \geq 0.$

The first constraint is the production possibility frontier (PPF), from equation (9.8), relating first and second period consumption. The second constraint gives the *lower* bound for first period consumption, from equation (9.10). The third constraint gives the *upper* bound for first period consumption, illustrate in Figure 9.15.

Here the constraints are linear, but the objective function is non-linear, so the problem is one of non-linear programming. This problem is particularly easy to solve if we assume that the solution appears on the *interior* of the production possibility frontier (PPF); i.e. in this chapter we assume that there is not a corner solution. (This implies that we assume the level of the capital good does not reach the maximal level of Lk_2/l_2.)

Then, for brevity, we express the PPF as in equation (9.9):

$$\alpha(1+S)/S = X(1) + X(2)/S \qquad\qquad (9.9)$$

Here:

$$\alpha \equiv L/l_1 + (K(1)/k_2)(1-l_2/l_1).$$

This is the maximum possible first period consumption.

Also, as introduced in Chapter 9 Section 9.5 above:

$S \equiv (l_1-l_2)/l_3k_2.$

This is the degree of superiority.

So our problem becomes:

Max $W(X(1),X(2))$
$X(1),X(2)$

Subject to:

$\alpha(1+S)/S = X(1) + X(2)/S.$

The inequality constraints no longer apply, as we assume that there is not a corner solution.

This problem is solved most easily by the method of LAGRANGE [BAUMOL 1977:Chapter 4]. That is, the constraint is reorganised as:

$\alpha(1+S)/S - X(1) - X(2)/S = 0.$

The left-hand side of this equation is multiplied by the Lagrange multiplier, P, and the whole expression is added to the objective function. This gives the Lagrangian:

$L = W(X(1),X(2)) + P[\alpha(1+S)/S-X(1)-X(2)/S].$[1]

We assume that W is strictly quasiconcave and sufficiently 'smooth' to allow differentiation of the Lagrangian. So maximization of the Lagrangian can be achieved by differentiating the Lagrangian with respect to $X(1)$, $X(2)$ and P. We get:

$\partial L/\partial X(1) = \partial W(X(1),X(2))/\partial X(1) - P = 0$ (10.1)

$\partial L/\partial X(2) = \partial W(X(1),X(2))/\partial X(2) - P/S = 0$ (10.2)

$\partial L/\partial P = \alpha(1+S)/S - X(1) - X(2)/S.$ (10.3)

---

[1] If the Lagrangian is maximised with respect to $X(1)$ and $X(2)$, and minimised with respect to P, the optimum of this non-constrained problem is the same as the optimum of the original constrained problem.

From equation (10.1) we have:

$$P = \partial W/\partial X(1) \tag{10.4}$$

and from equation (10.2) we have:

$$P = S \, \partial W/\partial X(2). \tag{10.5}$$

Now the optimal value of the Lagrange multiplier, P, can be interpreted as the opportunity cost of the constraint. Thus, from equation (10.4), a unit increment in $\alpha(1+S)/S$ (i.e. a unit outward shift in the PPF) gives rise to one extra unit of marginal utility in period 1.

Similarly, from equation (10.5), a unit increment to $\alpha(1+S)/S$ gives S units of marginal utility in period 2. This makes good sense, as S is the slope of the PPF, and so represents the 'trade-off' of present for future consumption.

To make further progress in solving the model, we need to specify a particular functional form for the utility/welfare function, $W(X(1),X(2))$. We do this in two stages.

First, we suppose that we can evaluate the utility of consumption, at any moment, with an 'instantaneous utility function', U(X). We then suppose that future utility is discounted at rate d. So the utility/welfare function can be written as:

$$W(X(1),X(2)) = U(X(1)) + U(X(2))/(1+d). \tag{10.6}$$

The second stage is to specify a functional form for U(X). We suppose that the instantaneous marginal utility of consumption is positive, but decreasing with consumption. This requirement is satisfied by numerous functions, but perhaps the simplest is:

$$U(X) = AX^{\beta}, \qquad A > 0, \quad 0 < \beta < 1. \tag{10.7}$$

So we can specify the functional form of the utility/welfare function as:

$$W(X(1),X(2)) = AX(1)^{\beta} + AX(2)^{\beta}/(1+d). \tag{10.8}$$

We can now evaluate the partial derivatives used in equations (10.4) and (10.5):

$$\partial W/\partial X(1) = A\beta X(1)^{\beta-1}$$

$$\partial W/\partial X(2) = A\beta X(2)^{\beta-1}/(1+d). \tag{10.8}$$

Substitution for these partial derivatives in equations (10.1) and (10.2) gives:

$$A\beta X(1)^{\beta-1} - P = 0 \tag{10.9}$$

$$A\beta X(2)^{\beta-1}/(1+d) - P/S = 0. \tag{10.10}$$

Eliminating P between equations (10.9) and (10.10) gives:

$$A\beta X(2)^{\beta-1}/(1+d) = A\beta X(1)^{\beta-1}/S$$

i.e. $(X(1)/X(2))^{\beta-1} = S/(1+d)$

i.e. $X(1) = (S/(1+d))^{1/(\beta-1)}X(2).$ $\tag{10.11}$

Substitution for $X(1)$ in (9.9) gives:

$$\alpha(1+S)/S - (S/(1+d))^{1/(\beta-1)}X(2) - X(2)/S = 0$$

i.e. $X(2)(1/S + (S/(1+d))^{1/(\beta-1)}) = \alpha(1+S)/S$

i.e. $X(2) = \alpha(1+S)/(1 + S(S/(1+d))^{1/(\beta-1)}).$ $\tag{10.12}$

Thence from equation (10.11):

$$X(1) = \alpha(1+S)/[S + (S/(1+d))^{1/(1-\beta)}]. \tag{10.13}$$

We can calculate these values for the same technology as used earlier. i.e.:

$l_1 = 10, l_2 = 1, k_2 = 1, l_3 = 5$, so $S = 1.8$.

If we specify initial capital as $K(1) = 10$, and the labour force as $L = 100$, as before, then $\alpha = 19$.

For the welfare function we use: $A = 1, \beta = 0.5, d = 0.1$.

This gives: $X(1) = 11.88, X(2) = 31.81$ and $P = 0.145$.

10.3 Shadow Prices in the Neo-Austrian Model

It is clear that the outputs in periods one and two are constrained by the initial labour force and the initial capital stock. For example, if we could increase the labour force used in the two periods, we could increase the output in either period, or in both periods. In particular, if we assume that there is no capital saturation, then an extra element of labour, δL, would be used in process R_1, to generate a further $\delta L/l_1$ units of output. So the extra welfare generated by the extra marginal δL units of labour is that which corresponds to $\delta L/l_1$ extra consumption.

Readers will recognize that this extra welfare, because of the marginal relaxation of the constraint on labour, is the 'shadow price' of labour [BAUMOL 1977:Chapter 6], that is, the opportunity cost of the constraint on labour. This is the valuation that society should put on labour because of its scarcity. We could similarly calculate the shadow price of capital. We note that these shadow prices may be used to decentralise the planning of an economy (see e.g. MALINVAUD [1953], KOOPMANS [1957]).

The calculation of the shadow prices emerges naturally if, instead of solving our optimization problem with a single constraint, the PPF, we use all of the relationships that contribute to the PPF as constraints. To this end, we write our problem as:

$$\underset{X(1),X(2)}{\text{Max}} \quad W(X(1),X(2))$$

Subject to:

$$X_1(1) + X_2(1) = X(1) \tag{10.14}$$

$$l_1 X_1(1) + l_2 X_2(1) + l_3 \delta K(1) = L(1) \tag{10.15}$$

$$k_2 X_2(1) = K(1) \tag{10.16}$$

$$X_1(2) + X_2(2) = X(2) \tag{10.17}$$

$$l_1 X_1(2) + l_2 X_2(2) = L(2) \tag{10.18}$$

$$k_2 X_2(2) = K(2) \tag{10.19}$$

$$K(2) = K(1) + \delta K(1) \tag{10.20}$$

$$X_1(1), X_2(1), X_1(2), X_2(2), L, \delta K(1) > 0.$$

Constraints (10.14) and (10.17) define total output in the two periods. Constraints (10.15) and (10.18) relate to labour availability, and constraints (10.16) and (10.19) relate to capital availability. We also note that constraint

(10.20) for period two recognizes that without capital deterioration, second period capital, $K(2)$, equals first period capital, $K(1)$, plus first period capital accumulation, $\delta K(1)$.

We now set up the Lagrangian for this constrained optimization problem. To do this, as before we first reorganise the constraints, so that zero appears on the right-hand side of the equations. i.e.:

$$-X(1) + X_1(1) + X_2(1) = 0 \tag{10.21}$$

$$L(1) - l_1 X_1(1) - l_2 X_2(1) - l_3 \delta K(1) = 0 \tag{10.22}$$

$$K(1) - k_2 X_2(1) = 0 \tag{10.23}$$

$$-X(2) + X_1(2) + X_2(2) = 0 \tag{10.24}$$

$$L(2) - l_1 X_1(2) - l_2 X_2(2) = 0 \tag{10.25}$$

$$K(2) - k_2 X_2(2) = 0 \tag{10.26}$$

$$\delta K(1) + K(1) - K(2) = 0. \tag{10.27}$$

We now associate a Lagrange multiplier with each constraint. We identify this with the constraining element, which is the left-most element of each constraint. So we associate the multiplier $P_{X(1)}$ with constraint (10.21), $P_{L(1)}$ with constraint (10.22), etc. We now form the Lagrangian as before, by taking the objective function and adding to it the left-hand side of each constraining equation, multiplied by the corresponding Lagrange multiplier. i.e.:

$$V = W(X(1), X(2))$$

$$+ P_{X(1)}[-X(1) + X_1(1) + X_2(1)]$$

$$+ P_{L(1)}[L(1) - l_1 X_1(1) - l_2 X_2(1) - l_3 \delta K(1)]$$

$$+ P_{K(1)}[K(1) - k_2 X_2(1)]$$

$$+ P_{X(2)}[-X(2) + X_1(2) + X_2(2)]$$

$$+ P_{L(2)}[L(2) - l_1 X_1(2) - l_2 X_2(2)]$$

$$+ P_{K(2)}[K(2) - k_2 X_2(2)]$$

$$+ P_{\delta K(1)}[\delta K(1) + K(1) - K(2)].$$

Optimization proceeds as usual, by maximising the Lagrangian with respect to the variables $X(1)$, $X_1(1)$, $X_2(1)$, $X(2)$, $X_1(2)$, $X_2(2)$ and $\delta K(1)$, and minimising it with respect to the Lagrange multipliers $P_{X(1)}$, $P_{L(1)}$, $P_{K(1)}$, $P_{X(2)}$, $P_{L(2)}$, $P_{K(2)}$ and $P_{\delta K(1)}$.

As usual, we assume that the objective function is strictly quasi-concave, and everywhere differentiable. Thus the optimization can be achieved by differentiation. As differentiating the Lagrangian with respect to the Lagrange multipliers will just give the constraints evaluated at the optimum, we simply differentiate with respect to the variables. We obtain:

$$\partial V/\partial X(1) = \partial W/\partial X(1) - P_{X(1)} = 0 \tag{10.28}$$

$$\partial V/\partial X(2) = \partial W/\partial X(2) - P_{X(2)} = 0 \tag{10.29}$$

$$\partial V/\partial X_1(1) = P_{X(1)} - l_1 P_{L(1)} = 0 \tag{10.30}$$

$$\partial V/\partial X_2(1) = P_{X(1)} - l_2 P_{L(1)} - k_2 P_{K(1)} = 0 \tag{10.31}$$

$$\partial V/\partial X_1(2) = P_{X(2)} - l_1 P_{L(2)} = 0 \tag{10.32}$$

$$\partial V/\partial X_2(2) = P_{X(2)} - l_2 P_{L(2)} - k_2 P_{K(2)} = 0 \tag{10.33}$$

$$\partial V/\partial \delta K(1) = P_{\delta K(1)} - l_3 P_{L(1)} = 0. \tag{10.34}$$

If we set:

$$W_1 \equiv \partial W/\partial X(1)$$

and:

$$W_2 \equiv \partial W/\partial X(2)$$

from equations (10.28) and (10.29) we get:

$$P_{X(1)} = W_1, \;\; P_{X(2)} = W_2.$$

Substituting in equations (10.30) and (10.32) gives:

$$P_{L(1)} = W_1/l_1, \;\; P_{L(2)} = W_2/l_1.$$

Further substitution in equations (10.31) and (10.33) gives:

$$P_{K(1)} = W_1(1-l_2/l_1)/k_2, \ P_{K(2)} = W_2(1-l_2/l_1)/k_2.$$

Finally, from equation (10.34) we have:

$$P_{\delta K(1)} = W_1 l_3/l_1.$$

We note that the Lagrange multiplier for $X(1)$, first period consumption, is simply the marginal utility of consumption in the first period. Now the marginal utility of consumption is exactly the extra benefit received from an increment of extra consumption. This shows clearly that one may interpret Lagrange multipliers as the shadow prices of the constraining variables.

The shadow price of labour in the first period, $P_{L(1)}$, is the shadow price of consumption divided by l_1. This is, of course, exactly in line with the reasoning in the introduction to this section. The shadow price of capital in the two periods can be similarly interpreted.

We can calculate values for these shadow prices, using the same welfare function and parameter values as used above. i.e:

$$l_1 = 10, l_2 = 1, k_2 = 1, l_3 = 5 \ (i.e. \ S = 1.8)$$

$$K(1) = 10, L = 100 \ (i.e. \ \alpha = 19)$$

$$A = 1, \beta = 0.5, d = 0.1.$$

From the differentiation of (10.8), using (10.7) we get:

$$W_1 \equiv \partial W/\partial X(1) = A\beta X(1)^{\beta-1} \tag{10.35}$$

$$W_2 \equiv \partial W/\partial X(2) = A\beta X(2)^{\beta-1}/(1+d). \tag{10.36}$$

At the optimum, from our calculations in Section 10.2, we know:

$$X(1) = 11.88, \ X(2) = 31.81.$$

So substituting for the above values, we get:

$P_{X(1)} = 0.1451 \quad P_{X(2)} = 0.0806$

$P_{L(1)} = 0.0145 \quad P_{L(2)} = 0.0081$

$P_{K(1)} = 0.1306 \quad P_{K(2)} = 0.0725$

$P_{\delta K(1)} = 0.0725.$

We note that the ratio of first to second period shadow prices are all the same [BERNHOLZ and FABER 1973:56]:

$$P_{X(1)}/P_{X(2)} = P_{L(1)}/P_{L(2)} = P_{K(1)}/P_{K(2)} = 1.8 = S.$$

Now the (own) rate of interest can be defined by (see e.g. BURMEISTER [1980:11], FABER [1979:77]):

$$r = P_{X(1)}/P_{X(2)} - 1.$$

Thus we see that in this example the own rates of interest of the goods are all equal, with $r = 0.8$.

We also note that $P_{K(2)} = P_{\delta K(1)}$. Both of these results are in line with intuition, and both can be derived by substituting the relationships for $X(1)$ and $X(2)$, given in equations (10.12) and (10.13), into the formulae for W_1 and W_2, given in equations (10.35) and (10.36).

10.4 The Model with More than Two Periods

To illustrate how this approach can be generalized to $3, 4, ..., n$, etc. periods, we shall restate the basics of the model. For simplicity of exposition we shall not include capital deterioration. We also assume there is no capital saturation in any period. So we have:

$$L(t) = L_1(t) + L_2(t) + L_3(t)$$

$$X_1(t) = L_1(t)/l_1$$

$$X_2(t) = K(t)/k_2 = L_2(t)/l_2$$

$$\delta K(t) = L_3(t)/l_3$$

$$K(t+1) = K(t) + \delta K(t).$$

For a three period model[2], making the usual substitutions we obtain:

---

[2] The same model, with n-periods and capital deterioration, is analysed in FABER [1979:Chapter 5].

$$X(1) = L/l_1 + (K(1)/k_2)(1-l_2/l_1) - (l_3/l_1)\delta K(1) \qquad (10.37)$$

$$X(2) = L/l_1 + \{[K(1)+\delta K(1)]/k_2\}(1-l_2/l_1) - (l_3/l_1)\delta K(2) \qquad (10.38)$$

$$X(3) = L/l_1 + \{[K(1)+\delta K(1)+\delta K(2)]/k_2\}(1-l_2/l_1). \qquad (10.39)$$

As before, we define:

$$\alpha \equiv L/l_1 + (K(1)/k_2)(1-l_2/l_1).$$

Again, α is the maximum possible consumption in period 1.

Substitution for α in equations (10.37), (10.38) and (10.39) gives:

$$X(1) - \alpha = -(l_3/l_1)\delta K(1) \qquad (10.40)$$

$$X(2) - \alpha = [\delta K(1)/k_2](1-l_2/l_1) - (l_3/l_1)\delta K(2) \qquad (10.41)$$

$$X(3) - \alpha = [\{\delta K(1)+\delta K(2)\}/k_2](1-l_2/l_1). \qquad (10.42)$$

We recall the definition:

$$S \equiv (l_1-l_2)/l_3k_2. \qquad (9.5)$$

Reorganisation of equations (10.40), (10.41) and (10.42), together with identity (8.5), yields:

$$X(1) + X(2)/(1+S) + X(3)/[(1+S)S] = \alpha(1+S)/S \qquad (10.43)$$

(cf. equation (9.9) for the n = 2 case).

We can plot the PPF surface represented by equation (16) in $(X(1),X(2),X(3))$ space. It has the shape shown in Fig. 10.1.

When the constraints on the system, described above, are imposed, the result is a quadrilateral of the form shown in Fig. 10.2. Optimization now requires the definition of three dimensional indifference surfaces, to give a unique optimum.

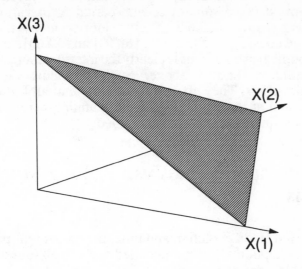

Fig. 10.1. The three-period PPF for a neo-Austrian model.

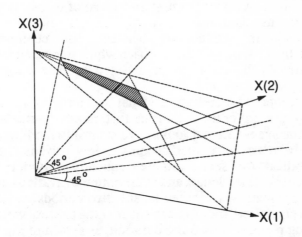

Fig. 10.2. The constrained three-period PPF for a neo-Austrian model.

Clearly, for four or more periods a geometric solution becomes impossible to draw. However, if the utility/welfare function is given a particular functional form, then the solution to an n-period optimization problem is possible, using matrix methods. Such solutions imply that the entire investment and consumption patterns, $\{\delta K(t)\}$ and $\{X(t)\}$, are determined at the same moment in time. This is clearly the interpretation of the 3-period geometric solution, shown above. Such problems are known as intertemporal models. They effectively assume that all future events are fully known, and at the beginning of the planning period all decisions relating to subsequent periods can be defined.

10.5 Intertemporal Plans vs. 'Rolling Myopic' Plans

From Parts I and II, on evolution and time, the reader will recognize that we feel the assumption of perfect knowledge about all future events to be an unacceptable way of proceeding. This is particularly the case when dealing with environmental matters. We simply cannot pretend to know everything about the natural world and how it interacts with economic activity, which is itself changing through the introduction of novel techniques. Scientific research is continually altering our knowledge about the natural world and also changing the nature of economic activity. We therefore do not use the 'once and for all' full intertemporal approach for modelling long-run interactions between the economy and the environment. Instead, we seek an approach which is more flexible, allowing decisions made in the future to be affected by new information, as it becomes available.

What we propose, therefore, is what we term a 'rolling myopic'[3] approach. We use 'myopic' to indicate that, at any particular moment in time, economic agents are not looking very far into the future, so that the decisions they make are related to only a few periods ahead. We use 'rolling' to indicate that such plans are frequently revised, to take account of alterations in our knowledge, and in the nature of available technologies. So if the decision period is limited to, say, two periods, and decisions are reassessed every period, then the decison making process would be a series of overlapping plans, of indefinite duration, as shown in Fig. 10.3.

---

[3] For similar approaches see DAY and CIGNO [1978], FULLERTON, HENDERSON and SHOVEN [1984], and BALLARD and GOULDER [1985]. There usually the term 'sequential myopic' plan is used instead of 'rolling myopic' plan. For an excellent discussion of seqential decision making, see SCHMUTZLER [1991].

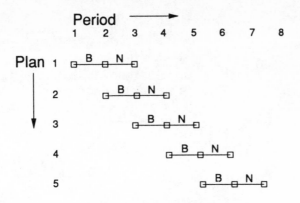

Fig. 10.3.   A two-period rolling myopic plan.

Plan 1 is made at the beginning of period 1, and covers periods 1 and 2. The planned activity for period 1 is 'binding', and is carried out. However, the planned activity for period 2 is 'non-binding', and only provisional.

When period 2 is reached, plan 2 is formulated. The outcomes of plan 1 now act as initial conditions for plan 2. Plan 2 is also over two periods, periods 2 and 3. The planned activities for period 2 are binding, and carried out, but those for period 3 are non-binding (provisional), etc.

It is quite feasible to have such plans over n periods (n > 2), with m periods binding (m < n). For example, plans over three periods, with one period binding, are shown in Fig. 10.4.[4]

So the full rolling myopic plan is a series of overlapping finite time-horizon plans. The planned outcomes from each plan act as the intial conditions for the succeeding plan. One interpretation of rolling myopic plans is that they reflect a desire for 'flexibility' in planning [KOOPMANS 1964; MAIER 1984]. We return to this issue in Chapter 12.

This notion of a rolling myopic plan we feel to be very realistic. For instance, it is well known that firms formulate plans with finite time-horizons, and review these plans reasonably frequently. Such plans also have the advantage that they are indefinite in duration, but their behaviour is only sensitive to the length of the myopic planning horizon.

---

[4] We are grateful to a reviewer of the first edition of this book [KLEPPER 1992] for pointing out an error in the original version of this figure.

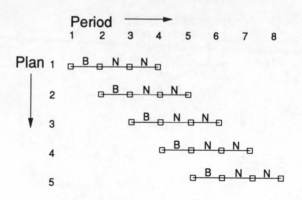

B - Binding   N - Non-Binding

Fig. 10.4. A three-period rolling myopic plan, with one period binding.

A rolling two-period myopic plan behaves the same over the first 19 periods, whether the overall duration is 20 periods or 20,000 periods. That is, the behaviour of the plan is insensitive to guesses about the nature of the distant future. In this, myopic rolling plans are quite unlike conventional intertemporal plans.

10.5.1 A Two-Period Rolling Myopic Plan

We now turn to a particular rolling myopic plan, with two planning periods, with only the first period decisions being binding. We take this as our example because, as we shall show, it is particularly easy to represent diagrammatically how such a plan is implemented. Also, it is straightforward to apply such a plan for simulation purposes. To proceed, we recall the nature of the PPF for a two period plan, without capital deterioration. This is as shown in Fig. 10.5.
We mark the axes $X(t)$ and $X(t+1)$ to reflect the fact that we are now considering a two-period plan as embedded in a much larger (flexible) plan, with a much longer duration. The optimization procedure employs a set of indifference curves, as in Fig. 10.6.

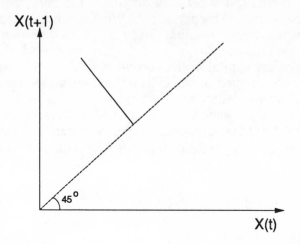

Fig. 10.5. The PPF for a neo-Austrian model, without capital deterioration.

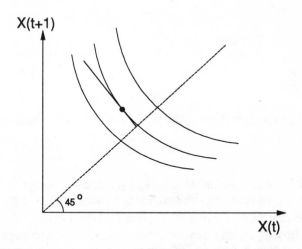

Fig. 10.6. The optimization procedure for a two-period rolling myopic plan.

Now the optimal point chosen gives the planned consumption in periods t and t+1. The consumption planned for period t is implemented. What of the planned consumption for period t+1? We do not implement this; instead it is now the maximum possible first period consumption for the next planning period. We see this is so, as in the two-period plan, we do not plan to accumulate capital in the second period. So the planned second period consumption must be the largest possible, and the planned second period capital accumulation must be zero.

So the non-implemented second-period consumption defines the maximum first period consumption for the next period. That is, it defines the point on the 45° line for the next plan's PPF. This is shown in Fig. 10.7.

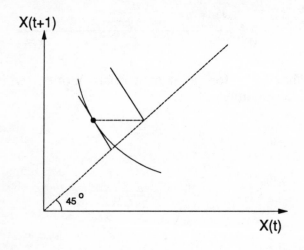

Fig. 10.7.   The construction of the next period's PPF with a rolling myopic plan

As the technology is constant (i.e. l_1, l_2, k_2, l_3 are unchanged), the slopes of the PPFs are the same for each successive two-period plan. The slope is, of course, the degreee of superiority, $S \equiv (l_1 - l_2)/l_3 k_2$.

The PPF, however, has moved upwards because the capital stock has increased. If we assume the indifference curves are also constant over time (i.e. the two-period utility/welfare function is unchanged), then we can use the same indifference map to construct the new optimal point. This allows the third PPF to be constructed, etc., as shown in Fig. 10.8.

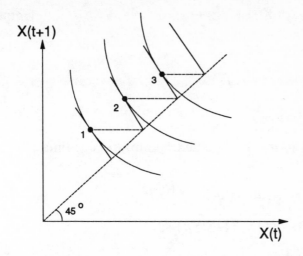

Fig. 10.8. The time structure of optimization with a rolling myopic plan.

The points in Fig. 10.8 marked '1', '2', '3', are the optimal points, giving rise to the consumption path $X(1)$, $X(2)$, ... , $X(t)$, etc. It is possible, of course, to derive the corresponding path of capital accumulation, $\delta K(t)$, etc, and also the corresponding paths of capital, $K(t)$, and labour use, $L_1(t)$, $L_2(t)$, $L_3(t)$. If one wished, one could even plot the path of output, $X(t)$, and labour used to produce the consumption good, $L_1(t)+L_2(t)$. This would give rise to a 'traverse' path on the production surface, as discussed in Chapter 9 (see Fig. 9.12).

10.5.2 Solving the Rolling Myopic Plan Model

The solution to the two-period rolling myopic plan is a straightforward extension of the solution of the two-period plan discussed above. We use the same welfare function (cf. equations (10.6) and (10.7)):

$$W(X(1),X(2)) = AX(t)^\beta + AX^*(t+1)^\beta/(1+d).$$

Here we use $X^*(t+1)$ to indicate that this is the *maximum possible* $X(t+1)$. It is the provisional, *non-binding* value. The *actual* $X(t+1)$ is decided at time $t+1$.

The constraints on the maximising of the objective function are:

$$\alpha(t)(1+S)/S = X(t) + X^*(t+1)/S \qquad \text{(cf. equation (9.9))}$$

where:

$$\alpha(t) \equiv L/l_1 + K(t)(1-l_2/l_1)/k_2$$

$$S \equiv (l_1-l_2)/l_3 k_2.$$

The solution to this constrained optimization at time t is (cf. equations (10.13) and (10.12)):

$$X(t) = \alpha(t)(1+S)/[S+(S/(1+d))^{1/(1-\beta)}]$$

$$X^*(t+1) = \alpha(t)(1+S)/[1+S(S/(1+d))^{1/(\beta-1)}].$$

Now here $\alpha(t)$ varies over time, as $K(t)$ varies. For a given $X^*(t)$ we can calculate $K(t+1)$ as follows.

We know that:

$$X_2(t) = K(t)/k_2 = L_2(t)/l_2$$

i.e. $L_2(t) = l_2 K(t)/k_2.$

Also: $X(t) = X_1(t) + X_2(t)$

i.e. $X_1(t) = X(t) - X_2(t)$

$$= X(t) - K(t)/k_2.$$

Now: $L_1(t) = l_1 X_1(t) = l_1(X(t)-K(t)/k_2).$

Also: $L = L_1(t) + L_2(t) + L_3(t)$

So: $\delta K(t) = L_3(t)/l_3$

$$= \{L - l_1(X(t)-K(t)/k_2) - l_2 K(t)/k_2\}/l_3$$

$$= L/l_3 - l_1 X(t)/l_3 + K(t)(l_1-l_2)/l_3 k_2$$

$$= L/l_3 - l_1 X(t)/l_3 + SK(t).$$

So: $K(t+1) = K(t) + \delta K(t)$

$$= L/l_3 - l_1 X(t)/l_3 + (1+S)K(t).$$

Thus the step-by-step solution to the two-period myopic rolling plan problem is as follows:[5]

1. Given $K(t)$, calculate $\alpha(t)$.

2. Thence calculate $X(t)$ and $X^*(t+1)$.

3. From $X(t)$ calculate $K(t+1)$.

4. Given $K(t+1)$, calculate $\alpha(t+1)$ ... etc.

Table 10.1. The outcome of a two period rolling myopic plan.

t	X(t)	X(t+1)	K(t)	$\delta K(t)$	$\%\delta K(t)/K(t)$
1	21.90	24.00	10.00	1.34	13.37
2	23.00	25.21	11.34	1.40	12.38
3	24.15	26.47	12.74	1.47	11.57
4	25.36	27.80	14.22	1.55	10.89
5	26.64	29.19	15.76	1.63	10.31
6	27.97	30.65	17.39	1.71	9.82
7	29.37	32.19	19.10	1.79	9.39
8	30.85	33.80	20.89	1.88	9.01
9	32.39	35.50	22.77	1.98	8.68
10	34.02	37.28	24.75	2.08	8.39

This type of calculation is illustrated in Table 10.1, using the following parameter values:

$l_1 = 7, l_2 = 1, k_2 = 1, l_3 = 5.$ (i.e. S=1.2).

---

[5] As the model presented is a discrete linear system, it is possible to find analytic solutions for all future states of the model. We do not follow this path for two reasons. First, the extension of this model presented in Chapter 10 is non-linear, so not amenable to such treatment. Second, by stressing the iterative, step-by-step, nature of the solution, we stress the openness of the model to decisions which make use of all information then available. That is, we stress the openness of the model to the emergence of novelty.

$K(1) = 10, L = 100, ß = 0.05, d = 0.1$.

Also illustrated in Table 10.1 is the capital accumulation in each period, $\delta K(t)$, and the proportional rate of growth of capital, $\delta K(t)/K(t)$. The time profiles of output and capital stock which result from this rolling myopic plan are shown in Fig. 10.9.

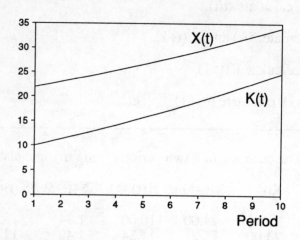

Fig. 10.9. Output and capital stock time profiles resulting from a rolling myopic plan.

10.5.3 Shadow Prices for a Rolling Myopic Plan

For a simple rolling myopic plan, the calculation of the shadow prices is straightforward.

If we use a two-period plan, then only the decisions relating to the first period are binding, so we do not need to calculate the shadow prices relating to the unrealized decisions for the second period. The shadow prices we need are therefore given by the formulae derived in Section 10.3. i.e.:

$P_{X(1)}(t) = W_1(t)$

$P_{L(1)}(t) = W_1(t)/l_1$

$P_{K(1)}(t) = W_1(t)(1-l_2/l_1)/k_2$

$P_{\delta K(1)}(t) = W_2(t)(1-l_2/l_1)/k_2$.

Table 10.2. The time profile of shadow prices derived from a two-period rolling myopic plan.

t	$P_{X(1)}(t)$	$P_{L(1)}(t)$	$P_{K(1)}(t)$	$P_{\delta K(1)}(t)$
1	0.145	0.015	0.131	0.073
2	0.112	0.011	0.101	0.056
3	0.087	0.009	0.078	0.043
4	0.067	0.007	0.060	0.033
5	0.052	0.005	0.047	0.026
6	0.040	0.004	0.036	0.020
7	0.031	0.003	0.028	0.015
8	0.024	0.002	0.021	0.012
9	0.018	0.002	0.017	0.009
10	0.014	0.001	0.013	0.007

The shadow prices for the same welfare functions and parameter values as for Table 10.1 are shown in Table 10.2.

We note that all of the shadow prices are falling over time. This is because capital is being accumulated, so output per unit labour is steadily increasing over time. As the welfare function exhibits diminishing instantaneous marginal utility of consumption (i.e. impatience to consume), the opportunity cost, in welfare terms, of all these factors is steadily decreasing.

10.6 The Innovation of a Novel Technique

To show the strength of the rolling myopic plan approach, when combined with a neo-Austrian approach to production, we shall now examine the effect of introducing a novel technique into the model.

We begin with our usual two technique model, with a two-period rolling myopic plan. We suppose this runs for a certain period of time, until at time τ a new technique begins to be innovated. We assume this is newly invented (i.e. economic genotypic change has occurred), and is made up of two further processes, as follows:

Process R_4 uses labour and capital to produce the consumption good. The capital good is specific to process R_4. As in most real world cases, the capital goods cannot be substituted between processes. We call this capital good K^4. (Here we use a superscipt rather than a subscript to remind us that, unlike labour and output, capital cannot be aggregated between processes.)

Process R_5 uses labour only to produce the capital good for process R_4. So the full technology available is now as follows:

R_1: l_1 units of labour $\rightarrow$ 1 unit of output. $\qquad\qquad\qquad$ } $\quad T_1$

R_2: l_2 units of labour $\oplus$ k_2 units of capital good 2 $\qquad$ }
$\qquad\qquad\qquad\rightarrow$ 1 unit of output. $\qquad\qquad$ } $\quad T_2$
$\qquad\qquad\qquad\qquad\qquad\qquad\qquad\qquad\qquad\qquad$ }

R_3: l_3 units of labour $\rightarrow$ 1 unit of capital good 2. $\qquad$ }

R_4: l_4 units of labour $\oplus$ k_4 units of capital good 4 $\qquad$ }
$\qquad\qquad\qquad\rightarrow$ 1 unit of output. $\qquad\qquad$ } $\quad T_3$
$\qquad\qquad\qquad\qquad\qquad\qquad\qquad\qquad\qquad\qquad$ }

R_5: l_5 units of labour $\rightarrow$ 1 unit of capital good 4. $\qquad$ }

We first note that, with a two-period model, technique T_3 will be innovated only if its degree of superiority over technique T_1 is greater than that of technique T_2 over technique T_1. i.e. For the innovation of technique T_3 we require, as a necessary condition:

$$(l_1\text{-}l_4)/l_5k_4 > (l_1\text{-}l_2)/l_3k_2$$

i.e. $S_3 > S_2$, where S_3 is the 'degree of superiority' of technique T_3, and S_2 is that of technique T_2, as defined in (9.5).

Supposing technique T_3 is superior to technique T_2, what will happen? What kind of phenotypic change will occur in response to the genotypic change, i.e. the invention of technique T_3? Supposing there is a reasonable degree of impatience to consume, one would expect that accumulation of capital for technique T_2 will cease, and accumulation of capital for technique T_3 will commence. In such a case, all the remaining capital specific to technique T_2 will continue to be used while there is sufficient labour left to do so, as the alternative to using this capital is to employ labour with the low productivity technique T_1.

In reality, the capital used by technique T_2 will deteriorate over time, so eventually only a vanishingly small amount of that type of capital will remain, and the technique will have been effectively terminated. As we wish to model this innovation of technique T_3, and the corresponding decline of technique T_2, it is necessary to reintroduce capital deterioration into the model.

This three-sector model is therefore described as follows:

$$R_1: L_1(t)/l_1 = X_1(t) \qquad\qquad \} \qquad T_1$$

$$R_2: L_2(t)/l_2 = K^2(t)/k_2 = X_2(t) \qquad \}$$
$$\qquad\qquad\qquad\qquad\qquad\qquad\qquad\qquad \} \qquad T_2$$
$$R_3: L_3(t)/l_3 = \delta K^2(t) \qquad\qquad\qquad \}$$

$$R_4: L_4(t)/l_4 = K^4(t)/k_4 = X_4(t) \qquad \}$$
$$\qquad\qquad\qquad\qquad\qquad\qquad\qquad\qquad \} \qquad T_3$$
$$R_5: L_5(t)/l_5 = \delta K^4(t) \qquad\qquad\qquad \}$$

$$L(t) = L_1(t) + L_2(t) + L_3(t) + L_4(t) + L_5(t)$$

$$K^2(t+1) = K^2(t) - cK^2(t) + \delta K^2(t)$$
$$\qquad\qquad = (1-c)K^2(t) + \delta K^2(t)$$

$$K^4(t+1) = K^4(t) - cK^4(t) + \delta K^4(t)$$
$$\qquad\qquad = (1-c)K^4(t) + \delta K^4(t)$$

$$K^4(t) = 0, \quad t \le \tau.$$

Our problem would then be to maximise the welfare function subject to the above constraining equations. Clearly, the solution will be in two parts; that up to time $t = \tau$, when only techniques T_1 and T_2 are available, and that after time $t = \tau$, when all three techniques are available. The former has already been dealt with, so we shall concentrate here on the second part, for $t \ge \tau$.

At time $t = \tau$, the stock of the capital good for technique T_2 is $K^2(\tau)$. The stock of the capital good for technique T_3 is zero; i.e. $K^4(\tau) = 0$. Accumulation of the capital good for technique T_2 is zero; i.e. $\delta K^2(t) = 0$, $t \ge \tau$.

We first proceed to construct the production possibility frontier between periods t and $t+1$. $(t > \tau)$.

Capital accumulation of the third technique capital good is $\delta K^4(t)$. This requires labour:

$$L_5(t) = l_5 \delta K^4(t).$$

We assume all capital stock of both types is fully utilized (i.e. there is no capital saturation).

So for process R_2:

$$X_2(t) = K^2(t)/k_2; \quad L_2(t) = l_2 X_2(t) = l_2 K^2(t)/k_2.$$

Similarly, for process R_4:

$$X_4(t) = K^4(t)/k_4; \quad L_4(t) = l_4 X_4(t) = l_4 K^4(t)/k_4.$$

As there is no capital accumulation of the first type of capital good:

$$\delta K^2(t) = 0, \text{ so } L_3(t) = 0.$$

Now we have:

$$L = L_1(t) + L_2(t) + L_3(t) + L_4(t) + L_5(t).$$

So: $L_1(t) = L - L_2(t) - L_3(t) - L_4(t) - L_5(t)$

$$= L - l_2 K^2(t)/k_2 - 0 - l_4 K^4(t)/k_4 - l_5 \delta K^4(t).$$

So: $X_1(t) = [L - l_2 K^2(t)/k_2 - l_4 K^4(t)/k_4 - l_5 \delta K^4(t)]/l_1.$

Now: $X(t) = X_1(t) + X_2(t) + X_4(t)$

$$= [L - l_2 K^2(t)/k_2 - l_4 K^4(t)/k_4 - l_5 \delta K^4(t)]/l_1 + K^2(t)/k_2 + K^4(t)/k_4$$

i.e. $X(t) = L/l_1 + K^2(t)(1 - l_2/l_1)/k_2 + K^4(t)(1 - l_4/l_1)/k_4 - l_5 \delta K^4(t)/l_1.$ (10.44)

In period two of the two-period planning horizon, we set:

$$\delta K^{*4}(t+1) = \delta K^{*2}(t+1) = 0$$

i.e. we plan no capital accumulation.

Also, we know the stock of the two types of capital good at time t+1, using:

$$K^2(t+1) = (1-c)K^2(t)$$

$$K^4(t+1) = (1-c)K^4(t) + \delta K^4(t).$$

Therefore, from equation (10.44), we can write:

$$X^*(t+1) \quad = L/l_1 + (1-c)K^2(t)(1-l_2/l_1)/k_2 + [(1-c)K^4(t)\delta K^4(t)](1-l_4/l_1)/k_4.$$

$$(10.45)$$

Further, reorganisation of (10.44) allows one to express $\delta K^4(t)$ as:

$$\delta K^4(t) = [L/l_1+K^2(t)(1-l_2/l_1)/k_2+K^4(t)(1-l_4/l_1)/k_4-X(t)]l_1/l_5. \qquad (10.46)$$

Substitution for $\delta K^4(t)$ from (10.46) in (10.45) gives the PPF as:

$$X^*(t+1) \quad = [L/l_1+K^2(t)(1-l_2/l_1)/k_2+K^4(t)(1-l_4/l_1)/k_4]\{1+(l_1-l_4)/l_5k_4\}$$

$$- cK^2(t)(1-l_2/l_1)/k_2 - cK^4(t)(1-l_4/l_1)/k_4 - X(t)(l_1-l_4)/l_5k_4.$$

We can compare this with the corresponding PPF before period $t = \tau$. With capital accumulation of the first capital good, and without the availablility of technique T_3, the PPF is as derived in Chapter 9, Section 9.6 (cf. equation (9.11)):

$$X^*(t+1) \quad = [L/l_1+K^2(t)(1-l_2/l_1)/k_2]\{1+(l_1-l_2)/l_3k_2\}$$

$$- cK^2(t)(1-l_2/l_1)/k_2 - X(t)(l_1-l_2)/l_3k_2.$$

If we consider the case at time $t = \tau$, then as the new technique will have just become available, none of its capital will have been accumulated. i.e. $K^4(\tau) = 0$. Thus the new PPF at time $t = \tau$ will be:

$$X^*(\tau+1) \quad = [L/l_1+K^2(\tau)(1-l_2/l_1)/k_2]\{1+(l_1-l_4)/l_5k_4\}$$

$$- cK^2(\tau)(1-l_2/l_1)/k_2 - X(\tau)(l_1-l_4)/l_5k_4.$$

If the new technique had not become available, then the PPF would have been:

$$X^*(\tau+1) \quad = [L/l_1 + K^2(\tau)(1-l_2/l_1)/k_2]\{1+(l_1-l_2)/l_3k_2\}$$

$$- cK^2(\tau)(1-l_2/l_1)/k_2 - X(\tau)(l_1-l_2)/l_3k_2.$$

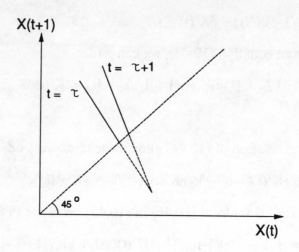

Fig. 10.10. The effect of innovating a new technique on the PPF in a neo-Austrian model.

We note that the slope of the new PPF is greater than that before the introduction of technique T_3, as:

$$(l_1-l_4)/l_5k_4 > (l_1-l_2)/l_3k_2.$$

Also, the new PPF has a larger intercept. Thus the effect of innovating the new technique is a rotation of the PPF. It is easy to show that the point of rotation lies below the 45° line, as illustrated in Fig. 10.10.

It is interesting to note that the slope of the PPF is determined by the nature of the best technique available, and switches to its new value as soon as the new technique becomes available, even though it has not yet been brought into use.

It is straightforward to simulate the effect of introducing a new technique in a rolling myopic model. We use the usual method with the following parameter values:

$$l_1 = 7, l_2 = 1, k_2 = 1, l_3 = 5, l_4 = 1, k_4 = 1, l_5 = 4.9$$

$$c_2 = 0.1, c_4 = 0.1, b = 0.05, d = 0.1$$

$$K^2(0) = 10, K^4(0) = 0, L = 100, \tau = 14.$$

In Fig. 10.11 we see the plots of total output, and output by each process, over twenty-five periods. We introduce the new technique, technique T_3, in period 14.

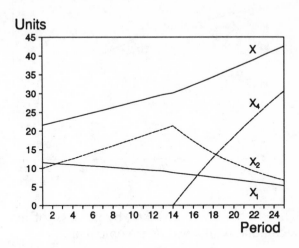

Fig. 10.11.   The effect on output of innovating a new technique in a rolling myopic model.

The use of the labour force over time, by all five processes, is shown in Fig. 10.12.

We note that the behaviour of the model seems very reasonable. Up until period 13 there is a steady accumulation of capital for technique T_2. After that time it is clearly not sensible to accumulate this form of capital, if there is a reasonable degree of impatience to consume. Instead, capital for technique T_3 begins to be accumulated, and the stock of the old type of capital steadily decreases through deterioration.

The reader will note that the path of total output of the consumption good has a slight "hiccough" in period 14. Up to period 14 total output is growing steadily, using just techniques T_1 and T_2. After period 15 a new growth path of output is established, using all three techniques. However, in period 14 there seems to be an adjustment which retards total output. This is because in this period the whole set of production possibilities alters, and a new pattern of capital accumulation is being established. That is, the PPF alters in shape and intercept, as discussed above, and the optimization procedure reflects this. This adjustment process is illustrated in Fig. 10.13.

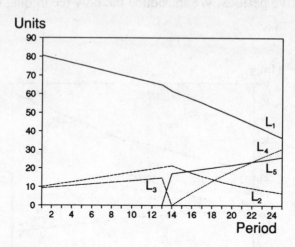

Fig. 10.12. The effect on employment, by process, of innovating a new technique with a rolling myopic plan.

We note that the optimum actually achieved in period 14 is substantially different from that which would have been achieved had the new technique not become available. In this case, with the techniques and welfare function we use, the effect is to reduce present consumption from the value that would have been optimal without the innovation. However, a different set of parameter values and/or a different welfare function, could have led instead to an increase. That is, the adjustment effect we observe is not a necessary outcome of the model. However, it is interesting that such a 'growth pause' can be thrown up by the model, and this further strengthens our view that myopic rolling plans offer a fruitful way of modelling long-run phenotypic economic evolution in a neo-Austrian framework.

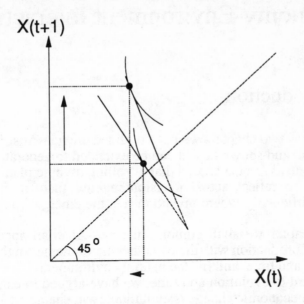

Fig. 10.13. The adjustment process caused by innovation of a new technique.

10.7 Summary

This chapter, and Chapter 9, have established the basic concepts and models of neo-Austrian capital theory. We have attempted to show that it offers a powerful technique for the modelling of phenotypic evolution of production in economies. In particular, the combination of the time structure of capital accumulation, and the use of rolling myopic plans, captures important long-run aspects of economic activity in the face of the emergence of novelty.

In the next chapter we shall extend this neo-Austrian approach to encompass the interactions of economic activity with the natural environment.

11 A Neo-Austrian Simulation Model of Economy-Environment Interactions

11.1 Introduction

In the previous two chapters we have outlined the neo-Austrian approach to production, and shown how it can be extended to generate the shadow prices of inputs. We also argued that a 'rolling myopic plan' approach is more likely to reflect actual decision making than an intertemporal approach, particularly where invention (i.e. the emergence of novelty) is anticipated.

In this chapter we shall combine the neo-Austrian approach to the modelling of production with the two other major themes of this book; viz. (i) evolution and time, and (ii) the natural environment.

With regard to evolution and time, we have argued in earlier chapters that long-run economic change is evolutionary in character. In particular, we have noted the difficulty of analysing long-run economic change because of the emergence of novelty (i.e. genotypic evolution). In what follows we shall, therefore, not attempt to model such genotypic evolution ex ante, as our contention is that such ex ante modelling is, in principle, impossible. Instead, we shall take the emergence of novelty, through invention, as exogenously given. This will allow us to concentrate on predictable, phenotypic change. That is, we shall concentrate on the process of innovation, to the modelling and simulation of which the neo-Austrian approach is so well-suited. In particular, we shall introduce an element of phenotypic evolution that we have not yet attempted to model. This is technical progress; we define this to be the incremental, and predictable, improvement in the efficiency of production processes with use.

Regarding the natural environment, we shall attempt to model two aspects of the interaction of this with the production process. First, the use of a non-renewable resource is included in the model; this resource is steadily depleted over time. The effect of this depletion is to increase the 'extraction cost' of the resource. Second, we suppose that the production process is polluting, and that pollution abatement is required. Both of these modelling extensions reflect the operation of the Second Law of Thermodynamics (i.e. the First Arrow of Time).

The structure of the rest of this chapter is as follows. In Section 11.2 we discuss the rationale for the simulation model in the light of the earlier chapters.

The modelling of technical change is then explored in Section 11.3. There we distinguish between 'invention', 'innovation' and 'technical progress'.

Section 11.4 constitutes the bulk of this chapter, and is a formal description of the simulation model we propose.

In Section 11.5 we discuss the possible interpretations of the model.

We present some simulation results in Section 11.6 and give a summary in Section 11.7. (The mathematical details of the simulation model are given in Appendix A11.1, and the model parameters used are shown in Appendix A11.2. Chapter 11 draws upon material originally developed in FABER, PROOPS, RUTH and MICHAELIS [1990]).

11.2 First Summary and Rationale for the Simulation Model

Before moving on to the details of the formal model, and its simulation results, it is worth outlining the model, and describing how it fits into the overall conceptual framework we have attempted to establish in the earlier chapters.

Our contentions in the earlier chapters can, briefly, be summarized as follows:

1. Evolution is a fundamental concept, applicable to all dynamic systems.

2. Important traits of evolutionary developments can be conceptualized as involving two distinct aspects. The first aspect we term 'phenotypic evolution' (the evolution of realizations). This relates to processes which do *not* involve the emergence of novelty; these processes are therefore predictable in broad terms. The second aspect we term 'genotypic evolution' (the evolution of potentialities). This relates to processes, which *do* involve the emergence of novelty; such processes are therefore unpredictable.

3. The economic system can be viewed as one with evolutionary characteristics. In the short-run, predictable, phenotypic processes are the appropriate object of study. However, in the long-run, genotypic processes dominate, making the long-run future inherently unpredictable.

4. Evolution is, by definition, a temporal process. Therefore, it is helpful to supplement the concept of evolution with the concept of time. The different statuses of the past and the future spring naturally from our different kinds of knowledge. The concept of 'time' can only be understood with respect to human knowledge, and therefore only with respect to human beings. Humans, however are intrinsically characterized by ignorance. Besides novelty, in terms of genotypic evolution and chaotic developments, this ignorance hinders human understanding of, and ability to predict, the course of evolution for any system.

5. The distinction between the two arrows of time can be regarded as partially reflecting the distinction between the different types of time irreversibility. We have distinguished between three different types of time irreversibility, which allow the differentiation of approaches in economics in terms of their use of these three different types of irreversibility.

6. A principal factor in economic evolution is the interaction of economic activity with the natural environment. In the short-run the natural environment is a 'given', acting as a boundary condition on economic activity.

7. However, the long-run effect of economic activity is, through the Second Law (the First Arrow of Time), to alter the natural environment. This in turn alters the boundary conditions of economic activity. This may lead to the search for invention, which constitutes the emergence of novelty.

8. Genotypic processes are inherently unpredictable, so the ex ante modelling of genotypic evolution is, in principle, impossible. However, the emergence of novelty may be understood in retrospect. That is, ex post modelling is possible. Therefore it is futile to attempt to predict the nature of inventions that may result from the impact of natural environmental constraints on economic activity. However, one may attempt to model and understand their nature once they have occurred. That is, historical analysis is feasible for systems exhibiting genotypic evolution.

9. Phenotypic processes are predictable in principle, albeit subject to the problem of ignorance, so the evolution of such systems can be modelled both ex ante and ex post. In particular, the evolution of production processes, particularly the innovation of new inventions,

can be well modelled ex ante with neo-Austrian capital theory. This concentrates upon the process of accumulation of capital goods, and hence offers richer insights than conventional models.

10. The use of a rolling myopic plan approach to decision making reflects the response of decision makers who are aware that the world they live in involves the emergence of novelty. This myopic approach also, fortuitously, makes the simulation of such models much more tractable than a full intertemporal optimization approach.

11.3 Modelling Technical Change

Throughout this book we have distinguished between predictable phenotypic evolution and unpredictable genotypic evolution. With regard to production processes, clearly both types of evolution occur, as technical change. In the light of this, we wish to emphasize the distinction between three aspects of the process of technical change in economic evolution.

1. *Invention* is the emergence of a new production process. This may or may not become embodied in a new technique of production, as defined in Chapter 8. This constitutes the upredictable emergence of new potentialities for the system, through genotypic evolution. Invention may be modelled only ex post.

2. *Innovation* is the process by which a new invention is brought into use through the restructuring of the entire economy; i.e. how the new potentialities of the economic system are realized. The process of innovation will be characterized by the bringing into use of new techniques, and the accumulation of the corresponding new types of capital. It will also involve the falling into disuse of old techniques, and the non-replacement of old types of capital. Innovation may be modelled both ex post and ex ante.

3. *Technical Progress* is the process by which new production techniques are brought to their full potential level of efficiency. This does not involve the emergence of novelty, as the potential level of efficiency is known from consideration of the thermodynamics of the technique, etc. Further, the development of efficiency over time follows a characteristic sigismoid (S-shaped) path, which is predictable in principle. Thus this would also constitute phenotypic evolution, and be capable of being modelled both ex post and ex ante.

It is clear that a simulation model could involve all three types of technical change. However, invention could only be included as an exogenous item, as the simulation model could not be formulated to generate the invention endogenously. Clearly, such endogenous modelling is equivalent to the prediction of the invention, which we disallow. On the other hand, the model would be allowed to model endogenously the innovation and technical progress elements of technical change.

11.4 A Long-Run Neo-Austrian Model: Resources and Pollution

The model discussed in this section is an extension and generalization of the neo-Austrian models explored in Chapters 9 and 10. Like those models, it takes the activity analysis approach, using only linear production processes. That is, within a process there can be no substitution of factors. However, there can be substitution between techniques, over time, through the accumulation of technique-specific capital goods. Also, for the reasons discussed in Chapter 10, we employ a rolling myopic plan approach, rather than assuming full intertemporal optimization.

We recognize that in simulation modelling, sensitivity analysis is often employed [FABER 1970:22-64]. Here, however, we do not consider sensitivity analysis to be useful, for two reasons. First, our model is meant to be illustrative rather than predictive. Second, as modifying the parameters is equivalent to altering the genotype, we would anticipate that the model would be sensitive to such parameter adjustments (as indeed we find it to be).

The simulation model we now offer differs from the earlier simple models in seven ways.

1. In technique T_2, capital is used not only for the production of the consumption good, but also for the production of the capital good itself.

2. The production of the capital good requires the input of a natural resource. This natural resource is exhaustible, which is reflected by its 'ore concentration' falling as its extraction continues.

3. The natural resource ore must be extracted by a separate process.

4. The 'cost' of extraction of the natural resource ore increases as its concentration declines.

5. The production of the consumption good with technique T_2 also generates 'pollution'.

6. The natural environment is assumed to be capable of degrading a certain proportion of this pollution, rendering it non-noxious. The pollution that remains in the natural environment accumulates, and the higher is the stock of accumulated pollution, the lower is the ability of the natural environment to degrade the pollution.

7. There is a process designed specifically to abate pollution emission. The intensity with which this process operates is assumed to be determined by 'pollution standards', which are socially determined. The higher is the accumulated stock of pollution in the natural environment, the more stringent are the restrictions governing the emission of further pollution, so the more intensively is the pollution abatement process operated.

11.4.1 The Production Side

We now proceed to an outline description of the simulation model.

The production side of this model involves five linear production processes, R_1 to R_5.

The single consumption good, which may not be stored, can be produced in process R_1 and process R_2. Process R_1 uses only labour, while process R_2 employs labour and a capital good.

The capital good can be manufactured in process R_3, where labour, the capital good itself, and a natural resource are the inputs.

The natural resource is exhaustible and can be extracted by use of process R_4, which utilizes only labour. The amount of labour necessary to extract one unit of the resource depends on the concentration of the resource ore in the ground in that period. The lower is the ore concentration, the higher is the necessary amount of labour.[1] The concentration in turn depends on the amount of the natural resource previously extracted: the higher this amount, the lower the concentration of the natural resource ore.

Pollution is also emitted by process R_2, and this is at least partially abated by process R_5, using both labour and the capital good.

---

[1] In FABER, NIEMES and STEPHAN [1987:Chapter 4] it is shown that under certain assumptions there is a relationship between the concentration of the resource, the energy used to extract it, and the entropy of the environment. See also FABER and WAGENHALS [1988], where examples from the copper industry are given.

As before, we note that we may say there exist two techniques to produce the consumption good. The first technique, T_1, consists only of one production process, namely R_1. The second technique, T_2, however, consists of R_2, R_3, R_4 and R_5. While it takes only one period to manufacture with T_1 it takes two periods with T_2, because first the resource has to be extracted with R_4 and the capital good must be produced in R_3 and only thereafter, in the second period, the consumption good is manufactured in R_2. It is easy to introduce more complicated structures, for instance by considering also a time lag between the extraction of the natural resource and the production of the capital good.

Let us assume that only technique T_1 is known and used in the first period, and that technique T_2 is newly invented. That is, genotypic evolution occurs in the first period, altering the potentialities of the production system by making new production processes available.

Then technique T_2 will, with adequate time preference present, be innovated from the second period on. That is, phenotypic evolution (evolution of the realizations of the system) occurs subsequent to the genotypic change. This is reflected by a substitution process taking place between the two techniques, which prevails as long as the superiority and roundaboutness implied by the new technique T_2 have not been fully exhausted [FABER, NIEMES and STEPHAN 1987:Chapter 6]. This initiates a structural change of the economy since the capital good, as well as the resource sector, have to be built up.

The production restrictions on the economy are upon labour, capital and the natural resource. In addition, we shall assume that certain changing environmental standards need to be fulfilled.

11.4.2 Technical Progress and Resource Use

We consider technical progress to take place only in the use of the resource in the production of the capital good. In this model technical 'search' for increases in the level of technical efficiency is made endogenous by combining two factors. First, the increase in the level of technical efficiency of using the resource is induced by the scarcity of the resource, as measured by the resource concentration. The lower is the concentration of the resource, the greater is the increase in the level of technical efficiency in using the resource. Second, the feasible increase in technical efficiency at that time varies directly with the 'efficiency gap' between the current level of technical efficiency and the maximum potential level of efficiency, which in general will be determined by technical/physical factors (e.g. thermodynamic efficiency limits in the use of fossil fuels).

The changes in technical efficiency described above are assumed to be continuous for the purposes of this chapter. It is recognized that, in reality, improvements in technical efficiency are usually associated with discrete improvements, consequent upon new discoveries, patents, etc. However, as this model is explicitly focussing on long-run changes, the representation of technical progress as a smooth and continuous process seems to be reasonable at this level of abstraction.

11.4.3 Pollution Production, Degradation and Abatement

In this model we assume that pollution is generated only by process R_2, the innovating process. The emission of pollution into the environment is assumed to be proportional to the level of output of R_2.

The natural environment can degrade pollution when it is in low concentrations, but the proportion of pollution that can be degraded in any period of time falls as the accumulated stock of pollutants increases.

Pollution abatement takes place in process R_5, using both labour and the capital good. The proportion of potential pollution emissions that is abated is also determined by the accumulated stock of pollutants. The higher is the accumulated stock of pollutants in the environment, the more stringent are the exogenously given emission abatement regulations, until at high levels of pollution, emission abatement is almost complete.

11.4.4 The Demand Side

As in Chapters 9 and 10, concerning the preferences of the individual we shall make as few assumptions as possible. These are:

A1.   At any time, more consumption is preferred to less.

A2.   Consumption in the present is preferred to an equal amount of consumption in the future, i.e. the rate of time preference is positive and therefore there exists impatience to consume (for a definition see e.g. BURMEISTER [1980:27-28] and for a general discussion of this concept KOOPMANS [1960]).

We also assume, as discussed in Chapter 10:

A3.   Individuals behave myopically, i.e. their maximization behaviour extends only over two periods.

However, for analytical tractability we need a method to aggregate the behaviour of individuals. For the sake of simplicity we use the following assumption, as used (implicitly) in Chapters 9 and 10:

A4.   The preferences of individuals can either be aggregated to give a strictly quasi-concave welfare function, or these preferences can be subsumed under the preference of a planning agency.

We shall therefore model the demand side of the economy by a non-linear welfare function, the arguments of which are the amounts of the consumption good in each period. The time preference of the consumers is aggregated in this welfare function. It is expressed by the employed rate of social discount [see e.g. LIND 1982]. This is, in formal terms, the procedure used throughout Chapter 10.

For the benefit of the reader not trained in economics, we note in passing that there is an extensive literature on the relationships between models of planned economies, as used in Chapters 9 to 11, and models of decentralized market economies. A decentralized interpretation of our type of model is given in FABER [1979:85-86]. For a general representation of the relationship of models of centralized and decentralized economies, see KOOPMANS [1957].

As before, we assume that there is a two-period rolling myopic maximization of this welfare function, i.e. the maximization behaviour extends only over two periods and the maximization procedure is repeated in each period. The decisions made at any time regarding the first period consumption/capital accumulation is binding, and is implemented, etc.

We determine for an interval of N periods the development of the following variables: the amount of extracted resources; the investment; the stock of the capital good; the consumption; the gross quantity of pollution emission; the amount of emission treated by the waste management process; the level of pollution; and the amount of natural pollution degradation. We also determine the shadow prices of labour; capital; output; the natural resource; and pollution abatement.

11.4.5 The Simulation Procedure

The detailed implementation of the model is described in Appendix A11.1, and is embodied in a Lotus 1-2-3 spreadsheet. This has the advantage that parameters can be adjusted and the resultant time profiles of the various activities immediately displayed and graphed. In particular, to ensure reasonably realistic outcomes, the model parameters can be specified in terms of required initial growth rates of output, capital, etc. (The parameter values used for the simulation discussed in this paper are shown in Appendix A11.2).[2]

11.4.6 The Welfare Function

Our use of the welfare function is based upon the assumptions A1, A2, and A4, stated in Section 11.4.4 above.

As in Chapter 10, we use an instantaneous utility function, $U(X)$, and a two-period welfare function:

$$W(X_1, X_2^*) = U(X_1) + U(X_2^*)/(1+D).$$

Here X_1 represents consumption in the first period, and X_2^* represents maximum possible consumption in the second period (i.e. assuming no capital accumulation in the second period). D is the discount rate.

It should also be noted that a time period must not necessarily be interpreted as a single year. For the innovation of some technologies a time period of 5, 10 or even 20 years may be appropriate. Suitable period discount and deterioration rates are calculated from the specified annual figures.

11.5 Interpreting the Model

The model is open to at least two different interpretations. Either we may regard process R_1 as 'subsistence agriculture', and processes R_2 and R_3 as 'industry', using an aggregate measure of capital. In this case 'resource' and 'pollution' would also be regarded as aggregate measures. In this case our model would offer an aggregated simulation of the industrial development process, with corresponding aggregate resource use and aggregate pollution.

---

[2] A Lotus 1-2-3 worksheet of the full model is available from the second author. Those desiring a copy should indicate whether they would like the worksheet on a 3.5in (720k) or 5.25in (360k) DOS format disc. To cover expenses and postage, they should also send a money order or Eurocheque for £10 (sterling) payable to Keele University.

Alternatively, the model can be regarded as representing a subsection of a wider industrial system, with several capital goods in use. In that case process R_1 can be regarded as the 'rest' of the industrial activities, using separate capital goods not described in the model, but still in competition for labour with processes R_2, R_3, R_4 and R_5. Process R_2 can then be interpreted as an industry producing a good which is being innovated, and process R_3 as the industry supplying the capital good for the production of the consumption good. Under this interpretation the resource and pollution may be regarded as industry specific, rather than aggregated.

11.6 Some Simulation Results

To illustrate the use of the model, it has been run with the parameter values shown in Appendix A11.2. It must be stressed that the parameter values chosen are not intended to represent any particular market, or any particular economy. Rather, the parameters used were chosen both because they are economically 'reasonable' and also generate a time structure of production, resource depletion and pollution which is intuitively reasonable, at least to the authors. In line with this being a long-run model, each time period is five years, and the simulation lasts for fifty periods, i.e. 250 years. It is not suggested that the innovation of a technique using a single resource will, in practice, be able to be represented by the relatively simple relationships in this model over such a time span. However, a fundamental attribute of this model is that production, resource use and pollution evolve together in the long-run, and the graphs to be discussed below are indicative of long-run trends that may be expected in the real world.

Before interpreting the behaviour of the model variables over time, it must be stressed that the model as it stands attempts to capture only certain facets of reality. In particular it explores the impact of invention (the introduction of technique T_2, embodying processes R_2, R_3, and R_4) on the structure of an economy as this new technique is innovated, in interaction with a limited resource base, endogenously determined improvements in the efficiency of resource use, the production of pollution, and the endogenously determined levels of pollution abatement. Obviously, the model so far is unrealistic; in particular this is true for its assumptions of a fixed labour force, which suffers no unemployment, and the absence of technical change outside of process R_3. We note further that the form of the simulation outcome depends critically on the parameter values and the stock of the capital good, of labour, and of resources in the first period.

The innovation of technique T_2 is clearly seen in Fig. 11.1.

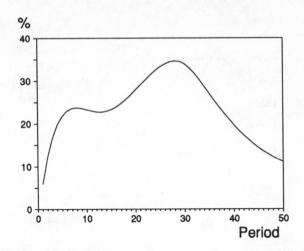

Fig. 11.1. The share of technique T_2 in output.

In the early stages the share of output of technique T_2 rises sharply, reflecting the superiority of roundaboutness. However, the production of the capital good requires the use of an exhaustible natural resource, and the growing scarcity of this resource leads to a reduction in the share of output. The increasing scarcity of the resource generates resource saving technical progress, which allows the resumption of growth by technique T_2. However, there is an upper limit to the efficiency of the use of the resource, and as that limit is approached the possibilities for further resource saving technical progress diminish rapidly. This leads to a new downturn in the share of output of technique T_2. This is exacerbated by pollution reaching such high levels that pollution abatement becomes very strict, leading to a rapid reduction in the degree of superiority of technique T_2, and its consequent long-term decline.

Fig. 11.2 indicates that the simulation illustrated is for the second of the interpretations discussed in Section 11.5. Here technique T_2 generates only a small proportion of overall output, so it may be regarded as representing a particular industry within a wider economy. It is apparent that the growth of technique T_2, through competition for the fixed factor labour, causes a reduction in the output by technique T_1.

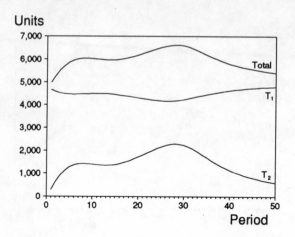

Fig. 11.2. Output of the consumption good by the two techniques, and overall.

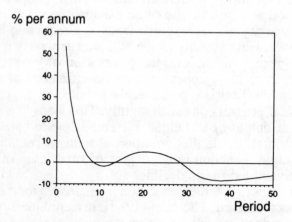

Fig. 11.3. The rate of growth of output of the consumption good by the innovating technique.

Fig. 11.3 illustrates that the rapid initial growth rate of the use of technique T_2 is rapidly reduced, for the reasons discussed above, and that apart from an interim period of increasing growth rate through improved technical capabilities, from periods 9 to 20 (i.e. years 45 to 100), the rate of growth of output of technique T_2 is steadily falling.

In this model the rate of return is given by the slope of the transformation curve, and its evolution over time is illustrated in Fig. 11.4. During the two periods of rapid capital accumulation, at the beginning and for an intermediate period, the interest rate is relatively high. On the other hand, at times of declining activity by technique T_2, and therefore low rates of capital accumulation, the interest rate is relatively low. It is noteworthy that the intermediate peak (period 24) in the interest rate occurs after the intermediate peak in the growth rate of the output by technique T_2 (period 20), but before the output by technique T_2 reaches a peak (period 28).

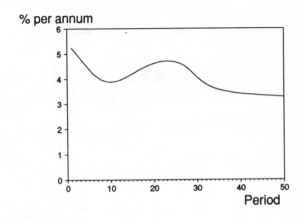

Fig. 11.4. The rate of return.

The labour use in production processes R_2 and R_3 is shown in Fig. 11.5. The shapes of these curves reflect the time structure of output and capital accumulation already discussed. Their convergence during the later periods reflects the increasing labour cost per unit of resource extracted, as the resource concentration and opportunities for further technical progress are both progressively reduced.

Pollution emission and abatement are shown in Fig. 11.6. Pollution emission follows the time path of output by process R_2. Pollution abatement does not begin until period 20, when accumulated pollution reaches a level sufficient to make abatement regulations effective. Pollution abatement

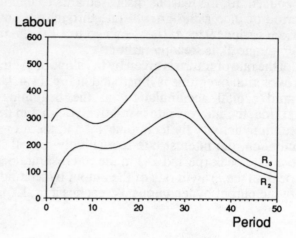

Fig. 11.5. The labour use in processes R_2 and R_3.

reaches a peak in period 34 as, despite steadily increasing abatement regulation, the fall in output by process R_2 rapidly reduces the pollution emission.

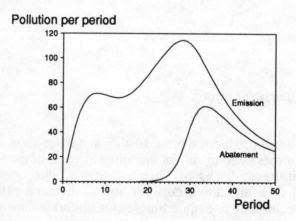

Fig. 11.6. Pollution emission and abatement.

Fig. 11.7 shows the use of labour in resource extraction and pollution abatement. It illustrates how, in the early years of the innovation of the second technique, up to period 20, a considerable quantity of labour is devoted to resource extraction but none to pollution abatement, while in the later years, when the industry is in terminal decline, the quantities of labour devoted to resource extraction and pollution abatement are nearly equal.

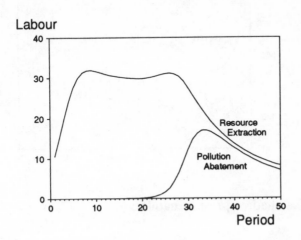

Fig. 11.7. The use of labour in resource extraction and pollution abatement.

We can now move to a discussion of the shadow prices implied by the model. It should be borne in mind that two sets of shadow prices can be calculated for a two-period horizon myopic model. The first set refer to the planned and implemented first period (t) decisions. The second set refer to the planned, but not implemented, second period (t+1) decisions. As only the first set of shadow prices are observable as market prices, only these current shadow prices will be presented and discussed. However, the second period shadow prices can also be calculated, as discussed in Appendix A11.1.

The shadow price trajectory of the capital good is shown in Fig. 11.8. This time profile is the inverse of the shape of the share of the innovating sector, as shown in Fig. 11.1. This reflects the altering value of capital in the light of its altering scarcity. Initially, capital becomes more abundant, so the shadow price of capital falls. Later there is a 'growth pause' because of resource scarcity, as discussed above. This causes a slowdown in capital accumulation, and through capital deterioration a fall in the capital stock.

This in turn causes the shadow price of capital to increase. As technical progress in resource use increases, capital accumulation resumes, and the shadow price again falls.

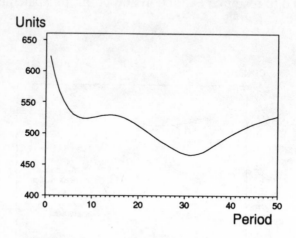

Fig. 11.8. The shadow price of capital.

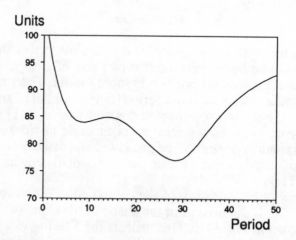

Fig. 11.9. The shadow prices of output and labour.

Finally, resource depletion and required pollution abatement lead to a fall in capital accumulation, a reduction in the capital stock through deterioration, and hence growing capital scarcity causes the shadow price to rise again.

The shadow prices of output and labour are shown in Fig. 11.9. These are identical, as the labour use coefficient for the first technique (l_1) is set at unity for this simulation run (see Appendix A11.1). Their time profiles closely match that of the shadow price of capital, except in the later periods. This is because in the later periods the high cost of resources means that, for the same 'degree of scarcity', capital is relatively less valued than in earlier periods. This is not the case for labour and output, as labour can be used to produce output without capital, with technique T_1.

The shadow price of pollution abatement is shown in Fig. 11.10.

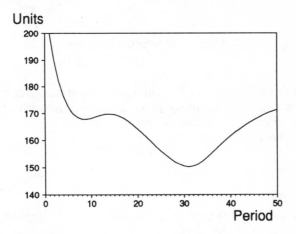

Fig. 11.10. The shadow price of pollution abatement.

It has the familiar shape, though in detail its shape lies somewhere between that of the shadow prices of labour and capital, as is demonstrated in detail in Appendix A11.1.

The shadow price of the natural resource is shown in Fig. 11.11. This reflects the steady depletion of the resource, and its consequent increasing scarcity.

We consider the results illustrated by these graphs to be encouraging. The rapid growth of innovating industries, followed by decline, but with the potential for later technology led rallies, has long been recognized [see

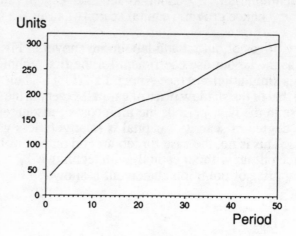

Fig. 11.11. The shadow price of the natural resource.

e.g. ROSENBERG 1976, 1982]. The time profiles of resource extraction and pollution abatement also seem to us to be consistent with observation, as do the time profiles of the shadow prices.

11.7 Summary

In this chapter we have attempted to implement the concerns and concepts discussed in the earlier chapters:

Following on from the discussions on evolution, time and ignorance, in Chapters 2 to 7, we have distinguished between phenotypic, predictable, processes, and genotypic, unpredictable, processes.

Further, our discussions on time irreversibility have led us to a model which includes the First Arrow of Time, through the depletion of a non-renewable resource and the emission of pollution, and also explicitly includes Teleological Sequence, through the neo-Austrian approach to capital accumulation. We introduce genotypic change, and allow for the ex post modelling of the emergence of novelty, via the assumption that invention has occurred, and a new technique has become available.

Also, the possible emergence of novelty naturally leads one away from the conventional full intertemporal optimization approach normally found in the environmental literature, towards a rolling myopic plan approach.

This explicitly recognizes the 'openness' of the future to novelty, and does not lock the economy into any particular long-term plan. Instead the plan allows for flexibility in the light of changing circumstances.

The approach embodied in this model seems to be promising. The simulation generates long-run time profiles of innovation, resource use, pollution and shadow prices that are consistent both with intuition and the historical record of industrialization.

However, the earlier conceptual discussions, and the simulation model presented in this chapter, are only early and tentative steps towards an understanding of the way economies and the natural environment mutually interact.

In Chapter 12 we seek to draw some conclusions from the analysis in Chapters 1 to 11. In particular we draw some lessons for policy making relevant to long-run economy-environment interactions. We also examine the role of, and necessity for, an interdisciplinary approach in economics in general, and in the understanding of long-run environment-economy interactions in particular.

Appendix 11.1

A Mathematical Description of the Model

A11.1.1 The Demand Side

The following model describes an economy composed of a large number of consumers and a central planning agency which has total knowledge about the social welfare function. The choice procedure within this model is a rolling myopic plan; i.e. there is a series of 2-period choices.

The intertemporal social welfare function, $W(X(t),X^*(t+1))$, represents the preferences between present consumption, $X(t)$, and maximum possible next-period consumption, $X^*(t+1)$. This welfare function remains unchanged over time.

With a one period social welfare function:

$$U(X(t)) = MX(t)^\beta, 0 < \beta < 1, M > 0.$$

The intertemporal social welfare function is:

$$W(X(t),X^*(t+1)) = U(X(t)) + U(X^*(t+1))/(1+D). \tag{A11.1}$$

For a single indifference curve of the intertemporal social welfare function, total differentiation gives:

$$dW = U'(X(t))dX(t) + [U'(X^*(t+1))/(1+D)]dX^*(t+1)$$

$$= 0. \tag{A11.2}$$

Here D denotes the (n-year) period discount rate. This can be calculated from the annual discount rate, d, using:[1]

---

[1] The period discount rate, D, can be calculated from the annual discount rate, d, as follows. We define:

$$1/(1+D) = (1/n) \sum_{i=1}^{n} 1/(1+d)^i$$

i.e. $D = n[(1/(1+d)-1]/[(1/(1+d)^{n-1})-(1/(1+d))] - 1 = nd/[1-(1/(1+d)^n)] - 1$

$D = nd/[1-(1/(1+d)^n)] - 1.$

From this we can infer the following general relation between the coordinates $(X(t),X^*(t+1))$ of a point and the absolute value of the slope w of the indifference curve at that point:

$$w \equiv dX^*(t+1)/dX(t) = (1+D)(X(t)/X^*(t+1))^{\beta-1}. \qquad (A11.3)$$

Rearrangement gives:

$$X^*(t+1) = [w/(1+D)]^{1/(1-\beta)}X(t). \qquad (A11.4)$$

A11.1.2 The Production Side

We shall describe the production side of the economy in full detail in Section A11.1.4. For the time being, we shall only give a brief summary so that we shall be in a position to outline the optimization procedure in Section A11.1.3.

Our assumptions on the production processes (cf. Section A11.1.4) will imply that the transformation curve in period t is of the form (see (A11.47) below):

$$X^*(t+1) = \phi(t) - \tau(t)X(t). \qquad (A11.5)$$

Here $X(t) \in [a(t),b(t)]$, $a(t) \geq 0$, $\phi(t) - \tau(t)b(t) \geq 0$.

Thus, in each period the transformation curve is a section of the straight line with slope $-\tau(t)$ and an intersection $\phi(t)$ on the ordinate $X^*(t+1)$.

It will also be shown in Section A11.1.5. that the coefficients $\tau(t)$ and $\phi(t)$, and the end points $[a(t),b(t)]$, can be calculated from the optimal values of $(X(t-1),X^*(t))$. This is possible because the choice of these values determines the sizes of all variables that are pertinent to the production possibilities in period t, such as: capital stock, natural resource concentration, the technical efficiency coefficient, and pollution stocks and flows.

A11.1.3 An Outline of the Optimization Procedure

Assume that the values of all the variables mentioned at the end of Section A11.1.2 are known for the beginning of period t. We shall now show how to obtain the optimal value of $(X(t), X^*(t+1))$.

Step 1:   Calculate the transformation curve, in particular the minimal and maximal values $[a(t), b(t)]$ of $X(t)$ (cf. Section A11.1.5 for details).

Step 2:   If the optimum is located in the range:

$a(t) < X(t) < b(t)$ (i.e. it is not a corner solution)

it must satisfy:

Slope of transformation curve = Slope of indifference curve

i.e. $\tau(t) = w$.   (A11.6)

Insert (A11.6) into (A11.4) to derive the relation:

$$X^*(t+1) = [\tau(t)/(1+D)]^{1/(1-B)}X(t) \tag{A11.7}$$

for an optimum in $[a(t), b(t)]$.

Step 3:   Use equation (A11.7) and equation (A11.5) of A11.1.2 to calculate $X(t)$:

$$\phi(t) - \tau(t)X(t) = [\tau(t)/(1+D)]^{1/(1-B)}X(t). \tag{A11.8}$$

Rearrangement gives:

$$(\tau(t) + [\tau(t)/(1+D)]^{1/(1-B)})X(t) = \phi(t). \tag{A11.9}$$

Therefore we have:

$$X(t) = \phi(t)/(\tau(t) + [\tau(t)/(1+D)]^{1/(1-B)}). \tag{A11.10}$$

Step 4:   Check whether $X(t)$ lies in $[a(t), b(t)]$. If so, $X(t)$ is optimal. If $X(t)$ does not lie in that range, then a corner solution is obtained. To find at which corner the solution occurs, the notional optimum, X(t), must be checked against the upper and lower boundaries for a true optimum. If $X(t) \geq b(t)$, then $b(t)$ is optimal; if $X(t) \leq a(t)$, then $a(t)$ is optimal.

Step 5: Calculate the optimal $X^*(t+1)$ from equation (A11.7) and (A11.10).

Step 6: Derive the values of the state variables for period $t+1$ from $(X(t),X^*(t+1))$. Return to Step 1 with t replaced by $t+1$.

A11.1.4 The Production Processes

There are five linear production processes, R_1 to R_5.

A11.1.4.1 Inputs

There are three potential inputs to the production processes; these are:

Labour (L) - used by R_1, R_2, R_3, R_4, R_5

Capital good (K) - used by R_2, R_3, R_5

Natural Resource (R) - used by R_3.

A11.1.4.2 Outputs

There are five potential outputs from the production processes; these are:

Consumption good (X) - produced by R_1, R_2

Capital good (δK) - produced by R_3

Natural Resource (R) - extracted by R_4

Pollution (dP^+) - produced by R_3

Pollution abatement (dP^-) - produced by R_5.

Labour is available throughout in fixed quantity; the quantities available of the capital good and the natural resource vary over time.

A11.1.4.3 Process R_1

Process R_1 uses labour, $L_1(t)$, as the only input for the production of the consumption good, $X_1(t)$. Since l_1 units of labour are necessary for the production of one unit of output in process R_1, we write:

R_1: l_1 units of labour $\rightarrow$ 1 unit of output.

So we can use:

$$X_1(t) = L_1(t)/l_1. \tag{A11.11}$$

A11.1.4.4 Process R_2

Process R_2 uses labour, $L_2(t)$, and capital, $K_2(t)$, for the production of the consumpton good, $X_2(t)$. This process also generates pollution, $dP^+(t)$, i.e.:

R_2: l_2 units of labour $\oplus$ k_2 units of labour $\rightarrow$ 1 unit of output
$$\oplus\ p_5 \text{ units of pollution.}$$

(The symbol '$\oplus$' indicates the combination of the two factors).

Here l_2 and k_2 are the production coefficients of capital and labour, respectively, and p_5 is the output coefficient of pollution. We can write:

$$X_2(t) = K_2(t)/k_2 = L_2(t)/l_2. \tag{A11.12}$$

A11.1.4.5 Pollution Production

The amount of pollution emitted to the environment, $dP^+(t)$, is proportional to the output of the consumption good produced in process R_2:

$$dP^+(t) = p_5 X_2(t). \tag{A11.13}$$

A11.1.4.6 Process R$_3$

In process R$_3$ labour, L$_3$(t), the capital good, K$_3$(t), and natural resources R(t) are used to produce the capital good, δK(t), i.e.:

R$_3$: l$_3$ units of labour $\oplus$ k$_3$ units of capital $\oplus$ q$_3$(t) units of natural resource
$\rightarrow$ 1 unit of new capital.

So we can write:

$$\delta K(t) = L_3(t)/l_3 = K_3(t)/k_3 = R(t)/q_3(t). \tag{A11.14}$$

A11.1.4.7 Technical Progress in Natural Resource Use

Here $q_3(t)$ represents the quantity of the natural resource necessary for the production of one unit of the capital good. Technical progress affects the efficiency of natural resource use in the production of new capital. The efficiency of natural resource use, Z(t), is used as an inverse weight in the determination of the natural resource coefficient $q_3(t)$:

$$q_3(t) = q_3(0)/Z(t) \qquad \text{for } t \geq 1.$$

The level of technical efficiency of natural resource use increases monotonically, and is bounded above by a specified maximum technical efficiency, Z^*. Technical progress allows an increase in technical efficiency, dZ(t), each time period, so that the next period level of technical efficiency is given by:

$$Z(t+1) = Z(t) + dZ(t). \tag{A11.15}$$

The increase in technical efficiency, dZ(t), increases with falling natural resource concentration, σ(t), and is proportional to the 'efficiency gap', Z^*-Z(t). The formula used for the increase in technical efficiency is:

$$dZ(t) = A\sigma(t)^{-1/a}B[Z^*-Z(t)]. \tag{A11.16}$$

Here A, a, B and Z^* are positive constants, and $0 < \sigma(t) < 1$.

A11.1.4.8 Process R_4

Process R_4 uses labour as the only input to extract the natural resource $R(t)$:

R_4: $l_4(t)$ units of labour $\rightarrow$ 1 unit of natural resource.

So we can write:

$$R(t) = L_4(t)/l_4(t). \tag{A11.17}$$

Here $l_4(t)$ is time dependent, i.e. the lower the concentration of natural resources, $\sigma(t)$, the more labour is necessary to extract them:

$$l_4(t) = -\phi\ln\sigma(t) \quad (\phi > 0), \tag{A11.18}$$

where $\sigma(t)$ is given by:

$$\sigma(t) = \sigma(0)\exp(-\mu CR(t)) \quad (\mu > 0). \tag{A11.19}$$

Here ϕ and μ are constants and $CR(t)$ denotes the cumulative extraction of natural resources up to period t. For a precise definition of the concentration of natural resources and a theoretical justification of equations (A11.18) and (A11.19), see FABER, NIEMES and STEPHAN [1987:136-9].

A11.1.4.9 Natural Pollution Degradation

It is assumed that there are natural pollution degradation processes at work in the environment. These are affected by the level of pollution, so that the proportion of pollution in the environment which is degraded in one time period decreases as the level of pollution increases. Pollution degradation in any period is given by:

$$DP(t) = [P(t)+dP^+(t)]\pi(t), \tag{A11.20}$$

where $\pi(t)$ is given by:

$$\pi(t) \equiv H_2/(1+\exp[\Theta_2(P(t)+dP^+(t)-y_2)]). \tag{A11.21}$$

Here $P(t)$ is the level of accumulated pollution at the beginning of period t, and $dP^+(t)$ the change of pollution during period t.

H_2, Θ_2 and y_2 are positive constants. So the ability of the environment to reduce both the stock of pollution and current pollution production decreases monotonically as environmental pollution increases.

A11.1.4.10 Process R_5

Process R_5 is used to at least partially abate the pollution due to process R_2. It uses labour and the capital good:

R_5: l_5 units of labour $\oplus$ k_5 units of capital $\rightarrow$ 1 unit of pollution abatement.

So we write:

$$dP^-(t) = L_5(t)/l_5 = K_5(t)/k_5. \tag{A11.22}$$

A11.1.4.11 Pollution Abatement Policy

The proportion of potential pollution emission which has to be abated (according to the plans of the central planning agency) also varies with the overall level of residual pollution, after natural degradation, two periods earlier. (This time lag is introduced because policy on pollution abatement generally lags behind observed pollution levels; it also makes the model more analytically tractable). Pollution abatement, $dP^-(t)$, is a proportion of pollution emission:

$$dP^-(t) = dP^+(t)f(t), \tag{A11.23}$$

where $f(t)$ is given by:

$$f(t) \equiv H_1/(1+\exp(\Theta_1(P(t-2)+dP^+(t-2)-DP(t-2)-y_1)) \quad \text{for } t \geq 2. \tag{A11.24}$$

Here H_1, Θ_1 and y_1 are positive constants. According to the plans of the central planning agency, pollution abatement in period t has to be more intense the higher was the environmental pollution in period $t-2$.

The level of pollution at the beginning of the next period is therefore given by:

$$P(t+1) = P(t) + dP^+(t) - DP(t) - dP^-(t). \tag{A11.25}$$

A11.1.4.12 Capital Deterioration

There is a unique rate of deterioration, C, of the capital stock. Hence, for the capital stock in time period t+1 we get:

$$K(t+1) = (1-C)K(t) + \delta K(t). \qquad (A11.26)$$

For an n-year period, the period deterioration rate, C, is derived from the annual deterioration rate, c, by:

$$C = nc/[1-(1/(1+c)^n]-1.$$

A11.1.5 Optimality Conditions

From (A11.7)-(A11.26) we are able to derive the optimality conditions, as shown below.

Total output is given by:

$$X(t) = X_1(t) + X_2(t) \qquad (A11.27)$$

$$= (L_1(t)/l_1) + X_2(t).$$

Total labour use is constant, and divided among the processes according to:

$$L = L_1(t) + L_2(t) + L_3(t) + L_4(t) + L_5(t). \qquad (A11.28)$$

Similarly, capital is divided among the processes according to:

$$K(t) = K_2(t) + K_3(t) + K_5(t). \qquad (A11.29)$$

Here we know:

$$L_2(t) = l_2 K_2(t)/k_2 \qquad (A11.30)$$

$$L_3(t) = l_3 \delta K(t) \qquad (A11.31)$$

$$L_4(t) = l_4(t)R(t) = l_4(t)q_3(t)\delta K(t). \qquad (A11.32)$$

Using (A11.22), (A11.23), (A11.13) and (A11.12) we get for $L_5(t)$:

$$L_5(t) = dP^-(t)l_5 = p_5f(t)l_5K_2(t)/k_2. \tag{A11.33}$$

From (A11.14) and (A11.22) we obtain:

$$K_2(t) = K(t) - K_3(t) - K_5(t) \tag{A11.34}$$

$$= K(t) - \delta K(t)k_3 - k_5dP^-(t)$$

$$= K(t) - \delta K(t)k_3 - k_5p_5f(t)K_2/k_2.$$

Rearrangement gives:

$$K_2(t) = [k_2/(k_2+k_5p_5f(t))][K(t)-\delta K(t)k_3]. \tag{A11.35}$$

Inserting (A11.30)-(A11.33) into (A11.28) and using (A11.35) we get:

$$L_1(t) = L - L_2(t) - L_3(t) - L_4(t) - L_5(t) \tag{A11.36}$$

$$= L - l_2K_2(t)/k_2 - l_3\delta K(t) - l_4(t)q_3(t)\delta K(t) - p_5f(t)l_5K_2(t)/k_2$$

$$= L - (K_2(t)/k_2)[l_2+p_5f(t)l_5] - \delta K(t)[l_3+l_4(t)q_3(t)]$$

$$= L - [(K(t)-\delta K(t)k_3)/(k_2+k_5p_5f(t))](l_2+p_5f(t)l_5)$$

$$\quad - \delta K(t)[l_3+l_4(t)q_3(t)].$$

From (A11.27) together with (A11.35) and (A11.36) we obtain:

$$X(t) = L_1(t)/l_1 + K_2(t)/k_2 \tag{A11.37}$$

$$= \{L-K(t)[(l_2+p_5f(t)l_5)/(k_2+p_5f(t)k_5)]$$

$$\quad - \delta K(t)[(l_3+l_4(t)q_3(t)) - k_3(l_2+p_5f(t)l_5)/(k_2+k_5p_5f(t))]/l_1]$$

$$\quad + K(t)/(k_2+k_5p_5f(t)) - k_3\delta K(t)/(k_2+k_5p_5f(t))$$

$$= L/l_1 - [K(t)/(k_2+p_5f(t)k_5)][(l_2+p_5f(t)l_5)/l_1-1]$$

$$\quad - \delta K(t)\{[(l_3+l_4(t)q_3(t))/l_1] - k_3(l_2+p_5f(t)l_5)/l_1(k_2+k_5p_5f(t))$$

$$\quad + k_3/(k_2+k_5p_5f(t))\}.$$

Let:

$$\alpha(t) \equiv L/l_1 + [K(t)/(k_2+p_5f(t)k_5)][1-(l_2+p_5f(t)l_5)/l_1] \tag{A11.38}$$

so X(t) can be written as:

$$X(t) = \alpha(t)-\delta K(t)\{[(l_3+l_4(t)q_3(t))/l_1] - k_3(l_2+p_5f(t)l_5)/[l_1(k_2+k_5p_5f(t))]$$

$$+ k_3/(k_2+k_5p_5f(t))\}. \tag{A11.39}$$

Since the optimization is a myopic one, the economy plans for:

$$\delta K(t+1) = 0.$$

Hence (A11.39) yields the maximum possible consumption in time period t+1. Therefore the maximum possible next period consumption is given by:

$$X^*(t+1) = L/l_1 + [K(t+1)/(k_2+p_5f(t+1)k_5)][1-(l_2+p_5f(t+1)l_5)/l_1].$$

$$\tag{A11.40}$$

Substituting $K(t+1) = (1-c)K(t) + \delta K(t)$ in (A11.40) gives:

$$X^*(t+1) = L/l_1 + [K(t)(1-c)/(k_2+p_5f(t+1)k_5)][1-(l_2+p_5f(t+1)l_5)/l_1]$$

$$+ [\delta K(t)/(k_2+p_5f(t+1)k_5)][1-(l_2+p_5f(t+1)l_5)/l_1]. \tag{A11.41}$$

From (A11.39) we have:

$$\delta K(t) = [\alpha(t)-X(t)]/\{[(l_3+l_4(t)q_3(t))/l_1]-[k_3(l_2+p_5f(t)l_5)/l_1(k_2+k_5p_5f(t))]$$

$$+k_3/(k_2+k_5p_5f(t))\} \tag{A11.42}$$

$$= [\alpha(t)-X(t)]l_1(k_2+k_5p_5f(t))/[(l_3+l_4(t)q_3(t))(k_2+k_5p_5f(t))$$

$$+l_1k_3-k_3(l_2+p_5f(t)l_5)].$$

Substituting for $\delta K(t)$ from (A11.42) in (A11.41) yields:

$$X^*(t+1) = L/l_1 + [K(t)(1-c)/(k_2+p_5f(t+1)k_5)][1-(l_2+p_5f(t+1)l_5)/l_1]$$

$$+ [(\alpha(t)-X(t))(l_1-l_2-p_5f(t+1)l_5)][k_2+k_5p_5f(t+1)]$$

$$/[\{(l_3+l_4(t)q_3(t))(k_2+k_5p_5f(t))+l_1k_3-k_3(l_2+p_5f(t)l_5)\}$$

$$(k_2+k_5p_5f(t+1))]. \qquad (A11.43)$$

In analogy with (A11.38) we define $\alpha'(t)$ as shown in (A11.44):

$$\alpha'(t) = L/l_1 + [K(t)(1-c)/(k_2+p_5f(t+1)k_5)] [1-(l_2+p_5f(t+1)l_5)/l_1].(A11.44)$$

Substitution from (A11.44) in (A11.43) gives:

$$X^*(t+1) = \alpha'(t) + [(\alpha(t)-X(t))[l_1-l_2-p_5f(t+1)l_5][k_2+k_5p_5f(t+1)]$$

$$/[\{(l_3+l_4(t)q_3(t))(k_2+k_5p_5f(t))+l_1k_3-k_3(l_2+p_5f(t)l_5)\}$$

$$(k_2+k_5p_5f(t+1))]. \qquad (A11.45)$$

It is now clear that the slope of the production possibility frontier is given by:

$$\tau(t) \equiv dX^*(t+1)/dX(t) \qquad (A11.46)$$

$$= [l_1-l_2+p_5f(t)l_5][k_2+k_5p_5f(t)]/[\{(l_3+l_4(t)q_3(t))(k_2+k_5p_5f(t))+l_1k_3$$

$$-k_3(l_2-p_5f(t+1)l_5)\}(k_2+k_5p_5f(t+1))].$$

Substituting for (A11.46) in (A11.45) gives:

$$X^*(t+1) = \alpha'(t) + \alpha(t)\tau(t) - \tau(t)X(t). \qquad (A11.47)$$

Now from the demand side we have:

$$X^*(t+1) = w(\tau(t))X(t). \qquad (A11.48)$$

Combining (A11.48) with (A11.47) gives:

$$w(\tau(t))X(t) = \alpha'(t) + \alpha(t)\tau(t) - \tau(t)X(t). \qquad (A11.49)$$

Rearrangement gives:

$$X(t) = [\alpha'(t)+\alpha(t)\tau(t)]/[w(\tau(t))+\tau(t)]. \qquad (A11.50)$$

A11.1.6 Calculation of Shadow Prices in the Model

The method used follows that described in Chapter 9. The only necessary extension is the introduction of constraints for natural resource use and for pollution abatement.
The problem may be written as follows:

$$\underset{X(t),X^*(t+1)}{\text{Max}}\ W(X(t),X^*(t+1))$$

Subject to:

$$X_1(t) + X_2(t) = X(t)$$

$$l_1X_1(t) + l_2X_2(t) + l_3\delta K(1) + l_4R(t) + l_5dP^-(t) = L(t)$$

$$k_2X_2(t) + k_3\delta K(t) + k_5dP^-(t) = K(t)$$

$$p_5X_2(t)f(t) = dP^-(t)$$

$$q_3\delta K(t) = R(t)$$

$$X_1^*(t+1) + X_2^*(t+1) = X^*(t+1)$$

$$l_1X_1^*(t+1) + l_2X_2^*(t+1) + l_5dP^{-*}(t+1) = L(t+1)$$

$$k_2X_2^*(t+1) + k_5dP^{-*}(t+1) = (1-C)K(t) + \delta K(t)$$

$$p_5X_2^*(t+1)f^*(t+1) = dP^{-*}(t+1).$$

As usual, we now form the Lagrangian, by introducing a shadow price associated with each constraint.

$$V = W(X(t),X^*(t+1))$$

$$+ P_{X(t)}[-X(t)+X_1(t)+X_2(t)]$$

$$+ P_{L(t)}[L(t)-l_1X_1(t)-l_2X_2(t)-l_3\delta K(t)-l_4(t)R(t)-l_5dP^-(t)]$$

$$+ P_{K(t)}[K(t)-k_2X_2(t)-k_3\delta K(t)-k_5dP^-(t)]$$

$$+ P_{dP^-}(t)[dP^-(t)-p_5X_2(t)f(t)]$$

$$+ P_{R(t)}[R(t)-q_3\delta K(t)]$$

$$+ P_{X^*(t+1)}[-X^*(t+1)+X_1^*(t+1)+X_2^*(t+1)]$$

$$+ P_{L(t+1)}[L(t+1)-l_1X_1^*(t+1)-l_2X_2^*(t+1)-l_5dP^{-*}(t+1)]$$

$$+ P_{K^*(t+1)}[(1-C)K(t)+\delta K(t)-k_2X_2^*(t+1)-k_5dP^{-*}(t+1)]$$

$$+ P_{dP^{-*}(t+1)}[dP^{-*}(t+1)-p_5X_2^*(t+1)f(t+1)].$$

Maximization, by differentiation with respect to the variables other than the shadow prices, gives the results required.

[We use: $W_t \equiv \partial W/\partial X(t)$, $W_{t+1} \equiv \partial W/\partial X^*(t+1)$].

$$\partial V/\partial X(t) = W_t - P_{X(t)} = 0 \tag{A11.51}$$

$$\partial V/\partial X_1(t) = P_{X(t)} - l_1P_{L(t)} = 0 \tag{A11.52}$$

$$\partial V/\partial X_2(t) = P_{X(t)} - l_2P_{L(t)} - k_2P_{K(t)} - p_5f(t)P_{dP-(t)} = 0 \tag{A11.53}$$

$$\partial V/\partial\delta K(t) = -l_3P_{L(t)} - k_3P_{K(t)} - q_3P_{R(t)} + P_{K^*(t+1)} = 0 \tag{A11.54}$$

$$\partial V/\partial R(t) = -l_4(t)P_{L(t)} + P_{R(t)} = 0 \tag{A11.55}$$

$$\partial V/\partial P^-(t) = l_5P_{L(t)} - k_5P_{K(t)} + P_{dP-(t)} = 0 \tag{A11.56}$$

$$\partial V/\partial X^*(t+1) = W_{t+1} - P_{X^*(t+1)} = 0 \tag{A11.57}$$

$$\partial V/\partial X_1^*(t+1) = P_{X^*(t+1)} - l_1P_{L(t+1)} = 0 \tag{A11.58}$$

$$\partial V/\partial X_2^*(t+1) = P_{X^*(t+1)} - l_2P_{L(t+1)} - k_2P_{K^*(t+1)} - p_5f(t+1)P_{dP-^*(t+1)}$$

$$= 0 \tag{A11.59}$$

$$\partial V/\partial dP^{-*}(t-1) = -l_5P_{L(t+1)} - k_5P_{K^*(t+1)} + P_{dP-^*(t+1)} = 0. \tag{A11.60}$$

From (A11.51): $P_{X(t)} = W_t$. $\tag{A11.61}$

From (A11.57): $P_{X^*(t+1)} = W_{t+1}$. $\tag{A11.62}$

From (A11.52): $P_{L(t)} = P_{X(t)}/l_1$. $\tag{A11.63}$

From (A11.55): $P_{R(t)} = l_4(t)P_{L(t)}.$ (A11.64)

From (A11.56): $P_{dP-(t)} = l_5P_{L(t)} + k_5P_{K(t)}.$ (A11.65)

Substituting for $P_{dP-(t)}$ from (A11.65) in (A11.53) gives:

$$P_{X(t)} - l_2P_{L(t)} - k_2P_{K(t)} - p_5f(t)[l_5P_{L(t)}+k_5P_{K(t)}] = 0.$$

Reorganisation gives:

$$P_{K(t)} = [P_{X(t)}-\{l_2+p_5f(t)l_5\}P_{L(t)}]/[k_2+p_5f(t)k_5].$$ (A11.66)

From (A11.54): $P_{K*(t+1)} = l_3P_{L(t)} + k_3P_{K(t)} + q_3P_{R(t)}.$ (A11.67)

From (A11.58): $P_{L(t+1)} = P_{X*(t+1)}/l_1.$ (A11.68)

From (A11.60): $P_{dP-*(t+1)} = l_5P_{L(t+1)} + k_5P_{K*(t+1)}.$ (A11.69)

A11.1.7 Implementation of the Simulation Model

The implementation of the simulation model has the following steps:

S1. $\alpha(t) = L/l_1 + [K(t)/(k_2+p_5f(t)k_5)][1-(l_2+p_5f(t)l_5)/l_1]$

S2. $\alpha'(t) = L/l_1 + [K(t)(1-c)/(k_2+p_5f(t)k_5)][1-(l_2+p_5f(t)l_5)/l_1]$

S3. $dZ(t) = A\sigma(t)^{-1/a}B[Z*-Z(t)]$

S4. $Z(t+1) = Z(t) + dZ(t)$

S5. $q_3(t) = q_3(0)/Z(t)$

S6. $\sigma(t) = \sigma(0)\exp(-\mu CR(t))$

S7. $l_4(t) = -\phi\ln\sigma(t)$

S8. $\tau(t) = [l_1-l_2+p_5f(t)l_5][k_2+k_5p_5f(t)]/[\{(l_3+l_4(t)q_3(t))(k_2+k_5p_5f(t))$

$\quad\quad +l_1k_3-k_3(l_2-p_5f(t+1)l_5)\}(k_2+k_5p_5f(t+1))]$

S9. $w(\tau(t)) = [\tau(t)/(1+D)]^{1/1-B}$

S10. $X(t) = [\alpha'(t)+\alpha(t)\tau(t)]/[w(\tau(t))+\tau(t)]$

S11. $X^*(t+1) = w(\tau(t))X(t)$

S12. $\delta K(t) = [\alpha(t)-X(t)]l_1(k_2+k_5p_5f(t))/[(l_3+l_4(t)q_3(t))(k_2+k_5p_5f(t))$
$$+l_1k_3-k_3(l_2+p_5f(t)l_5)]$$

S13. $K(t+1) = (1-c)K(t) + \delta K(t)$

S14. $K_2(t) = k_2[K(t)-\delta K(t)k_3]/(k_2+k_5p_5f(t))$

S15. $X_2(t) = K_2(t)/k_2$

S16. $dP^+(t) = p_5X_2(t)$

S17. $\pi(t) \equiv H_2/(1+\exp(\Theta_2(P(t)+dP^+(t)-y_2)))$

S18. $DP(t) = (P(t)+dP^+(t))\pi(t)$

S19. $f(t) \equiv H_1/(1+\exp(\Theta_1(P(t-2)+dP^+(t-2)-DP(t-2)-y_1)))$

S20. $dP^-(t) = dP^+(t)f(t)$

S21. $P(t+1) = P(t) + dP^+(t) - DP(t) - dP^-(t)$

S22. $L_5(t) = l_5dP^-(t)$

S23. $K_5(t) = k_5dP^-(t)$

S24. $L_3(t) = l_3\delta K(t)$

S25. $L_4(t) = l_4(t)q_3(t)\delta K(t)$

S26. $L_2(t) = l_2X_2(t)$

S27. $L_1(t) = L - L_2(t) - L_3(t) - L_4(t) - L_5(t)$

S28. $R(t) = q_3(t)\delta K(t)$

S29. $K_3(t) = k_3R(t)/q_3(t)$

S30. $CR(t+1) = CR(t) + R(t)$

S31. $X_1(t) = L_1(t)/l_1$

S32. $W_1 = M\beta X(t)^{\beta-1}$

S33. $W_2 = M\beta X^*(t+1)^{\beta-1}/(1+D)$

S34. $P_{X(t)} = W_1$

S35. $P_{X^*(t+1)} = W_2$

S36. $P_{L(t)} = P_{X(t)}/l_1$

S37. $P_{R(t)} = l_4(t)P_{L(t)}$

S38. $P_{K(t)} = [P_{X(t)} - \{l_2+p_5f(t)l_5\}P_{L(t)}]/[k_2+p_5f(t)k_5]$

S39. $P_{dP-(t)} = l_5P_{L(t)} + k_5P_{K(t)}$

S40. $P_{K^*(t+1)} = l_3P_{L(t)} + k_3P_{K(t)} + q_3P_{R(t)}$

S41. $P_{L(t+1)} = P_{X^*(t+1)}/l_1$

S42. $P_{dP-^*(t+1)} = l_5P_{L(t+1)} + k_5P_{K^*(t+1)}.$

Appendix 11.2

Parameter Values for the Simulation

Initial Conditions

$L = 5000.0$ $K(0) = 50.0$ $n = 5$

Labour Coefficients

$l_1 = 1.0$ $l_2 = 0.138$ $l_3 = 4.245$ $l_5 = 0.276$

Capital Good Coefficients

$k_2 = 0.138$ $k_3 = 0.069$ $k_5 = 0.276$ $c = 0.1$

Technical Progress Coefficients

$a = 0.7$ $A = 0.7$ $Z^* = 0.8$ $B = 0.001$

$q_3(0) = 0.08$ $Z(0) = 0.2$

Resource Coefficients

$\sigma(0) = 0.5$ $\mu = 0.008$ $\varphi = 0.561$ $CR(0)=0$

Pollution Coefficients

$p_5 = 0.05$ $P(0) = 0.0$ $H_1 = 0.95$ $y_1 = 1800.0$

$\Theta_1 = 0.005$ $H_2 = 1$ $y_2 = 100.0$ $\Theta_2 = 0.04$

$f(0) = 0$ $f(1) = 0$

Welfare Coefficients

$d = 0.05$ $\text{ß} = 0.083.$

Part VI

Final Thoughts

12 Policy Implications and the Need for Interdisciplinary Research

12.1 Introduction

We began this book by noting that we considered the preservation of the ecosystem to be the greatest challenge facing humankind. As a contribution to the methodology of ecological economics we have therefore examined, in some detail, how long-run economy-environment interactions can be conceptualized and modelled.

In this final chapter we seek to draw some conclusions and suggest what lessons for policy might be derived from our analysis. We do this in two ways.

First, in Section 12.2, we consider the implications for policy making on environmental matters. We especially note that a recognition of evolution, the emergence of novelty, and of ignorance, strongly constrains what can be regarded as 'reasonable' methods of policy analysis and planning.

In particular, in Section 12.3 we note that while planning for non-renewable resource use is quite straightforward, planning for pollution production and abatement is much more difficult.

In Section 12.4 we consider the importance of interdisciplinary research for ecological economics, and for economics more generally. (In this chapter we extend material originally developed in FABER and PROOPS [1985]).

12.2 The Policy Implications of Evolving Systems

What are the implications of a world which exhibits phenotypic and genotypic evolution for policy making? To answer this question we need to recall the definitions we have used earlier in this book.

The phenotypic evolution of a system is the change over time of the realization of its potentialities, where those potentialities are unchanging.

The genotypic evolution of a system is the change over time of its potentialities.

We also recall that we discussed at length three types of time irreversibility that may be exhibited. These are related to 'Risk', 'Uncertainty' and 'Teleological Sequence'. In this connection also, the notion of ignorance became important. The consideration of ignorance reveals that the behaviour of systems which exhibit only phenotypic evolution cannot always be predicted even though they are, in principle, predictable. On the other hand, systems which also exhibit genotypic change are, in principle, unpredictable because of the emergence of novelty. Clearly, systems which are unpredictable are going to be very difficult to plan to any degree. That is, while they may be modelled ex post, they cannot be modelled ex ante.

It is clear, from our discussion in earlier parts of this book, that we consider this emergence of novelty, and the appearance of subjective novelty because of ignorance, to be a central and incompletely addressed issue in economics. If it is to be addressed, and if its policy implications are to be assessed, the essential first step is its recognition. The one thing we know for sure is that we do not know *everything* for sure! Alternatively, the one thing that we can *always* predict is that we will encounter the *unpredictable* and our *ignorance*, because of the occurrence of either objective or subjective novelty.

Thus the emergence of novelty should not be an 'add-on' to policy making, but its cornerstone and central tenet. In particular, we feel the case for such a stance is overwhelming in considerations of economy-environment interactions in the long-run. This approach leads us to the following conclusions.

1. The use of infinite time-horizon models, both in practice and theory [MALINVAUD 1953; KOOPMANS 1957; STEPHAN 1986] has to be re-evaluated. Such models require that everything be known, at least stochastically, at the initial moment when the intertemporal plan is formulated.

2. Any plan formulation should be open to revision as and when novelty occurs. Planning should be a continuing process, taking into account emerging novelty and ignorance. This should not only be the case in practice, but it should also be embodied in models of planning and decision making.

3. One should value, and plan for, flexibility in response to currently unforeseen possibilities. For example, planning for systems to operate near the limits of their capabilities may be optimal in the short-run, but it severely limits flexibility of response for the long-run. (Here, of course, the paper by KOOPMANS [1964], mentioned in Chapter 4, Section 4.4.1, is of relevance.)

12.3 Policy Formulation in Environmental Matters

Having established some general principles for planning in the face of genotypic evolution, we now turn to the problem of economy-environment interactions in particular.

12.3.1 Sources of Novelty in Economy-Environment Interactions

When considering economy-environment interactions, we recognize three main sources of novelty.

1. The invention of new techniques of production. The emergence of the nuclear power industry and of microelectronics, over the past decades, are examples here.

2. The emergence of new types of interaction between economic activity and the global ecosystem. For example, the sudden appearance of a 'hole' in the ozone layer was not predicted, and is still not properly understood.

3. The alteration of social aims and norms. The Western attitude to the natural environment is quite unlike that of other cultures. Perhaps this attitude will change.

As our concern is with the unpredictable emergence of novelty, it would be worth asking whether we can establish the circumstances under which novelty is likely to arise. Regarding 1., the invention of new techniques, in several of the above chapters we argued that physical constraints are likely to lead to a search for invention, though of course effective inventions may not be found, and the technology, and indeed the culture, may founder as a result.

Regarding 2., the emergence of new economy-environment interactions, these are likely to emerge through the emission of new types of polluting wastes into the global ecosystem, or through the emission of greater quantities of already produced wastes.

Concerning 3., social attitudes to the natural environment, these may be affected by increased awareness of the long-term damage that can be inflicted, irreversibly, on the natural world by casual economic activity.

12.3.2 Resource Depletion vs Pollution

The two main areas of concern, and of economic analysis, in economy-environment interactions are the depletion of natural resources, and the production of pollution.

Our impression is that many authors, especially economists, see pollution as the lesser of these two evils. This is because one may view pollution as an 'externality', where its non-market nature leads to its over-production. If, somehow, one were to 'internalize' this externality then pollution would cease to be a problem.

On the other hand, most economists recognize that non-renewable resources are just that; once used up they must be substituted with other resources, which may or may not become available.

From our analysis of the emergence of novelty and the consequences of ignorance, our position is that pollution is a much greater threat in the long-run than the depletion of non-renewable resources. To show why we view the world this way, let us begin with the problem of resource depletion in a world exhibiting genotypic evolution.

Suppose we are exploiting a natural resource, which we know to be non-renewable. That is, there is a certain known, finite 'quantity' available. More usually, there is a finite quantity above a certain minimum 'useful' concentration. Supposing property rights are well defined, then economic agents will value the resource in terms of its scarcity, as discussed in Chapter 8. Thus as the resource is used up, its price will rise. This will generate a search for further reserves of the resource (prospecting), a search for techniques using less of the resource (resource-saving invention), and a search for techniques using other, cheaper, resources (which may eventually lead to resource-substituting invention; see also SCHMIDTCHEN [1989]).

Thus, any novelty that is induced by increasing prices will tend to be beneficial, and move the economy further away from any natural constraints on its activity. It should be said, as noted in Chapter 8, that the prospect of the emergence of novelty will mean there will be incomplete futures markets, so prices will tend to be lower than those which are necessary for an 'optimal' allocation of the production factors. However, even so prices will rise over time, so prospecting and invention will still be undertaken, although to a lesser degree than with 'intertemporally optimal' prices.

Let us now consider pollution. Here, the novelty that emerges is in terms of new relationships between economic activity and the natural environment. This novelty is potentially, and usually, deleterious. Examples include the hole in the ozone layer, mentioned above, algal bloom from fertilizer run-off, acid rain and its effects on lakes, air pollution and forest death, etc. All of these are relatively new phenomena, and they were unexpected and unwelcome.

Countering the effects of pollution by 'internalizing' it within the market system would certainly help, ex post. However, this is unlike the case of market-led resource depletion, as the effect of a new pollutant is initially unknown, because of ignorance. Therefore, the 'price' of the pollutant would only be knowable ex post.

Thus resource use can be said to generate scarcity, which is reflected in a rising market price. This rising price is, in turn, likely to generate beneficial novelty. On the other hand, new pollutants are themselves a source of deleterious novelty. This novelty will, at best, generate a search for a system of market pricing to encourage the reduction of their emission.

That is, resource use is a known problem that tends to generate, at least to some extent, its own, novel, solution. On the other hand, a new form of pollution is a novel problem, for which a solution must be constructed. Clearly, the former sort of problem is far easier to deal with than the latter.

In summary, there exists an inherent asymmetry in the recognition of problems of natural resource depletion and the degradation of the environment. The above is not meant to imply that a profligate use of resources is to be encouraged. Rather, it aims to indicate that pollution, especially novel forms of pollution, should be avoided as far as possible.

12.4 The Place of Interdisciplinary Research in Economics

During recent years economics has exhibited two divergent trends. One trend is towards ever greater formalization and 'mathematization'. More and more economic theory has become a type of 'what if' speculation. The range of concepts has expanded, but all too often without reference to the economic and social meaning of those concepts. For example, one sees publications on contract theory and labour economics clearly written by economists who have only a passing acquaintance with how trade unions and employers actually reach agreements.

The explosive growth of rational expectations modelling is a further sign of this approach to economics that does not make reference to the real phenomena. It is, of course, impossible to formulate a rational expectation in the anticipation of the emergence of unpredictable novelty and ignorance.

The other trend, especially in the field of environmental economics, has been much healthier. Here at least some economists have started to address problems of pollution and resource use, not only in the narrow sense of 'internalising' their external effects, but in the light of the Second Law of Thermodynamics, and the impossibility of 'costless' recycling. However, even here there have been models which reflect more the wishful thinking of their creators, rather than the reality of the natural world. For example, commenting on a paper discussing optimal growth with a depletable natural resource, KOOPMANS [1982:322] said:

"... I feel the work not only in this paper, but in similar literature over the last ten years is rather lacking in the realistic representation of technological feasibility ... I submit that there is no practical experience pertaining to a situation in which the ratio of resource use to capital is very low."

In our view, if economics is to make good progress, it must open itself to a greater extent to work in other disciplines, be it politics, law, sociology, psychology, physics, chemistry or biology. This is especially true for work on environmental matters. It is in this sense that we agree with HAHN's [1987:111] advice:

"... no really drastic changes are needed in the manner in which much economic research proceeds at present although it would be a great advantage if it were to encompass a great deal more than it does of the knowledge of society other disciplines have provided."

That this interdisciplinary approach is still not being widely practised can be instanced by reference to a new book on resource economics by HARTWICK and OLEWILER [1986]. This thorough and modern text, likely to become a standard reference work, contains not one mention of the Second Law of Thermodynamics.

If the problems of resource depletion, and especially of pollution, are to be confronted, we feel sure that an interdisciplinary approach is necessary. In particular, the growing relationship between economics and the physical sciences offers a direction worthy of further exploration. Before considering how such interdisciplinary work can be encouraged, we briefly review the interaction of economics and the physical sciences to date.

12.4.1 Economists and Physical Science

There are many widely accepted models and concepts which use analogies between physical theory and economics. However, we do not consider such use of analogy to be truly interdisciplinary, as this involves the sharing of concepts between disciplines and not just the borrowing of ideas and methods. Indeed, analogical reasoning can even be misleading if concepts from physical science are incorporated into social and economic models but not fully understood and internalized by the researcher.

12.4.1.1 Physical Analogies

Economics has a long tradition of employing concepts and methods from the physical sciences [MIROWSKI 1984, 1988, 1989; PROOPS 1985, 1987]. Explicit use of analogies with aspects of physical theory was made by WALRAS [1874] and EDGEWORTH [1881]; FISHER [1892] made an early attempt to express an isomorphism between concepts in economics and thermodynamics. In more modern times SAMUELSON [1947] has expressed certain economic results in the same form as LE CHATELIER's principle from thermodynamics.

The central concept from thermodynamics, entropy, has also been widely used in economics [see e.g. THEIL 1967]. The entropy concepts was originally derived from 'classical' thermodynamics. It can also be derived from statistical mechanics, where the 'orderliness' or 'concentration' of a system is expressed in terms of a suitable set of probabilities or frequencies. It is this formulation that has been extensively exploited in economics, for such diverse applications as measuring industrial concentration, inequalities of income and employment, and geographic concentration.

This use of pure analogy is exemplified by the use of 'gravity models' in regional economics [see e.g. ISARD 1975]. In such models interaction between population centres is assumed to vary with their size and distance apart.

Recently THOBEN [1982] has suggested that the use of mechanical analogy in economics should be supplanted by the use of 'organistic' analogy, recognizing that a complex economic system is more akin to a self-regulating and developing organism than to a mechanical system. A similar exploration of organistic analogy is due to FEHL [1983], who draws an analogy between economies and 'dissipative structures', which are discussed in more detail in Section 12.4.1.3 below. In a similar vein

HANNON [1985] has argued for the analogy between economies and ecosystems to be recognized, with ecosystems offering the potential for an experimental systems basis for economics.

12.4.1.2 Physical Limits

Such drawing of analogies has not been the only method of conjuncture of economics with the physical sciences. Perhaps JEVONS [1865] was the most eminent of the early economists who examined the physical nature of economic activity, when he considered the importance of coal to the British economy. More recently GEORGESCU-ROEGEN [1971] has stressed the importance of thermodynamic entropy to understanding the functioning of economies. The concern of both authors has been the physical limits to social activity. For JEVONS, it was the possible future shortage of coal that he saw as a constraint upon industrial activity, while GEORGESCU-ROEGEN stressed the wider problem of the irreversibility of productive activity and the constraints this places on economic activity in the long run because of finite exhaustible resources. Thus the concerns about fuel reserves have also found expression in the field of Energy Analysis, which developed rapidly following the oil 'crisis' of 1973 [see e.g. SLESSER 1978]. The aim of energy analysis is to map the direct and indirect energy use of an economy through the productive process.

The problem of environmental pollution has also become of great interest in recent years [see e.g. DALES 1968; DORFMAN and DORFMAN 1977; KNEESE 1977]. Again, interest among economists and other scholars has centred upon how pollution may act as a physical limitation on human economic activity.

12.4.1.3 Dissipative Structures

Recently, a third and more general relationship between economics and thermodynamics has been developed, based on the work of PRIGOGINE [1980] and the Brussels School of Thermodynamics. This approach distinguishes between static structures, such as crystals, and dynamic structures, such as convection cells[1], flames and organisms. A static structure is in equilibrium with its environment, its structure being maintained by internal stasis. A dynamic structure, on the other hand, maintains a constant relationship with its environment via active internal

---

[1] Convection is the transmission of heat through a fluid by the movement of mass within the fluid.

processes, in particular processes which generate entropy and dissipate energy. Such dynamic systems have been described as being far from thermodynamic equilibrium, and under certain circumstances may demonstrate not simply self-maintenance, but also 'self-organization', and thereby generate further structuring [PROOPS 1983].

The classic example of a dynamic structure is a convection cell, which develops when a liquid is subject to a temperature gradient. If the temperature gradient is small the liquid will transport energy through its bulk solely by conduction; but if the temperature gradient is increased, regularly shaped convection cells will form spontaneously, increasing the rate of heat transport through the liquid. These convection cells correspond to a more 'structured' state of the system, with the energy flux acting as an ordering agent for this 'dissipative structure'. Now economies are such complex structures, maintaining themselves by 'consuming low entropy' to use the phrase of SCHRÖDINGER [1944]. Ordered, low entropy fuels are used up and high entropy waste heat is dissipated in all the productive processes by which economies maintain themselves.

12.4.2 Physical Scientists and Economics

Although economists have made liberal use of physical science, dialogue between economists and physical scientists over matters of energy use, resource depletion, and pollution has also helped the understanding of physical scientists. For example, in the early days of concern over energy shortage (i.e. the 1970s), a common theme among physical scientists was that economic value must derive from energy [e.g. GILLILAND 1975], as energy is the only factor of production that is in principle non-substitutable. However, many economic studies have shown that energy can, to some extent, be substituted by capital or by labour, and also it can be augmented in production by technical progress.

This assumption of a single factor of production is reminiscent of the Labour Theory of Value of RICARDO and MARX. The problem of how the 'costs' of a single input can be transformed into the 'prices' of outputs has long been an area of debate in economics and the limits of this approach are very narrow [see e.g. SAMUELSON 1971].

It is our view that many physical scientists took this narrow stance on the role of energy in the production process because energy plays a central role in the physical scientists' world view. At the time when the problem of energy supply became an issue it was not unnatural that economists took the view that this was a problem of market operation, while physical scientists saw as the root of the problem an imminent absolute shortage of energy.

It is pleasing to note that the debate over the importance of energy as a productive factor not only caused many economists to adjust their stance and come to accept that economic activity has a physical foundation, it also brought many physical scientists to the view that although energy is a central factor for modern economies, it is not the only factor worthy of study.

The debate on energy and value also revealed much about the problems of interdisciplinary research between economists and physical scientists. In particular, it revealed how difficult it is to have discussions across the economics/physical science divide when the parties involved are conversant only with their own disciplines. A common language alone does not allow mutual comprehension when the conceptual frameworks employed by discussants are very different.

12.4.3 Interdisciplinary Research: Difficulties and Some Tentative Solutions
12.4.3.1 Difficulties

There is little tradition of interdisciplinary collaboration between economists and physical scientists. However, as KOOPMANS [1979:1] noted in his presidential address to the American Economic Association:

> "With increasing frequency natural and social scientists are indeed finding themselves thrown together in the study of new problems that are of great practical importance for society, and essentially interdisciplinary in character. Prominent among these are problems of environmental policy... Another class of problems concerns a desirable long-range mix of technologies of energy supply, conversion and use."

A notable development of an interdisciplinary research centre is the Santa Fe Institute, under the direction of Brian ARTHUR [POOL 1989]. A particular concern of this centre is the application of physical models of 'complex systems' to economic behaviour. While we applaud this development, we fear that the apparent concentration on mathematical modelling, rather than conceptual analysis, may cause the centre to be less fruitful that it might otherwise be.

Thus, although the urgency of interdisciplinary work is generally accepted there is as yet little progress. We believe that the reason for this is that, besides the circumstances already mentioned above, there are obstacles of a psychological and institutional nature which impede such cooperation:

1. Research undertaking interdisciplinary work may face discouragement from the peer group of their fellow economists or physical scientists. Work across disciplines is often regarded as less 'serious' than work within a single discipline.

2. If one undertakes interdisciplinary research, one is almost bound to make certain blunders. One needs the courage to expose oneself not only to the critique of one's own discipline, but also to that of others. We found that these critiques are often rather harsh. One reason for this circumstance seems to be that the criteria which are used to evaluate research in a long established and specialized field are also used for interdisciplinary work, which is in its infancy.

3. It is often difficult to find someone who wants to cooperate, since one does not know those who would be willing. Those relatively few who have some standing are often too occupied with other things, while young scholars have first to specialize themselves in their own field in order to become recognized, so as to obtain a permanent position [KOOPMANS 1979:13].

4. The specialization of modern science has led to language barriers, normal terms being given specialized meanings to meet certain needs of expression. For example, the terms 'core', 'game', 'capital' and 'indifference' have specialized meanings for economists, as do the terms 'field', 'ensemble' and 'cycle' for physicists. But even more of a barrier to dialogue is the separation of what is perceived as important and valid as an explanatory device within different disciplines. For economists it tends to be 'the market' and 'optimizing behaviour' that are the concepts considered most appropriate, while physical scientists' concerns seem to be with the notion of transformation and time.

5. Having undertaken interdisciplinary work, research must then seek a publication outlet for their findings. Established fields have established journals, which is not the case for emerging interdisciplinary fields. Single discipline journals are often reluctant to accept interdisciplinary papers, as they feel them to be inappropriate to their readership.

6. A prerequisite for truly interdisciplinary work is a certain familiarity with the other's discipline. Since the knowledge available to individual participants will often not be sufficient, interdisciplinary research cooperation demands, to a large extent, teaching and learning on both sides. Compared to joint research within one area this is rather cumbersome. It is one thing to lecture students and quite another to give an elementary introduction to a specialist of another field, or to

be taught perhaps even by someone who is much younger than oneself, and sometimes not even established in his own discipline. Such discourse is, however, a sine qua non of interdisciplinary study. Only when the economist has mastered the relevant area of physical science (and not just read an introductory text), and only when the physical scientist is familiar and comfortable with the relevant economic theory, can truly fruitful dialogue and research take place. This is a tiresome and time consuming procedure, and can be a disincentive to interdisciplinary work. Given the publication pressure there will be a great temptation to work exclusively in one's own discipline.

12.4.3.2 Tentative Solutions

Our conclusion from the above discussion is that it is necessary to dissolve some established conceptual frameworks and to establish a wider vision [BOULDING 1970; DALY 1973; KÜMMEL 1980]. However, it will be some time before there are many researchers with as wide a background as we are recommending. In the meantime the following suggestions may help to aid the progress of interdisciplinary studies.

1. Workers in interdisciplinary fields are few in number and scattered over several different disciplines, such as mathematics, systems theory, physics, chemistry, engineering, geology, biology, ecology, regional science, planning, sociology, law and economics. In addition, these researchers are dispersed among many institutions and are therefore isolated. From our own experience the prime means of combating this isolation is through interdisciplinary conferences, symposia and seminars. As such meetings are almost the only opportunities for interdisciplinary dialogue, they need to be held more frequently than in established fields.

2. We have suggested that successful interdisciplinary research requires researchers to have studied and internalized both economics and physical science, at least to some degree. We feel that preparation for interdisciplinary research can take place at three levels. First, established researchers in a single field might benefit from directed reading in the appropriate complementary field for their interdisciplinary work. Second, if greater encouragement were given to the joint study of economics and physical science at undergraduate level, this would greatly assist the erosion of the conceptual boundaries that divide these branches of scholarship. Third, interdisciplinary

training at graduate school level would help to establish a body of scholars whose orientation would be naturally towards interdisciplinary work.

Some progress has already been made, with courses being offered in Engineering Economics at both graduate and undergraduate level. However, these courses are generally designed to produce skilled engineering managers, and while we support this aim, we do not feel that such courses offer the complete background for interdisciplinary research which we wish to promote.

12.5 Concluding Remarks

The course of modern scholarship and research has been of increased intellectual division of labour with, for example the defining of physics as distinct from chemistry and economics as distinct from political science. This division of labour has been enormously fruitful, but it has also led to specialization by scholars that may become counter-productive. In particular, such specialization has led scholars in different fields to evolve conceptual frameworks that are incompatible and mutually incomprehensible. There are a wide range of problems, which are of pressing nature, where the economists' and physical scientists' frameworks for analysis are, individually, insufficient for the task. Only by breaking down these conceptual barriers and establishing a wider and more open framework for discourse is progress likely to be made.

References

ALCHIAN, A.A. [1950] "Uncertainty, evolution, and economic theory", Journal of Political Economy 58:211-222.

ALLEN, P.M. and M. SANGLIER [1981] "Urban evolution, self-organisation, and decision making", Environment and Planning A 13:167-183.

ARROW, K. [1968] "Optimal capital policy with irreversible investment", in: J.N. WOLFE (ed.), Value and Capital and Growth: Papers in Honour of Sir John Hicks. Edinburgh University Press, Edinburgh.

ARROW, K. and A.C. FISCHER [1974] "Environmental preservation, uncertainty and irreversibility", Quarterly Journal of Economics 88:312-320.

ARROW, K. and F.A. HAHN [1970] Competitive General Equilibrium Analysis. Holden Day, San Francisco.

ARTHUR, W.B. [1984] "Competing technologies and economic prediction", Options (April):10-13.

ARTHUR, W.B. [1989] "Competing technologies, increasing returns and lock-in by historical events", Economic Journal 99:116-131.

AUGUSTINE, A. [1961] Confessions. Penguin, Middlesex; translated, R.S. PINE-COFFIN.

BAKKER, R.T. [1983] "The deer flees and the wolf pursues: incongruencies in predator-prey coevolution", in: D.J. FUTUYAMA and M. SLATKIN (eds.), Coevolution. Sinauer, Sunderland, Mass.

BALLARD, C. and L. GOULDER [1985] "Consumption taxes, consumer foresight and welfare", in: J. PIGGOTT and J. WHALLY (eds.), New Developments in Applied General Equilibrium Analysis. North-Holland, Amsterdam.

BAUMOL, W.J. [1977] Economic Theory and Operations Analysis (4th edn.). Prentice-Hall, Englewood Cliffs.

BAUMOL, W.J. and J. BENHABIB [1989] "Chaos: significance, mechanism, and economic applications", Journal of Economic Perspectives 3:77-105.

BELTRAMI, E. [1987] Mathematics for Dynamic Modelling. Academic Press, New York.

BENHABIB, J. and R.H. DAY [1980] "Erratic accumulation", Economics Letters 6:113-118.

BENHABIB, J. and R.H. DAY [1981] "Rational choice and erratic behaviour", Review of Economic Studies 48:459-471.

BENHABIB, J. and R.H. DAY [1982] "A characterization of erratic dynamics in the overlapping generations model", Journal of Economic Dynamics and Control 4:37-55.

BERNANKE, B.S. [1983] "Irreversibility, uncertainty and cyclical investment", Quarterly Journal of Economics 98:85-106.

BERNHOLZ, P. [1971] "Superiority of roundabout processes and positive rate of interest: a simple model of capital and growth", Kyklos 24:687-721.

BERNHOLZ, P. and M. FABER [1973] "Technical productivity of roundabout processes and positive rate of interest: a capital model with depreciation and n-period horizon", Zeitschrift für die gesamte Staatswissenschaft 129:46-61.

BERNHOLZ, P. and M. FABER [1976] "Time consuming innovation and positive rate of interest", Zeitschrift für Nationalökonomie 36:247-367.

BERNHOLZ, P., M. FABER and W. REISS [1978] "A neo-Austrian two period multisector model of capital", Journal of Economic Theory 17:38-50.

BINSWANGER, H.C., M. FABER and R. MANSTETTEN [1990] "The dilemma of modern man and nature: an exploration of the Faustian imperative", Ecological Economics 2:197-223.

BLAINEY, G. [1975] The Triumph of the Nomads: A History of Ancient Australia. Macmillan, Melbourne.

BLISS, C.J. [1975] Capital Theory and the Distribution of Income. North-Holland, Amsterdam.

BLISS, C.J. [1976] "Capital theory in the short-run", in: M. BROWN, K. SATO and P. SAREMBKA (eds.), Essays in Modern Capital Theory. North-Holland, Amsterdam.

BÖHM-BAWERK, E.V. [1889/1891] Kapital und Kapitalzins. Zweite Abteilung: Positive Theorie des Kapitalls, Innsbruck 1889; translated, W. SMART: The Positive Theory of Capital, 1890. Macmillan, London.

BOLAND, L.A. [1978] "Time in economics vs. economics in time: the 'Hayek Problem'", Canadian Journal of Economics 11:240-262.

BOULDING, K.E. [1970] Economics as a Science. McGraw-Hill, New York.

BOULDING, K.E. [1981] Evolutionary Economics. Sage, Beverly Hills.

BROCK, W. [1986] "Distinguishing random and deterministic systems: abridged version", Journal of Economic Theory 40:168-195.

BROWN, G.M. and R.W. JOHNSON [1982] "Pollution control by effluent charges: it works in the Federal Republic of Germany, why not in the USA?", Natural Resources Journal 22:929-966.

BURMEISTER, E. [1980] Capital Theory and Dynamics. Cambridge University Press, Cambridge.

BURMEISTER, E. and A.R. DOBELL [1970] Mathematical Theories of Economic Growth. Macmillan, New York.

CASS, D. [1972] "On capital overaccumulation in the aggregative neoclassical model of economic growth", Journal of Economic Theory 4:224-340.

CHEN, P. [1984] "A possible case of an economic attractor", Department of Physics, University of Texas (mimeo).

CLARK, C.W. [1976] Mathematical Bioeconomics. Wiley, New York.

CLARK, C.W., F.H. CLARK and G.R. MUNRO [1979] "The optimal exploitation of renewable resource stocks: problems of irreversible investment", Econometrica 47:25-47.

CLARK, N. and C. JUMA [1987] Long-Run Economics: An Evolutionary Approach to Economic Growth. Pinter, London.

COLLET, P. and J. ECKMANN [1980] Iterated Maps on the Interval as Dynamical Systems. Birkhauser, Basel.

COSTANZA, R. (ed.) [1991] Ecological Economics: The Science and Management of Sustainability. Columbia University Press, New York.

CROSBY, A.W. [1986] Ecological Imperialism. Cambridge University Press, Cambridge.

CROSS, J.G. [1983] A Theory of Adaptive Economic Behaviour. Cambridge University Press, Cambridge.

CUSA, Nicolas of [1964] "De Docta Ignorantia (Die belehrte Unwissenheit)". P. WILPERT (ed.), Verlag von Felix Meiner, Hamburg.

CYERT, R.M. and J.G. MARCH [1963] A Behavioral Theory of the Firm. Prentice-Hall, Englewood Cliffs.

DALES, F.H. [1968] Pollution, Property and Prices. University of Toronto Press, Toronto.

DALY, H.E. [1973] Toward a Steady State Economy. Freeman, San Francisco.

DASGUPTA, P.S. [1983] The Control of Resources. Harvard University Press, Cambridge, Mass.

DASGUPTA, P.S. and G.M. HEAL [1979] Economic Theory and Exhaustible Resources. Cambridge University Press, Cambridge.

DAY, R.H. [1982] "Irregular growth cycles", American Economic Review 72:406-414.

DAY, R.H. [1983] "The emergence of chaos from classical economic growth", Quarterly Journal of Economics 98:201-213.

DAY, R.H. and A. CIGNO [1978] Modelling Economic Change: A Recursive Approach. North-Holland, Amsterdam

DEBREU, G. [1959] Theory of Value. Wiley, New York.

DEBREU, G. [1974] "Excess demand functions", Journal of Mathematical Economics 1:15-23.

DIXIT, A. [1977] "The accumulation of capital theory", Oxford Economic Papers 29:1-29.

DOLAN, E.G. (ed.) [1976] The Foundations of Modern Austrian Economics. Sheed, Andrews and McMeel, Kansas City.

DORFMAN, R. and N. DORFMAN (eds.) [1977] Economics of the Environment. Norton, New York.

DORFMAN, R., P.A. SAMUELSON and R.M. SOLOW [1958] Linear Programming and Economic Analysis. McGraw-Hill, New York.

EDGEWORTH, F.Y. [1881] Mathematical Psychics. Kegan Paul, London.

EHRLICH, P.R. [1989] "The limits to substitution: meta-resource depletion and a new economic-ecological paradigm", Ecological Economics 1:9-16.

EPPLER, D. and L. LAVE [1980] "Helium investments in the future", The Bell Journal of Economics 11:617-630.

FABER, M. [1979] Introduction to Modern Austrian Capital Theory. Springer-Verlag, Heidelberg.

FABER, M. [1985] "A biophysical approach to the economy: entropy, environment and resources", in: VAN GOOL and BRUGGINK [1985].

FABER, M. (ed.) [1986a] Studies in Austrian Capital Theory, Investment and Time. Springer-Verlag, Heidelberg.

FABER, M. [1986b] "On the development of Austrian capital theory", in: FABER [1986a].

FABER, M. and J.L.R. PROOPS [1985] "Interdisciplinary research between economists and physical scientists: retrospect and prospect", Kyklos 38:599-616.

FABER, M. and J.L.R. PROOPS [1986] "Time irreversibilities in economics: some lessons from the natural sciences", in: FABER [1986a].

FABER, M. and J.L.R. PROOPS [1989] "Time irreversibility in economic theory: a conceptual discussion", Seoul Journal of Economics 2:109-129.

FABER, M. and J.L.R. PROOPS [1991a] "Evolution in biology, physics and economics: a conceptual discussion" in: S. METCALFE and P. SAVIOTTI (eds.) Evolutionary Theories of Economic and Technological Change. Harwood, London.

FABER, M. and J.L.R. PROOPS [1991b] "National accounting, time and the environment: a neo-Austrian approach" in: COSTANZA [1991].

FABER, M. and J.L.R. PROOPS [1991c] "The innovation of techniques and the time-horizon: a neo-Austrian approach", Structural Change and Economic Dynamics 2:143-158.

FABER, M. and J.L.R. PROOPS [1993] "Natural resource rents, economic dynamics and structural change: a capital theoretic approach", Ecological Economics (forthcoming).

FABER, M. and G. WAGENHALS [1988] "Towards a long-run balance between economics and environmental protection", in: W. SALOMONS and U. FÖRSTNER (eds.), Environmental Impact and Management of Mine Tailings and Dredged Materials. Springer-Verlag, Heidelberg.

FABER, M., R. MANSTETTEN and J.L.R. PROOPS [1992a] "Towards an open future: ignorance, novelty and evolution", in: R. COSTANZA, B. NORTON and B. HASKELL (eds.), Ecosystem Health: New Goals for Environmental Management, Island Press, New York.

FABER, M., R. MANSTETTEN and J.L.R. PROOPS [1992b] "An anatomy of surprise and ingnorance", Environmental Values 1:217-241.

FABER, M., H. NIEMES and G. STEPHAN [1983] Umweltschutz und Input-Output-Analyse. Mit zwei Fallstudien aus der Wassergütewirtschaft. Mohr (Paul Siebeck), Tübingen.

FABER, M., H. NIEMES and G. STEPHAN [1987] Entropy, Environment and Resources: An Essay in Physico-Economics. Springer-Verlag, Heidelberg.

FABER, M., G. STEPHAN and P. MICHAELIS [1989] Umdenken in der Abfallwirtschaft (2nd edn.). Springer-Verlag, Heidelberg.

FABER, M., J.L.R. PROOPS, M. RUTH and P. MICHAELIS [1990] "Economy-environment interactions in the long-run: a neo-Austrian approach", Ecological Economics 2:27-55.

FEHL, U. [1983] "Die Theorie dissipativer Strukturen als Ansatzpunkt für die Analyse von Innovationsproblemen in alternativen Wirtschaftsordnungen", in: A. SCHÜLER, H. LEIPOLD and H. HAMEL (eds.), Innovationsprobleme in Ost und West. Schriften zum Vergleich von Wirtschaftsordnungen. Gustav Fischer Verlag, Stuttgart.

FISHER, F.M. [1981] "Stability, disequilibrium awareness, and the perception of new opportunities", Econometrica 49:279-317.

FISHER, I. [1892] "Mathematical investigations in the theory of value and prices", Transactions of the Connecticut Academy of Arts and Sciences 9:11-126.

FLOOD, R. and M. LOCKWOOD [1986] The Nature of Time. Blackwell, Oxford.

FULLERTON, D., Y.K. HENDERSON and J. SHOVEN [1984] "A comparison of methodologies in equilibrium models", in: H. SCARF and J. SHOVEN (eds.), Applied General Equilibrium Analysis. Cambridge University Press, Cambridge.

FUNTOWICZ, S.O. and J.R. RAVETZ [1990] "Global environmental issues and the emergence of second order science", in: COSTANZA [1991].

GEORGESCU-ROEGEN, N. [1971] The Entropy Law and the Economic Process. Harvard University Press, Cambridge, Mass.

GILLILAND, M.W. [1975] "Energy analysis and public policy", Science 189:1051-1056.

GLEICK, J.W. [1988] Chaos: Making a New Science. Heinemann, London.

GRANDMONT, J.-M. [1985] "On endogenous competitive business cycles", Econometrica 53:995-1045.

GÖDEL, M. [1931] "Über formal unentscheidar Sätze der *Principia Mathematica* und verwandte Systeme", Monatsh. für Math. u. Phys. 38:173-198.

GUCKENHEIMER, J. and P. HOLMES [1983] Nonlinear Oscillations, Dynamical Systems and Bifurcations of Vector Fields. Springer-Verlag, Heidelberg.

HAHN, F.A. [1966] "Equilibrium dynamics with heterogeneous capital goods", Quarterly Journal of Economics 80:633-646.

HAHN, F.A. [1970] "Some adjustment processes", Econometrica 38:1-17.

HAHN, F.A. [1987] Review of D.N. MCCLOSKEY "The Rhetoric of Economics", Journal of Economic Literature, 25:110-111.

HANEMANN, W.M. [1989] "Information and the concept of option value", Journal of Environmental Economics and Management 16:23-37.

HANNON, B. [1985] "Conditioning the ecosystem", in: VAN GOOL and BRUGGINK [1985].

HARTWICK, J.M. and N.D. OLEWILER [1986] The Economics of Natural Resources. Harper and Row, New York.

HAWKING, S.W. [1988] A Brief History of Time. Bantam, London.

HAYEK, F.A. [1972] Die Theorie komplexer Phänomene. Mohr (Paul Siebeck), Tübingen.

HEINER, R.A. [1983] "The origin of predictable behaviour", American Economic Review 73:560-595.

HEIDEGGER, M. [1927/79] Sein und Zeit. Max Niemeyer Verlag, Tübingen.

HENRY, C. [1974] "Investment decisions under uncertainty: the irreversibility effect", American Economic Review 64:1006-1012.

HICKS, J.R. [1939/1946] Value and Capital. Oxford University Press, Oxford.

HICKS, J.R. [1965] Capital and Growth. Oxford University Press, Oxford.

HICKS, J.R. [1970] "A neo-Austrian growth theory", Economic Journal 80:257-281.

HICKS, J.R. [1973a] "The Austrian theory of capital and its rebirth in modern economics", in: J.R. HICKS and M. WEBER (eds.), Carl Menger and the Austrian School of Economics. Oxford University Press, Oxford.

HICKS, J.R. [1973b] Capital and Time: A Neo-Austrian Theory. Oxford University Press, Oxford.

HICKS, J.R. [1976] "Some questions of time in economics", in: A.M. TANG, F.M. WESTFIELD and J.S. WORLEY (eds.), Evolution, Welfare, Time in Economics: Essays in Honour of Nicholas Georgescu-Roegen. Lexington Books, Toronto.

HOFSTADTER, D.R. [1979] Gödel, Escher, Bach. Hassocks, London.

HOSKINS, W. [1973] The Making of the English Landscape. Penguin, Middlesex.

HIRSHLEIFER, J. [1977] "Economics from a biological viewpoint", Journal of Law and Economics 20:1-52.

ISARD, W. [1975] Introduction to Regional Science. Prentice Hall, Englewood Cliffs.

JAKSCH, H.-J. [1975] "Die Mehrergiebigkeit längerer Produktionsumwege in einem linearen Vielsektorenmodell", Zeitschrift für die gesamte Staatswissenschaft 131:92-105.

JENSEN, R.V. and R. URBAN [1984] "Chaotic behaviour in a non-linear cobweb model", Economics Letters 15:235-240.

JEVONS, W.S. [1865] The Coal Question. Macmillan, London.

KADANOFF, L.P. [1983] "Roads to chaos", Physics Today (December):46-53.

KANT, I. [1956] "Kritik der reinen Vernunft", in: W. WEISSCHEDEL (ed.) I. Kant: Werkausgabe, Vol. 3. and 4. Suhrkamp, Frankfurt.

KATZNER, D.W. [1986] "Potential surprise, potential confirmation, and probability", Journal of Post Keynesian Economics 9:58-78

KEAST, A. (ed.) [1981] Ecological Biogeography of Australia. Junk, The Hague.

KETTLEWELL, H.B.D. [1973] The Evolution of Melanism. Oxford University Press, Oxford.

KIRZNER, I.M. [1973] Competition and Entrepreneurship. Chicago University Press, Chicago.

KIRZNER, I.M. (ed.) [1982] Method, Process and Austrian Economics: Essays in Honour of Ludwig von Mises. Lexington Books, Lexington.

KLEPPER, G. [1992] "Review of: M. Faber and J.L.R. Proops; Evolution, Time Production and the Environment (1st edn.)", Journal of Economics, 55:319-321.

KNEESE, A.V. [1977] Economics and the Environment. Penguin, Middlesex.

KNIGHT, F. [1921] Risk, Uncertainty, and Profit. Houghton Mifflin, Boston.

KOESTLER, A. [1967] The Ghost in the Machine. Hutchinson, London.

KOOPMANS, T.C. [1951] "Analysis of production as an efficient combination of activities", in: T.C. KOOPMANS (ed.), Activity Analysis of Production and Allocation. Wiley, New York.

KOOPMANS, T.C. [1957] "Allocation of resources and the price system", in: T.C. KOOPMANS, Three Essays on the State of Economic Science. McGraw-Hill, New York.

KOOPMANS, T.C. [1960] "Stationary utility and impatience", Econometrica 28:287-309.

KOOPMANS, T.C. [1964] "On flexibility of future preferences" in: M.W. SCHELLY II and G.L. BRYAN (eds.), Human Judgements and Optimality. Wiley, New York.

KOOPMANS, T.C. [1974] "Is the theory of competitive equilibrium with it?", American Economic Review (Papers and Proceedings) 64:325-329.

KOOPMANS, T.C. [1979] "Economics among the sciences", American Economic Review 69:1-13.

KOOPMANS, T.C. [1982] "Comment", in: LIND [1982].

KÜMMEL, R. [1980] Growth Dynamics of the Energy Dependent Economy. Mathematical Systems in Economics, Athenäum, Königstein.

KURZ, M. and D. STARRETT [1970] "On the efficiency of a competitive program in an infinite horizon model", Review of Economic Studies 37:571-584.

LAYZER, D. [1976] "The arrow of time", Astrophysical Journal 206:559-564.

LEIJONHUFVUD, A. [1984] "Hicks on time and money", Oxford Economic Papers 36 (Supplement):26-46.

LEONTIEF, W. [1982] "Academic economics", Science 217:104-107.

LEVINS, R. and R. LEWONTIN [1985] The Dialectical Biologist. Harvard University Press, Cambridge, Mass.

LI, T. and J.A. YORKE [1975] "Period three implies chaos", American Mathematical Monthly 82:985-992.

LIND, R.C. (ed.) [1982] Discounting for Time and Risk in Energy Policy. Johns Hopkins University Press, Baltimore.

LORENZ, E.N. [1963] "Deterministic non-period flows", Journal of Atmospheric Sciences 20:130-141.

MAIER, G. [1984] Rohstoffe und Innovation. Eine dynamische Untersuchung. Mathematical Systems in Economics, Athenäum, Königstein.

MALINVAUD, E. [1953] "Capital accumulation and efficient allocation", Econometrica 21:233-268.

MANTEL, R. [1974] "On the characterization of aggregate excess demand", Journal of Economic Theory 7:348-353.

MANTEL, R. [1976] "Homothetic preferences and community excess demand functions", Journal of Economic Theory 12:197-201.

MANTEL, R. [1977] "Implications of microeconomic theory for community excess demand functions", in: M. INTRILIGATOR (ed.), Frontiers of Quantitative Economics, Vol. III. North-Holland, Amsterdam.

MARSHALL, A. [1890] Principles of Economics. Macmillan, London.

MATTHEWS, R.C.O. [1984] "Darwinism and economic change", Oxford Economic Papers 36 (Supplement):91-117.

MAY, R.M. and G.F. OSTER [1976] "Bifurcations and dynamic complexity in simple ecological models", American Naturalist 110:573-599.

MENGER, G. [1871/1950] Grundsätze der Volkwirtschaftlehre. Wien; (trans.) Principles of Economics. The Free Press, Glenco, Ill.

MIROWSKI, P. [1984] "Physics and the marginalist revolution", Cambridge Journal of Economics 4:361-379.

MIROWSKI, P. [1988] "Energy and energetics in economic theory: a review essay", Journal of Economic Issues 22:811-830.

MIROWSKI, P. [1989] "How not to do things with metaphors: Paul Samuelson and the science of neoclassical economics", Studies in the History and Philosophy of Science 20:175-191.

MUTH, J.F. [1961] "Rational expectations and the theory of price movements", Econometrica 29:315-335.

NEGISHI, T. [1989] History of Economic Theory. North-Holland, Amsterdam.

NELSON, R.R. and S.G. WINTER [1982] An Evolutionary Theory of Economic Change. Harvard University Press, Cambridge, Mass.

NICKELL, S.J. [1978] The Investment Decisions of Firms. Cambridge University Press, Cambridge.

NICOLIS, C. and G. NICOLIS [1984] "Is there a climatic attractor?", Nature 311:529-532.

NICOLIS, G. and I. PRIGOGINE [1977] Self-Organization in Non-Equilibrium Systems. Wiley, New York.

NIEMES, H. [1981] Umwelt als Schadstoffempfänger: Die Wassergütewirtschaft als Beispiel. Mohr (Paul Siebeck), Tübingen.

NORGAARD, R. [1984] "Coevolutionary development potential", Land Economics 60:160-173.

O'CONNOR, M. [1985] "Prices in far from equilibrium economic system: an open system approach in environmental economics", Department of Economics, University of Auckland, New Zealand (mimeo).

O'DRISCOLL, G.P. and M.J. RIZZO [1984] The Economics of Time and Ignorance. Basil Blackwell, Oxford.

PELLENGAHR, I. [1986a] "Austrians versus Austrians I: a subjectivist view of interest", in: FABER [1986a].

PELLENGAHR, I. [1986b] "Austrians versus Austrians II: a subjectivist view of interest", in: FABER [1986a].

PENROSE, E.T. [1952] "Biological analogies in the theory of the firm", American Economic Review 42:804-819.

PERRINGS, C. [1991] "'Reserved Rationality' and the 'Precautionary Principle': technological change, time and uncertainty in environmental decision making", in: COSTANZA [1991].

PERRINGS, C. [1991] "Review of: M. Faber and J.L.R. Proops; Evolution, Time Production and the Environment (1st edn.)", Structural Change and Economic Dynamics 2:407-409.

PINDYCK, R.S. [1988] "Irreversible investment, capacity choice, and the value of the firm", American Economic Review 78:969-985.

POOL, R. [1989] "Research news. Strange bedfellows", Science 245:700-703.

POPPER, K.R. [1959] The Logic of Scientific Discovery. Hutchinson, London.

PRIGOGINE, I. [1962] Introduction to Non-Equilibrium Thermodynamics. Wiley, New York.

PRIGOGINE, I. and I. STENGERS [1984] Order out of Chaos. Heinemann, London.

PROOPS, J.L.R. [1983] "Organization and dissipation in economic systems", Journal of Social and Biological Structures 6:353-366.

PROOPS, J.L.R. [1985] "Thermodynamics and economics: from analogy to physical functioning", in: VAN GOOL and BRUGGINK [1985].

PROOPS, J.L.R. [1987] "Entropy, information and confusion in the social sciences", Journal of Interdisciplinary Economics 1:224-242.

PROOPS, J.L.R. [1989] "Ecological economics: rationale and problem areas", Ecological Economics 1:59-76.

PROOPS, J.L.R., M. FABER and G. WAGENHALS [1992] Reducing CO_2 Emissions: A Comparative Input-Output Study for Germany and the UK. Springer Verlag, Heidelberg.

RAVETZ, J.R. [1986] Usable knowledge, usable ignorance; incomplete science with policy implications, in: W. CLARK and R. MUNN (eds.), Sustainable Development of the Biosphere, Cambridge University Press, Cambridge.

REISS, W. [1981] Umwegproduktion und Positivität des Zinses: eine neo-österreichische Analyse. Duncker und Humbolt, Berlin.

REISS, W. and M. FABER [1982] "Own rates of interest in a general multisector model of capital", in: M. DEISTLER, E. FÜRST and G. SCHWÖDIAUER (eds.), Games, Economic Dynamics and Time Series Analysis. Physica-Verlag, Wien.

ROSENBERG, N. [1976] Perspectives on Technology. Cambridge University Press, Cambridge.

ROSENBERG, N. [1982] Inside the Black Box. Cambridge University Press, Cambridge.

SAMUELSON, P.A. [1947] Foundations of Economic Analysis. Harvard University Press, Cambridge, Mass.

SAMUELSON, P.A. [1971] "Understanding the Marxian notion of exploitation: a summary of the so-called transformation problem between Marxian values and competitive prices", Journal of Economic Literature 9:399-431.

SAMUELSON, P.A. [1983] "Rigorous observational positivism: Klein's envelope aggregation; thermodynamics and economic isomorphisms", in: F.M. ADAMS and B.G. HICKMANN (eds.), Global Econometrics: Essays in Honour of Lawrence R. Klein. MIT Press, Cambridge, Mass.

SCHELLING, T.C. [1978] Micromotives and Macrobehavior. Norton, New York.

SCHMIDTCHEN, D. [1989] "Preise und spontane Ordnung: eine evolutionstheoretische Perspektive", Discussion Paper A8902. University of Saarland.

SCHMUTZLER, A. [1991] Flexibility and Adjustment to Information in Sequential Decision Problems. Springer-Verlag, Heidelberg.

SCHRÖDINGER, E. [1944] What is Life? Cambridge University Press, Cambridge.

SCHUMPETER, J.A. [1912/1934] Theorie der wirtschaftlichen Entwicklung. Duncker und Humbolt, Berlin; (trans.) The Theory of Economic Development. Harvard University Press, Cambridge, Mass.

SCHUMPETER, J.A. [1954] History of Economic Analysis. George Allen & Unwin, London.

SHACKLE, G.L.S. [1955] Uncertainty in Economics. Cambridge University Press, Cambridge.

SHACKLE, G.L.S. [1972] Epistemics and Economics: A Critique of Economic Doctrines. Cambridge University Press, Cambridge.

SIMON, H.A. [1967] "Theories of decision-making in economics and behavioral science", in: Surveys of Economic Theory III, Resource Allocation. Macmillan, London.

SIMON, H.A. [1972] "Theories of bounded rationality", in: C.B. MCGUIRE and R. RADNER (eds.), Decision and Organisation. North-Holland, Amsterdam.

SLESSER, M. [1978] Energy in the Economy. Macmillan, London.

SMITHSON, M. [1988] Ignorance and Uncertainty: Emerging Paradigms. Springer Verlag, Heidelberg.

SMITHSON, M. [1989] The changing nature of ignorance. Paper presented at the INES/ACDC-Workshop: Risk Perception in Australia, Victoria.

SOLOW, R.M. [1985] "Economic history and economics", American Economic Review 75:328-331.

SONNENSCHEIN, H. [1972] "Do Walras' identity and continuity characterize the class of community excess demand functions?", Journal of Economic Theory 6:345-354.

SONNENSCHEIN, H. [1973] "Market excess demand functions", Econometrica 40:549-563.

STEGMÜLLER, W. [1969] Hauptströmungen der Gegenwartsphilosophie (2nd ed.). Kröner, Stuttgart.

SANGIANCHEIN, H. [1972] "Do Walras' identity and continuity characterize the class of community excess demand functions?", Journal of Economic Theory 6:345-354.

STEPHAN, G. [1980] Preise und Zinsen in Modellen mit unendlichem Horizont. Fischer, Frankfurt.

STEPHAN, G. [1983] "Roundaboutness, non-tightness and Malinvaud prices in multisector models with infinite horizon", Zeitschrift für die gesamte Staatswissenschaft 139:660-667 (reprinted in: FABER [1986a]).

STEPHAN, G. [1985] "Competitive finite value prices: a complete characterization", Zeitschrift für Nationalökonomie 45:35-54 (reprinted: in FABER [1986a]).

STEPHAN, G. [1986] "A neo-Austrian approach to the open-endedness of the future", in: FABER [1986a].

STEPHAN, G. [1987] "Economic impact of emission standards: a computational approach to waste water treatment in Western Europe", in: D. BÖS, M. ROSE and C. SEIDEL (eds.), Welfare and Public Economics. Springer-Verlag, Heidelberg.

STEPHAN, G. [1988] "A neo-Austrian approach to computable equilibrium models: time to build technologies and imperfect markets", Schweizerische Zeitschrift für Volkswirtschaft und Statistik 124:49-63.

STEPHAN, G. [1989] Emission Standards, Substitution of Techniques and Imperfect Markets: A Computable Equilibrium Approach. Springer-Verlag, Heidelberg.

STUTZER, M. [1980] "Chaotic dynamics and bifurcation in macro models", Journal of Economic Dynamics and Control 32:334-361.

THEIL, H. [1967] Economics and Information Theory. North-Holland, Amsterdam.

THOBEN, H. [1982] "Mechanistic and organistic analogies in economics reconsidered", Kyklos 35:292-306.

THOMPSON, J.N. [1982] Interaction and Coevolution. Wiley, New York.

UBBELOHDE, A.R. [1947] Time and Thermodynamics. Oxford University Press, Oxford.

VAN GOOL, W. and J.J. BRUGGINK (eds.) [1985] Energy and Time in the Economic and Physical Sciences. North-Holland, Amsterdam.

VEBLEN, T. [1902] "Why is economics not an evolutionary science?", Quarterly Journal of Economics 4:373-397.

WALRAS, L. [1874] Eléments d'Economie Politique Pure. Corbaz, Lausanne.

WEIZSÄCKER, C.C. VON [1971] Steady State Capital Theory. Springer-Verlag, Heidelberg.

WHITE, R.W. [1985] "Transitions to chaos with increasing system complexity: the case of regional industrial systems", Environment and Planning A 17:387-396.

WITT, U. [1980] Marktprozesse: Neoklassische Versus Evolutorische Preis-Mengendynamik. Athenäum, Königstein.

WITT, U. [1987] Individualistische Grundlagen der Evolutorischen Ökonomik. Mohr, Tübingen.

WITT, U. [1989] "Subjectivism in economics: a suggested reorientation", in: K.G. GRUNNERT and F. ÖLANDER (eds.), Understanding Economic Behaviour. Kluwer, Dordrecht.

WITT, U. and J. PERSKE [1982] SMS: A Programme Package for Simulation and Gaming of Stochastic Market Processes and Learning Behaviour. Springer-Verlag, Heidelberg.

WITTGENSTEIN, L. [1922/69] Philosophische Untersuchungen. Suhrkamp, Frankfurt.

WITTMANN, W. [1968] Produktionstheorie. Springer-Verlag, Heidelberg.

WODOPIA, F.-J. [1986a] Intertemporale Produktionsentscheidungen: Theorie und Anwendung auf die Elektrizitätswirtschaft. Mathematical Systems in Economics, Athenäum, Königstein.

WODOPIA, F.-J. [1986b] "Flow and fund approaches to irreversible investment", in: FABER [1986a].

YORKE, J.A. and E.D. YORKE [1981] "Chaotic behaviour and fluid dynamics", in: H.L. SWINNEY and J.P. GOLLUB (eds.), Hydrodynamic Instabilities and the Transition to Turbulence. Springer-Verlag, Heidelberg.

Subject Index

Author Index

Printing: Weihert-Druck GmbH, Darmstadt
Binding: Verlagsbuchbinderei Georg Kränkl, Heppenheim